HIROHITO

HIROHITO
THE EMPEROR AND THE MAN

EDWIN P. HOYT

New York
Westport, Connecticut
London

Copyright Acknowledgments

The author and publisher are grateful for permission to reprint from the following source:

All photographs are from *The Japanese Emperor through History* (The International Society for Educational Information: Tokyo, 1984), copyright © 1984, The International Society for Educational Information, Inc., and are reproduced by permission.

Library of Congress Cataloging-in-Publication Data

Hoyt, Edwin Palmer.
    Hirohito : the emperor and the man / Edwin P. Hoyt.
       p.   cm.
    Includes bibliographical references and index.
    ISBN 0-275-94069-1 (alk. paper)
    1. Hirohito, Emperor of Japan, 1901–1989. 2. Japan—Emperors—
Biography.   3. Japan—History—Shōwa period, 1926–1989.   I. Title.
DS889.8.H69   1991
952.03'3'092—dc20
[B]   91-4189

British Library Cataloguing in Publication Data is available.

Copyright © 1992 by Edwin P. Hoyt

Library of Congress Catalog Card Number: 91-4189
ISBN: 0-275-94069-1

First published in 1992

Praeger Publishers, One Madison Avenue, New York, NY 10010
An imprint of Greenwood Publishing Group, Inc.

Printed in the United States of America

The paper used in this book complies with the Permanent Paper Standard issued by the National Information Standards Organization (Z39.48-1984).

10 9 8 7 6 5 4 3 2 1

Contents

Photographs follow page 126.

in the postwar years between the Emperor and Hidenari Terasaki, a foreign office diplomat who also served Hirohito as advisor and translator in the postwar years. These notes had been completely unknown to the world. After Terasaki's death his widow, an American, had settled in Wyoming. After her death in 1990, their daughter was going through papers in the house and discovered the notes, which contain thoughts and recollections of the Emperor as far back as the Manchuria period. These notes provided the basis for several long articles in *Bungei Shinju.*

All of this material tends to indicate that Emperor Hirohito was very much the prisoner of the imperial system. While some of those around him, particularly his family members, believed that he should have broken out of the mold set by precedent, which he did do a few times, nevertheless, beginning in the 1920s, it became apparent that the army had seized control of the government and was itself out of control. Hirohito's main concern was preservation of the Meiji Constitution and the imperial legacy, both of which were threatened by the army's rash behavior.

Never, in the picture drawn from these diaries of men close around the Emperor, is there indication of the swashbuckling conspirator that several books have made Hirohito out to be, a man intent on conquering the world and using the Imperial Army as his major weapon in so doing. Instead there emerges the picture of a troubled man, given enormous responsibility but not nearly so clear a line of authority, who attempted time and again to thwart the Japanese army's headlong drive to war, but who in the end was defeated by events, bad luck, and the Western misunderstanding of the Japanese character. This misunderstanding is shown in the message sent by U.S. Secretary of State Cordell Hull to Tokyo in the fall of 1941, a message so harsh that veteran Japanese diplomats who were friends of the West referred to it as a "virtual declaration of war," and by the diversion of that all-important eleventh-hour message from President Roosevelt directly to the Emperor, which was tied up in U.S. Army channels and lay unnoticed until after the attack on Pearl Harbor had been carried out and the war had begun.

So through this material, published within two years of the Showa Emperor's death, a clearer picture emerges of Hirohito as a Japanese patriot and a strong believer in the destiny of Japan to lead Asia out of the wilderness of colonialism to independence. He is seen not as a man of war, but as someone who recognized the good qualities and leadership of the West as well as its failings. What is shown more clearly than ever is that the Meiji Constitution, which was reputed to give so much power to the Emperor, actually made him a prisoner of the imperial system, which the Imperial Army, in its wicked selfishness, turned into the emperor worship of the Imperial Way. All of these new "finds" illustrate that, beginning in the 1920s, the period in which the Japanese Imperial Army began to run amok, the Showa Emperor developed a distrust of the army that he retained until that army was disbanded in 1945. His efforts were turned to trying to divert Japan from that course of Asian empire which the army wanted.

Acknowledgments

The author is indebted to many people in Japan, Britain, and the United States for assistance in the preparation of this book. They include Etsuko Ishida; Kenji Koyama of the War History Room of the Japanese Defense Agency; Masataka Chihaya; Kanehisa Hoshino; Tsuneo Misawa; Hiroko Hattori; Fumio Kitamura, managing director of the Japan Foreign Press Center; Seiichi Soeda, media coordinator of the Japan Foreign Press Center; Takao Ueda of the Japan Foreign Press Center; Kumiko Murata, then a student at London University; Yoshitomo Sano, of the Komeito political party; Taeko Miyano; Doreen Simmons; Ian Mutsu, president of the International Motion Picture Company of Tokyo; Sheila Phalon; Junko Yamazaki of London; and the librarians at the National (Diet) library, at Tokyo International House, Japan, at the Foreign Correspondents' Club of Tokyo, at the Westminster public library in London, and at the Mathews Memorial Library in Virginia. He is also grateful to Olga G. Hoyt for editing and many other chores in connection with the book and to Diana P. Hoyt for typing.

HIROHITO

Introduction

Long the Imperial Way

The wall of secrecy that surrounds the Imperial Palace in Tokyo is so dense that it makes the regulations of MI5 look like the covenants of an open marriage contract.

It is November 1988 in Tokyo. Emperor Hirohito is dying and all the world knows it. Yet the Imperial Household Agency, which controls all the information about anything and everything that happens inside the palace moat, refuses to accept any telephone calls from outside or to respond to any letters. Since the Emperor's illness became acute two months ago, the agency has gone into a state of shock and is inaccessible to the outside world. Neither Japanese nor foreign journalists have been able to break through the wall of silence, which is opened daily only long enough for a household spokesman to give a vague report to the media describing the imperial body functions and virtually nothing else.

By mid-November the journalists were reduced to any sort of speculation, including one that the Emperor was dead and that this fact was being withheld from the public because the agency did not know what to do next. In the mystic atmosphere that surrounded the Imperial Palace, even this ridiculous impertinence was given due consideration by the reporters.

What was known to be true, and had been true since September, was that the Emperor was bleeding to death. His weight had reportedly dropped to 25 kilograms. His body was so punctured by holes from blood transfusions that the doctors had been forced to fix a permanent transfusion path into a blood vessel in his neck. The Emperor was dying from lacerations caused by his internal cancer, and there was nothing to be done about it but use all the appurtenances of modern medicine to keep him alive until his body finally rejected everything.

More than a year earlier, it had been known that Emperor Hirohito suffered from pancreatic cancer. But after surgery and some worrisome weeks in the spring of 1988, he seemed to recover. Photographs and television films showed him walking a little and relaxing on the veranda in the secluded imperial quarters, behind the great stone walls of the moat that surrounds three hundred acres of the most valuable land in the world, deep in the heart of Tokyo.

Now, in the autumn of 1988, suddenly the people of Japan learned something about themselves, and about the intense feeling for the Emperor that lies deep in the heart of Japan. For some Japanese this was a surprise. As soon as it became apparent on September 19 that the Emperor was mortally ill, people by the hundreds of thousands flocked to the gates of the Imperial Palace to pay homage to a man whom many foreigners, and even many young Japanese, had believed to be irrelevant to the Japanese society of the 1980s. In those last two weeks of September they braved the downpours of the typhoon season to say their prayers for Hirohito's recovery, although it had to be apparent that his recovery would be virtually a miracle.

Two weeks after the announcement of the illness, it had become equally apparent that the Emperor was dying. Why was modern technology being strained to keep Hirohito alive when there was no hope for recovery? Because there was no alternative. What man, what doctor, would decide to stop prolonging the life of the Son of Heaven, the semideity of Japan, whose own announcement of his mortality nearly forty years earlier had still not convinced many Japanese? The Emperor occupied a role in Japan perhaps best explained to outsiders as akin to that of the Pope to the world's Roman Catholic community: not a god, but certainly not a mere mortal—a being who assumes infallibility as he dons the robes of the office. So it was with Hirohito, the emperor of Japan, and, above that, the essence of Japan.

So the drama played itself out, as Japan moved into a culture shock that the outside world was unable to understand. Parliament stopped, the cabinet cancelled meetings. Visits of state to and from Japan were abandoned or delayed, festivals and conventions were put aside, and the nation assumed a state of mourning so pervasive that one newspaper commentator suggested that the cancellation of events and programs was going to have an adverse effect on the national economy through 1989.

Slowly, as the weeks passed, Japan returned to a semblance of normality, but the newspapers continued to give front-page news of the imperial health every day, and the television stations broadcast the imperial vital signs as a regular part of every newscast. Japanese life continued beneath the shadow of the imperial waning, with the realization that after the death of Hirohito nothing in Japan would ever be quite the same again.

The shock was the greatest felt in Japan since thirty-eight years before, when from the Emperor of Japan had emanated another sudden change that presaged new developments in the lives of the people. On August 15, 1945, the shock had been the Emperor's announcement that Japan had lost the Pacific war and his order to the armed forces to lay down their arms. Now, in 1988, after so many years of benign imperial reign, came another shock, and the realization that the future economic, social, and political development of Japan was open to question.

And from a not particularly friendly world came all the old bitter charges: that Japan and Japan alone was responsible for the great Pacific war, and that the Emperor, exonerated of criminality by the supreme allied commander, General Douglas MacArthur, and by the war crimes court, was really a war criminal after all.

To propitiate the foreign press, even to try to explain to the world public through that press the role of the Emperor in Japanese society, the government of Japan, through the semiofficial Foreign Press Center of Tokyo, arranged to hold a series of briefings for foreign correspondents, and three prominent Japanese historians and publicists appeared to discuss the Emperor and his role. But after the briefings the foreign press seemed both unimpressed and no wiser than before. The big question was: What is and was the role of the Emperor in Japanese society? From that question emanated all others, including the one that seemed so important to the press: What was Hirohito's role, and how great was his responsibility, in the events of the Pacific war?

As Hirohito lay on his deathbed, the reporters clustered like flies, hurling the same old questions, and sometimes outright accusations. The implication was always the same: Hirohito had been responsible for the war on China, beginning with the 1928 murder of the Manchu warlord Zhang Zoulin and the rape of Manchuria, which became the Japanese puppet state of Manchukuo. The theory that Hirohito had been at the bottom of a Japanese conspiracy to conquer the world had been advanced long before. Its prinicipal exponent, author David Bergamini, had written a long book twenty years earlier linking Hirohito, usually by slender evidence and often by farfetched innuendo, to all the aggressions and cruelties of the war. The Bergamini book, *Japan's Imperial Conspiracy*, was denounced by most responsible Japan scholars for its reckless innuendo and careless reporting of fact.

Now, in 1988, the British Broadcasting Corporation became party to the conspiracy theory, and in a careless and inaccurate documentary (one

British scholar counted more than fifty errors of fact) repeated all the old charges. The documentary also became the basis for a biography of Hirohito, which aped the charges once again.

Emperor Hirohito died on January 7, 1989, and immediately his son Crown Prince Akihito took over. The time frame of Japan changed. It had been Showa 63, the sixty-third year of the Emperor Hirohito's reign "of enlightened peace" that had proved so warlike. The new era starting immediately became Heisei 1 (year one of the era "of achieving peace").

At Akihito's first press conference, the reporters began the same questioning: What was your attitude toward the Pacific war? Akihito replied evenly that he scarcely recalled the Pacific war, because he was a child at the time. It is true. Akihito has never worn a military uniform, although his father often posed in the rig of general or admiral as the occasion demanded, just as does the monarch of England. To please the army, Hirohito also used to ride his white horse, Spring Snow, for pictures. If Akihito has a horse, he keeps it out of sight.

With the death of Hirohito, the ghosts of the China and Pacific wars had to be laid to rest. There was no longer anywhere for the accusers to direct their attention. Prime Minister Toshiki Kaifu, also, was too young at the time of the war to have been involved. Finally, Japan's long ordeal of guilt began to come to an end. In the next year or so, Akihito apologized on behalf of the throne to the Chinese and the Koreans and others who had been mistreated by Japan during 1932–45. Prime Minister Kaifu also apologized, on behalf of the people, and by the beginning of 1991 the issue of Japan's war guilt was fairly well behind the country. But not quite—in 1991 the North Koreans demanded apologies and reparations from Japan for the treatment of their half of Korea during the Japanese occupation that began in 1910 and lasted until 1945. The Japanese, who had grown wise to the ways of finance, gave the apologies but refused the reparations.

The question of the war remained. What seemed obvious, and had been admitted by Hirohito openly when General MacArthur began the U.S. occupation of Japan in 1945, was that as head of the Japanese state, the Emperor was responsible for the Pacific war, as he was responsible for the Mukden Incident and the Marco Polo Bridge Incident, which had become the China war. There has never been any question about that. But there has been question as to whether Hirohito himself was opposed to the idea of war with China and with the United States and Britain, and, if so, why he did not stop it.

In the postwar years the Japanese have been very reluctant to come to grips with their twentieth-century past. Japanese textbooks do not refer to the Rape of Nanking but to the Nanking Incident, and the whole episode is given about a half page in the junior high school history text. The rest of the war is treated in the same relative way. Some educators have pressed for fuller treatment of the war to show the details of Japan's guilt, but almost always these attempts have been frustrated by the Ministry of Education, which must approve all textbooks.

In 1989 and 1990, however, more attention was given in Japan to the events of the 1930s. One indication was a docudrama movie, *Five Days of Blood and Snow*, which tells the story of the attempt of junior army officers on February 26, 1936, to take over the Japanese government and install an army prime minister and army dictatorship—an attempt put down by the Emperor personally. Another was a series of articles in *Mainichi Shimbun*, one of the three enormous national newspapers, entitled "Facing the Past." A similar series was published by the *Japan Times*, an English-language newspaper, but the readership of that newspaper is heavily foreign, and its publication there was not nearly so meaningful as the articles in Japanese.

Two other links with the past came to light. One was the August 1990 publication in two parts, in the influential intellectual magazine *Chuo Koron*, of an account of Hirohito's reactions and actions during the army's finally successful attempt to wrest Manchuria away from China. The other was the publication in two parts in the magazine *Bungei Shunju* of a long account of Hirohito's thoughts and actions during the Pacific war by Hidenari Terasaki, a wartime diplomat and translator of English who was close to the throne. This account indicates, among other matters, the Emperor's very real fear that if he attempted to face down the army on the eve of war, he would be assassinated or discarded and his brother put in his place.

These materials cast new light on the role played by Emperor Hirohito in the critical periods of the 1930s and 1940s and should do much to reveal the truth of Japan's behavior and commitment to the Pacific war. Still, to understand these matters, one must have a glimpse of Japanese history. According to Japanese legend and history, which are closely intertwined, Hirohito and Akihito are from the unbroken line of the first emperor, Jimmu. So strong is this tradition that the royal family, unlike others, has no family name. The royal family *is* Japan and always has been.

All of the story about Jimmu and his descent from the sun goddess is legend, of course, and so is the rest of Japanese history up until about the year A.D. 539, when Emperor Kimmei, twenty-ninth in the line, ascended the throne.

Thereafter came a series of emperors, each reigning only a few years, and virtually none ruling in the sense of Charlemagne or a Caesar. Nevertheless, the emperors were and are the symbols of Japan, and have been since Jimmu. Akihito, when formally crowned in February 1991, became the 125th emperor in an unbroken line that has lasted more than two thousand years.

More is known about Emperor Hirohito than about any other emperor, since he reigned for more than sixty years. The nearest competitor in longevity was Hirohito's grandfather, Meiji, who reigned for forty-four years.

Such is the ambience of the imperial tradition that very little is known about Emperor Hirohito's personal life, and if the imperial household has its way, so it will always be. The mystique of imperial rule has been maintained over the centuries by silence. In the old days, the occasional courtesan would write her memoirs, revealing the most intimate of relations with some emperor, but these would never be published until many years later, or even centuries after the deaths of those involved. So when we read the memoirs of Lady Murasaki, with her myriad revelations of the bedroom habits of an imperial household of days gone by, we are getting a keyhole view that has no equivalent in modern times.

An editor, complaining about the paucity of "inside information" in the present work, wrote, "Even if Hirohito has not given you exclusive first look at his diaries, surely there are other sources (foreign visitors, etc.) who may have some personal comments to make about the Emperor, his family. There are barely any descriptions, even of his surroundings."

This is true, because Emperor Hirohito's privacy was so carefully guarded by his courtiers that only once in his life did he grant an interview to journalists. And that came under the most remarkable of circumstances, shortly after the occupation of Japan by the U.S. Army began. On January 1, 1946, Hirohito had declared himself to be merely a mortal man (which few Japanese believed), and the foreign journalists were clamoring for interviews. So Hirohito gave an interview to Miles W. Vaughan, of the (then) United Press Associations, and one or two others. It was held in the Imperial Palace, and the journalists had a look at the imperial surroundings, with the imperial library, which includes busts of Napoleon, George Washington, and Charles Darwin, and its English writing desk and English overstuffed furniture. And that is about all.

Preface

This book was begun in the mid-1980s, when it appeared likely that the time of the Showa Emperor, Hirohito, had almost run out, but for one reason and another the book was not finished in 1988, when it was learned that the Emperor was mortally ill and living on borrowed time. In the next year or so a number of books about Hirohito were published, in Japan and abroad. I felt that none of them did justice to Hirohito, who was neither the unworldly professional scientist that he has sometimes been portrayed to be, nor the scheming Machiavellian Prince of the school of conspiracy.

It is true that Hirohito loved to go to the ocean and dive and search for specimens of marine life, to which he then devoted hours of study in his private laboratory, with the assistance of a distinguished scientist. And it is true that he was a Japanese patriot, one who espoused the cause of Pan Asianism and Asia for the Asiatics, as an Asian must do. He was as hurt and annoyed by American and Australian anti-Oriental racism as the next Asian, and just as resentful. But it is also true that Hirohito was an Anglophile, who always treasured the memory of his short visit to England and his stay at Buckingham Palace as Crown Prince. More important, Hirohito dreaded the possibility of war with the West and agreed with such men as Admiral Isoroku Yamamoto that it should be avoided, because the chances of its bringing disaster to Japan were very great.

To me the picture of the real Hirohito is of a man of good will and peaceful intentions, caught up in the swirl of events of a turbulent period and trapped by the Japanese governmental and social system into becoming a symbol used by the Gunbatsu, the military and naval conspirators of the 1920s, who seized control of the Japanese government in 1932. Only three times in Hirohito's reign was he able to break the bonds of the imperial system that imprisoned him and lash out against the Gunbatsu; the third time, he brought about the surrender of Japan after she had exhausted her resources in August 1945. Even then, he was acting over the objections of the Gunbatsu, who had to be out-maneuvered by Hirohito and his allies.

To some extent I had already written about these events, using the sources then available, but in 1990, before the manuscript could be published, the highly regarded magazine *Chuo Koron* published two major revelations about the life of the Showa Emperor. The first of these, in August, came from the previously secret diary of Nobuaki Makino, a man who had risen high in the councils of the Empire, which dealt in detail with the 1928 murder by the Kwantung Army of the Manchurian warlord Zhang Zoulin, the manner of the Emperor's discovery of the facts, and the Emperor's angry reaction and the strong action he took. This was all new material, which among other things blows to pieces the theory that Hirohito himself planned the march of Japan, from the Manchurian incidents right through the planning for the Pacific war.

The second revelation of important new historical material about the Showa Emperor came in the following month's issue of *Chuo Koron*, and it, too, was from the previously unpublished Makino diary. The same issue contained material from another diary, kept by General Takeji Nara in the 1930s, after the period in which General Shigeru Honjo, former commander of the Kwantung Army, served as the Showa military aide.

The Nara revelations dealt with the Mukden Incident, in September 1931, in which the Kwantung Army actually seized control of Manchuria, and the Emperor's reactions and attempts to bring the Kwantung Army under control, which became impossible because of the collusion of virtually every senior officer in the Imperial Army. The Mukden Incident predated the uprising of the young army officers, in what was known as the 2–26–36 Incident, by more than five years, but in all that time between, the Imperial Army was in ferment and was a constant source of violence and disregard of constitutional parliamentary government. The Emperor, cleverly made captive in the army scheme of things, squirmed and tried to escape, but was not served well by such counselors as Prince Kinmochi Saionji, a major figure in these diaries, who contin-ually reminded Hirohito about his responsibilities under the imperial system—responsibilities to the military that were separate from his re-sponsibilities to the civil government, under Japan's strange, split Meiji Constitution.

The next element that changed the picture of the Showa Emperor was the publication in the winter of 1991 by *Bungei Shunju*, another eminently respectable magazine, of accounts of a number of conversations

The interview produced nothing world-shaking or even interesting for world readers. The Emperor was as careful in his statements and as colorless as ever. So it has always been.

Even when the man who was closer to Hirohito than any other for more than half a century, Grand Chamberlain Yoshihiro Tokugawa, consented to give me an interview on condition that it would remain secret until the book was published, the chamberlain would answer no direct personal questions about Hirohito. The Emperor's privacy, unlike that of virtually any other world figure in the new era of total communication, was preserved until the last. Through a family connection, I have known for a number of years a person who was once part of the imperial household, the royal master of archery. But when I sought information about Hirohito, I drew a blank.

As far as I know there is no oath of office taken by people in the imperial household when they sign on, but the silence from the palace behind the moat has persisted for generations in spite of the diligence of the Japanese and foreign press.

Therefore, unfortunately, there are no "informed foreign sources" for information about Hirohito. A handful of Japanese, such as Prince Kimmochi Saionji, the Marquis Koichi Kido, and a few others, were close to the Emperor and in their writings made some revelations. But as to Hirohito, as a personality, these sources carry the secret beyond his grave. Hirohito was a real man, however, and if not like every other man, at least a man who put on his trousers one leg at a time. He had his own hopes and own ambitions, some of which he managed to achieve.

Hirohito also interfered at least twice in the processes of Japanese government and reversed them. These actions were revolutionary, a staggering departure for a Japanese emperor, whose life by custom is more sequestered than that of any other head of state. In a way, a Japanese monarch has always been like a queen bee, surrounded by courtiers willing to give their lives for him but unwilling to allow him freedom of action outside the palace, or freedom to rule.

Although in the early Hirohito years much was made of the term Imperial Rule, there was never any imperial rule, by Hirohito, by his father, Taisho, or by Meiji. The concept of Imperial Rule was a carefully constructed program devised by the Japanese oligarchy to control the people of Japan, and the Emperor was their symbol of authority. Whenever Hirohito stepped out of his role, his advisors and courtiers were quick to force him back into his position as symbol, but not source, of authority. That is a major truth about Japan's imperial system that has never been understood by the Western world.

1

The Emperor Speaks

On two major occasions in his life, Emperor Hirohito violated the provisions of the constitution of Japan to save the nation from disaster. For the constitution provided that the Emperor should "rule" but that his actions must be approved by the Privy Council, and that all laws, imperial ordinances, and imperial rescripts must be countersigned by a minister of state.

To the world, the more important of these two occasions came on the night of August 14, 1945, when the Pacific war was still raging and atomic weapons had been used against Japan.

The scene was the underground bomb shelter on the grounds of the Imperial Palace of Japan, behind its splendid, stone-walled moat, where Emperor Hirohito had lived for most of his adult life like a captive bird.

It was a hot and muggy night, with the moon high and fireflies flickering in the green shrubbery up above.

Assembled in the shelter were the members of Japan's Supreme Defense Council, which included the prime minister; the foreign minister; the ministers of war, navy, and home affairs; and several other counsellors to the Emperor. They were seated in two long rows, running almost the length of the bomb shelter. The emergency lights above them flickered yellowly on the long tables covered with expensive fabric bearing the imperial crest. Before each man was a pile of papers. In spite of the heat in the uncooled shelter, all were dressed in full uniform or in formal civilian wear with high collars. The heat was oppressive, and they sat sweating.

One of those present was Vice Admiral Zenjiro Hoshino, a naval counsellor who had been attending these meetings for four years, as a member and then as the chairman of the Imperial Defense Assistance Committee.

All this time, privately, Admiral Hoshino had opposed the war against the United States and Britain. He had attended the Air War College in the United States and had studied for his doctorate in engineering in that country. He knew the United States and its military and industrial potential as did few Japanese, and he had agreed with admirals Isoroku Yamamoto and Mitsumasa Yonai back in the 1930s, when they had opposed the radicals of the navy, trying to stop the rush to war.

But for the past four years, of course, Admiral Hoshino had been careful to keep his private views very private, for in the framework of the military oligarchy any opposition to the war was a ticket to oblivion. He had watched as General Tojo and the army led Japan from victory upon victory to defeat upon defeat.

Tojo had bulldozed his way until the summer of 1944, when the inner line of empire was breached in the Marianas. The fall of Saipan had been an enormous shock. Saipan was a colony, to be sure, but a very old one, the Japanese presence dating back to the first world war. The Japanese people had for years regarded Saipan as an integral part of Japan, and many Japanese had made their homes there. The consequence of the fall of Saipan had been the collapse of the cabinet of General Hideki Tojo, which had rashly promised the nation that the empire would never be invaded.

The Emperor, sitting here on this evening of August 14, in his uniform as a general of the army, was white-faced and serious. He had been as shocked as anyone at the long series of military disasters, although since Guadalcanal he had recognized that the war had turned around and Japan was on the defensive. In the last days of Guadalcanal he had demanded action from the army to match that of the navy, but he had not gotten it. The fall of Saipan was proof positive to him that Tojo and the generals were lying to him. Hirohito had not granted Tojo the usual reward for good service given to former prime ministers: Tojo was not invited to join the council of advisors, although every prime minister up until his day had been. Tojo had gone out in disgrace.

But while Tojo had gone in July 1944, the tradition and the thinking of the army had remained, to control Japan's destiny. Even as late as a week before this historic meeting of August 14, the army had pledged to fight on to victory.

In spite of the army's intransigence, Emperor Hirohito had been quietly making some preparations to bring the war to a close. Some of his advisors had been putting out feelers through diplomatic channels for several months. For a time the work was done through Geneva, but nothing came of it; the Allied demand for unconditional surrender stood in the way. Until very recently it had seemed that there might be hope in dealing through Moscow, with which Japan had retained an uneasy neutrality over the last few years, in spite of the Berlin-Rome-Tokyo alliance.

Over these past few months the Emperor had become ever more concerned. He had been shocked by the events of March 10, 1945, when Tokyo had been hit by the Saipan-based B–29 bombers of the U.S. Air Force in an enormous raid (involving three hundred aircraft) which had come on a blustery night. The leading aircraft had dropped large clusters of incendiary bombs, and these had started a fire storm. The following planes, loaded with smaller incendiaries, had sown them across the city like a farmer sowing wheat. The result from the one night's bombing was the destruction of thousands of houses and the killing of perhaps two hundred thousand people. Nobody ever did know the real number of the dead, but the evidence the next day had been grim. Bodies were stacked like cordwood on the banks of the Sumida River in Central Tokyo, blackened corpses that looked like nothing more than burned logs.

The Emperor had heard the grisly tales, and he had insisted on going to see the results. After viewing the devastation, he had returned to the palace visibly shaken, convinced even more firmly than before that Japan could not stand many more of such savage attacks. But the army, it seemed, had an answer for everything, and the answer was always the same: Fight on to victory—a victory the Emperor knew was no longer possible.

The Japanese had already missed a chance to end the war. In February 1942, when Hirohito had heard the report of the Japanese capture of Singapore, he had indicated to General Hajime Sugiyama, the chief of staff, that this was the proper moment to bring the war to an end. The victory had been impressive. Moving like a tiger, General Tomoyuki Yamashita had slashed through the British defenses with an army only a third as large as Britain's and had so thoroughly confused his enemies that they had quickly surrendered. Japan had thus achieved basically what she wanted, control of Malayan tin and rubber and Dutch East Indies oil, and the Allies were in disarray. In spite of the American fury at the "infamy" of Pearl Harbor, there really might have been a chance for peace.

But the generals never looked back, and never listened, and Hirohito had not pursued the issue. Half a century later, as the Emperor lay dying, Western newspapers offered this instance as proof that Hirohito could have ended the war had he been so inclined. It was a part of the revival of the cry of "war criminal."

Admiral Hoshino knew about all this. At the time he had been chief of the War Preparations Bureau of the navy, and he moved in the inner circle of the navy ministry. All the way, the army had deluded itself. General Sugiyama had been giving the Emperor false information since the day the China war began, which he promised would be over in six months. The falsehoods continued through the movement into Indochina, which he said would force the Americans to back down, and the beginning of the move south, which he said would resolve Japan's problems in less than a year.

General Tojo had fooled himself completely. When the nation's petroleum shortage had become serious and the navy had wondered when the bombed-out refining facilities would be repaired, Tojo had said, "Do it by hand!" In those halcyon days of 1942, when the Germans, Italians, and Japanese seemed to be winning almost everywhere, Tojo had prophesied to the people and the Emperor an early victory for all the Axis powers.

But times changed. And the Emperor knew. Even before Saipan, the Emperor had called meetings of the six chief officers of the various services. On the part of the Emperor, this was an unprecedented act, and it annoyed General Tojo and the general staff. On June 8 these operational chiefs had declared that Japan would fight to the end. This was not the answer the Emperor had wanted, so on June 22, he had called another meeting, this time of the supreme war council, which included the prime minister, the war and navy ministers, and several others. At that time Admiral Hoshino was naval affairs bureau chief, and so he was one of those asked to attend.

"We have heard enough of this determination of yours to fight to the last soldiers," Hirohito had said. "We wish that you, leaders of Japan, will strive now to study the ways and means to conclude the war. In doing so, try not to be bound by the decisions you have made in the past."

This had been an enormous shock to the assemblage. Never before had the Emperor openly questioned the actions of the government to such a large group. Here was the most serious indictment of the government's war policies that he had ever made. The men of the military oligarchy did not know it, but the Emperor had been checking up on their statements. He might be confined to the palace, but his brothers and sisters were not, and he sent them out on private intelligence missions. The generals told him that the whole nation was eager to fight to the end, but when one of his sisters went to Yokohama she saw women and children marching with staves, and learned that these women and children would be expected to fight on the beaches with rifles and hand grenades, against tanks and machine guns. Remembering her words, at the June meeting the Emperor asked for concrete suggestions as to how the war might be brought to an end. The result of that meeting was the approach to the Soviets to intervene.

When the Potsdam Declaration had been announced early in August, because of a mistranslation it had been violently rejected by the Japanese establishment. The problem was the fate of the Emperor, and the rejection was based on the "cries of the silent dead," lest all that they had died for be destroyed with the passing of the imperial system. But that mistranslation had been straightened out, and while the Potsdam Declaration still called for "unconditional surrender" there was indication that there was actually room for some conditions. The prime consideration was the fate of the Emperor and the whole system. Some of the Allies, at least, had begun to understand this.

More and more it had become apparent in the past few hours, as the pressures mounted, that the Emperor and only the Emperor would have to make the decision. On him must rest the fate of the Imperial system and the people of Japan. The wording of the Potsdam Declaration was not that clear; certainly there was the danger (particularly in dealing with the Russians, the army believed) that no matter what was said, the enemy actions would be vicious. And by now, August 14, the Soviets were in the war, and were driving furiously into Manchuria and Korea.

Yes, the decision was the Emperor's, and that night the whole assemblage in the bomb shelter understood that. Even if the generals resisted, there were other factors at work: Prime Minister Kantaro Suzuki and Foreign Minister Shigenori Togo had decided for peace, and outside Japan hundreds of thousands of enemy soldiers were moving toward Tokyo from the north and south.

Admiral Hoshino kept a memorandum of the proceedings of that fateful meeting. Present were Prime Minister Suzuki, Navy Minister Mitsumasa Yonai, War Minister Korechika Anami, Foreign Minister Shigenori Togo, Privy Council President Hiranuma Kiichiro, the cabinet secretary, the army and navy affairs bureau chiefs, the composite plans officer, and the grand chamberlain.

In courtly language, writing in a magazine a few years after the war, Admiral Hoshino described what happened inside the bomb shelter that night: "Humbly let me state the facts," as a Japanese author would write.

The Potsdam declaration by the Allies was first read aloud by Foreign

Minister Togo. Prime Minister Suzuki then proposed that it be accepted, and the opinions of all concerned were called for.

The first clause, which Foreign Minister Togo said had unacceptable implications, concerned the imperial family and succession. The second clause called for the withdrawal and demobilization of the armed forces of Japan. The third defined "war crimes" and provided for the prosecution of "war criminals." The fourth called for the occupation of Japan.

Prime Minister Suzuki asked for opinions on the four clauses. The cabinet previously had been unable to agree. Six members had said that the declaration should be accepted, but General Anami and the army and navy chiefs of staff, General Umezu and Admiral Soemu Toyoda, had been violently opposed. Foreign Minister Togo now said that, undesirable though the proposal was, it would be most unprofitable not to accept. All the other matters to which the generals objected, particularly the war crimes clause, could be dealt with. The matter of the Emperor's status was the problem.

Navy Minister Yonai agreed with the prime minister.

Then spoke War Minister Anami. He was entirely opposed to the prime minister's view, he said. The Cairo Conference had threatened to destroy Manchuria, and the Japanese nation could not morally accept such a stricture. (What Anami meant was that the Japanese army had labored mightily to create Manchukuo, and to let it go now would be to sacrifice everything they had been fighting for.) He also agreed with the other objections to the declaration. Japan must go on and fight the decisive battle against the Americans in the homeland, declared the general. Life should be made so difficult for the enemy that the people of America and the other countries would grow weary of the war, and civil war might even break out in these countries.

General Umezu agreed with Anami. The only way was to fight the decisive battle on the shores of the homeland. To do anything less would be to dishonor the war dead.

The cabinet meetings also had been drawn along just those lines; the hard-line military men held out for every citizen of Japan to fight to the death, and the peace faction, led by the prime minister and the foreign minister, held out for acceptance of the Potsdam agreement.

Privy Council President Kiichiro Hiranuma, whose influence depended largely on the enormous prestige of the council with the Emperor, now spoke. In fact, his was the voice of Emperor Hirohito. It would have been out of character for the throne if Hirohito had himself conducted the questioning of the cabinet members and other officials. Everyone in the bomb shelter understood precisely that this was the case.

"Shouldn't we consider the tangible proposals?" Hiranuma asked.

Foreign Minister Togo said the tangible proposal was to send a special ambassador.

"So be it!" replied the privy council minister. "And how do we justify the Soviet declaration of war?"

There was more talk but Hiranuma broke it off with "It seems to me the Soviet situation is very clear indeed. On the 26th of July they joined the three-power alliance against us." And he quizzed the others on their attitude toward the war crimes charges that were being made, and on the Allied demand for forcible disarmament of the Japanese military.

The military men were wriggling to show their displeasure, but Councillor Hiranuma, the voice of the Emperor, put them down. Japan was being bombed day and night, he declared, and the military could do nothing to stop it. Because of the air raids, homeland transportation facilities had been seriously disturbed. What was to be done about that?

Chief of Staff Umezu said, "It's true we have not done very well against the air raids, but from now on our methods are going to be improved. But anyhow, just because of the air raids we're certainly not going to surrender to the enemy."

Councillor Hiranuma then wanted to know what the navy could do; everyone knew he was talking about Admiral William F. Halsey's rampage with the U.S. Third Fleet along the shores of Japan, where he was attacking at will.

Admiral Toyoda said what everyone expected, that the navy had to save its planes for the big battle for the homeland.

The discussion went on and on, as Hiranuma questioned each man about his area of responsibility. The army men claimed they could put a hundred new divisions into the field, that they could build a hundred fortified areas on the beaches.

Finally, Hiranuma summed it up. Again he was speaking with the voice of the Emperor. "There is little room for further deliberation by this government. Let me say that I am already impressed by the serious nature of the distress of the nation."

And the Emperor sat stolidly on; he seemed to be scarcely listening. He could see that in fact the problems were insoluble, and that it was not in the interest of the people of Japan to continue this war.

Admiral Toyoda spoke up again. "The navy high command, the war minister, and the army chief of staff all share the same opinion. The prospects of actual victory are not great, but we can battle the enemy so fiercely that we destroy his self-confidence. We can destroy his fighting spirit. The fighting spirit of our people is great."

Here the prime minister finally interrupted. "We have been discussing this matter now for a very long time without you [military] people offering any truly cogent suggestions. The fact that this is a very serious matter, as attested to by the words of the president of the Privy Council. Since the opposition is so great, we must depend on nothing less than an imperial decision in this matter. [For "imperial" he used the term *Mimae*, which means God.]

"The honorable imperial decision we now humbly request," he said.

And now, at long last, Emperor Hirohito spoke.

"There is no chance of victory," he said. "The confidence we had earlier in the plans presented to us no longer exists. Furthermore, if, as the War Minister said, he could finish building ninety-nine fortified coastal areas by the end of the month, this is still not enough. The new divisions he talks about arranging could not be equipped. Moreover, I do not trust his boast of all sorts of new weapons that will win the victory over the Americans and the British.

"Furthermore, I have listened to my military advisor, who tells me that all this talk about the enormous number of people who will be taken as war criminals is not to be trusted.

"The same sort of situation existed in the Meiji Era with the three-power intervention, which was supposed to bring total disaster to the country but instead enhanced the welfare of the people."

The Emperor then made a worshipful and sympathetic gesture with his gloved white hands. That was all.

The imperial decision had already been made on August 10 at two o'clock in the morning after a long supper, when the Emperor was relaxing in the midst of a party of his close friends and courtiers. He brought forth a paper and cleared his throat. His friends knew, because he had done this many times before, that he was about to read to them one of the brief poems for which he was celebrated, as his grandfather had been celebrated before him—a poem that would indicate to the people of Japan the imperial attitude.

The time of righteousness had come, according to this poem, a tanka poem, which the Emperor now recited, his voice rising with deep-seated emotion. Everyone around him at the time cried, including Admiral Hoshino. For here the Emperor was showing his sadness, his sympathy for all Japan. From Admiral Hoshino's vantage point, the poem seemed to be a vision of a new Japan rising from the ashes of the old—a "triumphant shout," throwing off the fetters.

So five days before the surrender Hirohito was already framing the construction of a new Japan. Never before in his reign had the issues been so clear.

Now, on the night of August 14, Admiral Hoshino saw his Emperor sitting there, and Hoshino's heart was moved. He could see that Hirohito was fully aware of the importance of the decision he had made, and of its consequences to Japan and to the world.

The decision was made official on this night. The generals sat at the long tables, apparently impassive, although their world of army authority had suddenly come to an end.

Immediately after the conference, the emperor sent Jiju Hasunuma, his military aide, to see the chief of the military affairs bureau of the army. He also sent a message to imperial headquarters. He was prescient enough to know from where the trouble would come; he cautioned the army and navy leaders not to cause any difficulty or try to subvert the decision to end the war. Specifically, he ominously warned the imperial headquarters that if there were trouble, "we will most certainly hear of it and we will do something drastic about it."

Admiral Hoshino heard the rest later. The chief of the military affairs bureau of the army and the other leaders of both services had decided to accede to the Emperor's demands.

When the admiral visited the U.S. naval high command, he learned that at the time of the surrender the Americans were strongly in favor of forcing the dethronement of the Emperor, holding him equally responsible for the war, with the generals. That attitude hung dormant in some American quarters for nearly half a century, and gained new life in 1988 as the Emperor lay dying. The Americans and some Britons still did not realize how tight were the bonds that tied Hirohito to the military oligarchy, or how he had burst these bonds, four days before he managed to manipulate events to bring off the surrender.

A recording was made that night of the speech the Emperor would make at noon the next day to the Japanese people. As will be described later in the book, a number of ardent young officers tried to rebel and take over the government, but were put down. The next day at noon, the Emperor's broadcast announcing the surrender was made to the nation and to the world.

2

Perfect Harmony

昭和 Showa! These two Japanese characters together mean "perfect harmony." It is one of the ironies of history that an era conceived in the search for tranquillity and enlightenment should have turned into one of the bloodiest and most volatile periods in world history. But that is what happened.

In 1926 Showa was the name chosen by the young Emperor Hirohito's counsellors to signify his reign, in the Japanese fashion of offering promise for the new era. The name was not the first choice; the first choice of the counsellors was Kobun, which means "brilliant light and literary accomplishment." But when someone close to the Imperial Palace leaked the name of the new era to *Mainichi Shimbun*, the big national newspaper, the counsellors were aghast. It would be a most unpropitious beginning, a real cultural disaster, to muddy the prospects of the Emperor's reign with publicity. So an emergency meeting of the counsellors burned the midnight lamps, and next day a different name for the era was announced, much to the chagrin of the editors of *Mainichi*.

Showa.* The prospects seemed bright for the future of a young emperor who wanted to model his historical period on the grace of the British Empire, who wanted to be a constitutional monarch, who reigned, but did not rule.

For a short time, from 1926 to 1929, the name seemed completely appropriate. The world was prosperous and at peace. Japan, for once, seemed to be at one with its neighbors and with the superpowers of the sea, Britain and the United States. But at the end of 1929 all that changed. The moving force was the international depression and mon-

---

*Showa also means peace, reconciliation, and unity.

etary collapse, which brought down Japan's fragile economy and led to one national crisis after another. In the search for a remedy, the military, already dissatisfied because of the series of cutbacks and repressions in the post–World War I years, found an opportunity to make a drive for power. Within two years the vision of a halcyon Japan, something perhaps out of the pages of Gilbert and Sullivan, had been replaced with a fierce warrior mask that was synonymous with aggression abroad and repression at home. With the lightning conquest of Manchuria, Japan was on her way to power and then ignominy.

Then, twenty years after the opening of the Hirohito era, the world changed once again. For the first time in history, Japan was totally subjugated. The Imperial Way was completely changed. Hirohito, who had ascended to godhood in the 1930s, was reduced to being an ordinary citizen who took his wife to baseball games. It appeared then that the Showa era might well mark the end of Japanese empire.

But as twenty more years passed, Japan began her economic "miracle." Her industry, much of which had been destroyed by the Americans, was completely rebuilt—ironically, by those same Americans. They supplied the capital, and the Japanese supplied the brains and the initiative and the slogging work. Japan emerged with the most modern industrial plant in the world. At this point Japan was challenged, not by the Americans, but by the West Germans, who were also basking in the aftermath of total military defeat at the hands of a generous enemy.

In the 1970s, in virtually every industrial field—steel, autos, appliances, electronics—the Japanese began to challenge the world, and Showa came to symbolize a new economic aggressiveness. The old *zaibatsu*, the wealth combine or trust of the 1930s, became the *zaikai*, which means world of wealth. The zaikai of Japan are a hundred times more powerful than the old *zaibatsu*. In the 1980s Japan emerged as the most important industrial power in the world, challenging in every way a faltering United States.

By the 1980s Japan had become banker to the world, thus buttressing her own economic power. In 1988, of the ten most powerful banks in the world, two were American, one was British, one French, and six Japanese—owned, controlled, and allied with the *zaikai*.

But the challenge of the 1980s was very different from that of the 1940s. There was no open aggression, no military muscle shown except under the mantle of "defense." The "defense" combine of the Pacific, obviously aimed at the Soviet Union, was an alliance of the United States, Australia, and Japan, with New Zealand relegating itself to an independent role, as France had already done in Europe. China voiced concern that Japanese economic power was being buttressed by a growing military power, pushed on the Japanese people by a government essentially under the control of the same elements that had controlled Japan for a hundred years. And these were the elements that had given rise to the militarism of the 1930s.

To understand the story of Showa, the reign of Emperor Hirohito, and secure a glimpse of the future of Japan under Akihito, Hirohito's eldest son, one must study the emergence of modern Japan. The Japan of the 1850s was a truly feudal society. Since the seventeenth century the shogun had sat in Edo (now Tokyo), in a great palace behind a moat near the city that is now Yokohama. Meanwhile, a succession of emperors lived in the historic capital of Kyoto, where they and their court dallied and wrote poetry and considered the universe, while the shogun in Edo wielded military power and maintained order in the country. Japan then was divided into great fiefs, and the barons, or *daimyo*, owed their allegiance to the shogun, but only piety to the Emperor. Each daimyo maintained his power in the barony through the *samurai*, or warrior class, with each samurai pledging his loyalty to some lord, who in turn provided the samurai with a good living.

Contact between Japan and the outside world was held to a minimum; all foreigners except a handful of missionaries were relegated to Dejina, an island off the port city of Nagasaki, which is on the island of Kyushu—far from the source of power, Edo, on the Kanto plain of central Honshu Island.

In the days of Edo, every aspect of Japan's technology was primitive. Literature and art flourished at Kyoto, but to get there from Edo one took the Tokkaido road, which winds along the coastal plain, traveling by horse, palanquin, or ricksha or on foot, at considerable danger from the marauding bands of *ronin*, or masterless samurai, and highwaymen who preyed upon the travelers. There was no electricity, no gas. If one had to go out at night, which was always dangerous, one lighted one's way with a paper lantern. On the road the traveler passed samurai, always girt with swords and daggers, and if a traveler offended a samurai, perhaps by failing to get out of his way as he rode or strode forward, the warrior might draw his sword and cut the offender down and leave the corpse in the roadway.

The samurai concept—*bushido*, or the code of the knights—demanded absolute loyalty of the samurai to his master, to the point of death. When a daimyo died, some or all of his samurai might commit ritual suicide. Their code called for the samurai to live with constant thought of death.

They rose every morning with the idea that they might not survive the day. This is important because it explains much about modern Japan. The code of bushido was abandoned under the rule of the Meiji Emperor, but it lingered in the hearts of the members of the warrior class, who became the modern generals and admirals, and ultimately it was restored to honor in the 1930s by the militarists, for purposes of their own.

Although the whole idea of bushido and ritual suicide was again apparently abandoned by the modern Japan established under the U.S. occupation of the late 1940s, it still has adherents. In 1957, when President Dwight D. Eisenhower planned a trip to Japan, despite a wave of anti-Americanism brought on by the Japanese American defense alliance plans, Prime Minister Nobusuke Kishi demanded that Eisenhower abandon the trip. When Secretary of State John Foster Dulles indicated that this was not feasible or desirable, Kishi warned him that if Eisenhower did come to Japan, he, the prime minister, would commit ritual suicide. The Eisenhower trip was abandoned.

A few years later, popular novelist Yukio Mishima did commit suicide, standing on a portico overlooking the new fountainhead of Japan's military power, the euphemistically named Self-Defense Agency. Mishima's suicide was in protest against the abandonment of the old values of bushido by government and society. He cut his belly, and was assisted in the time-honored way by a follower who made sure that the ritual was completed.

Mishima was a misfit, a bisexual, and a cultist. Yet his followers are powerful enough to have prohibited the showing in Japan of a motion picture of Mishima's life made by a French producer. They did this by threatening to burn down any theater that showed the film.

Other extremists have contained several books that were unfavorable studies of the growing Japanese defense effort; the extremists threatened to burn the publishing houses and perhaps murder the publishers. Thus, anyone who would consider the life and times of Emperor Hirohito must bear in mind that the old ways of Japan still lurk dangerously in the background.

In the middle of the nineteenth century Japan was a small and mysterious nation, a cluster of islands lying on the edge of the Pacific Ocean, just close enough to China to have aroused the cupidity of the Mongol emperors, but with a population so fiercely independent that two Chinese attempts at conquest had failed. So the Japanese had been left to go their own way for five hundred years.

The government was a dictatorship operating under a shogun, or general, in the name of an emperor who had no direct power. The shogun was Iesada Tokugawa. Like the other Tokugawa shoguns, who had ruled by inheritance since 1603, Iesada ruled over the Japanese home islands of Honshu, Kyushu, Shikoku, and Hokkaido, and also over the Tsushima Islands and the Ryukyus, of which the most important was Okinawa. The population of Japan was approximately twenty-seven million, kept more or less stable by a series of famines that struck the country in the seventeenth and eighteenth centuries. As we have seen, the center of government, where the shogun ruled in his palace behind a huge moat, was Edo, and the cultural capital, where the Emperor lived, was Kyoto.

Foreigners, and particularly Westerners, were discouraged from visiting Japan and almost invariably were imprisoned and mistreated if they washed up on the Japanese shores. The single exception to this rule existed at Nagasaki, where trade was permitted. But the traders were confined to Dejina in Nagasaki harbor, and needed shogunal permission even to make a trip to Edo.

Jesuit and Franciscan missionaries from Portugal and Spain had been permitted into Japan in the sixteenth and seventeenth centuries, but the missionaries had annoyed the Tokugawas, who had then proceeded to stamp out Christianity in the islands. The first move was the crucifixion of six Franciscan priests in 1597; the last was the slaughter of the last remaining Christians in the castle at Shimabara in the middle of the seventeenth century. In all some 280,000 Japanese Christians were killed or driven into exile. At Shimabara the struggle also had political overtones. Masuka Tokisada, an enemy of the Tokugawa clan, gathered 33,000 Christians in the castle of Amakusa and prepared to resist the shogunate. They did resist, very successfully, until the shogunate persuaded the Dutch to send warships and cannon to batter down the castle wall. The shogun's troops swarmed in, massacred all the Christians, and forced any who denied that they were Christian to trample on images of Christ and the Virgin Mary. Thereafter the Christians were hunted down, and killed or forced to swear that they were Buddhists.

The expulsion of the Christians was part of the antiforeign sentiment which developed in Japan in the sixteenth century. At first the Westerners had been so generally welcomed that the lord of Omura granted the Jesuits title to the port of Nagasaki. But in the wars between the powerful nobles, the Westerners changed the Japanese attitude.

Furthermore, a new element entered the picture. The shogun Ieyasu Tokugawa died in 1616, and his successor, Hidetada, was persuaded to espouse Buddhism, newly brought over from China. The native Japanese religionists, the Shinto priests, did not approve, but some of them joined the Buddhists and the others came to an accommodation with them. They agreed on one matter: the other foreign religions must be driven out of Japan. Soon this attitude moved beyond religion, to be applied to every kind of foreign influence.

Foreigners had been trading at various ports, but by 1639 all foreigners except the Chinese and Dutch were expelled, and the Chinese and Dutch traders were confined to Nagasaki. Thirty Chinese ships and two Dutch ships each year were authorized to bring in merchandise.

In the beginning of the nineteenth century, however, winds of change were blowing in Japan. The major factor of change was an increasing spread of educational opportunity. Until the middle of the eighteenth century, education had been the prerogative of the upper classes. But at the end of that century the seignorial schools began to open their doors to some people of lower rank than the samurai. Also, as the number of daimyo decreased in a sort of centralization of power, more of the *ronin* were thrown into living by their wits. Since the samurai had been prohibited from engaging in business or agriculture and had only the occupations of soldier, scholar, and priest to sustain them, to support themselves the samurai began exposing the children of well-to-do peasants to education.

Also, as the nineteenth century began, Japan found herself ever more pestered by foreigners. The waters off Japan were important whaling grounds, and as Western shipmasters discovered this, they began to poke around the edges of Japan. In the 1820s the shogunate became so concerned over unauthorized landings that the masters of the coastal forts were instructed to fire without warning on any foreign ships that approached the shore. So the period 1825–50 was notable for the strong efforts of the Europeans and Americans to penetrate the wall of Japan, and the equally strong efforts of the Japanese government to keep them out.

Nagasaki was the key. The Dutch were the only Europeans popular with the shogunate, because of the incident at Shimabara and because during the rebellions of the peasants in the eighteenth century the Dutch had fought the revolutionaries. So they alone among Europeans were welcomed to Nagasaki. They strengthened their position by making much of the fact that they were Protestants, not Catholics, as if this were some different sort of religion. The shoguns were not really fooled, however; they kept a constant vigilance to prevent foreign religion from contaminating the Japanese people and forbade any foreign religious services, but they tolerated the presence of the Dutch. So Dutch scholars and some others came to Nagasaki, and soon had Japanese students who wanted to learn medicine and other skills of the West.

A Bavarian surgeon named Philip Siebold passed himself off as a Dutchman and was allowed to open a school at Nagasaki. He was expelled when the governor of Nagasaki learned that Siebold possessed a detailed map of all Japan.

In the 1820s every European nation was trying to pry loose the lid that enclosed Japan. The French, the British, the Russians were all on the move, and so were the Americans. As early as the 1820s American whalers appeared off the Japanese coast. Inevitably some of them were wrecked and the sailors swam ashore, where they were always imprisoned.

This was a period in which U.S. naval policy was very strong, under the principal later enunciated by Commander Alfred Thayer Mahan: "Trade follows the flag." So in 1846, with the knowledge that a number of American sailors were moldering in Japanese prisons, Commodore James Biddle was sent with two warships to get them out and stop this practice. He anchored his two warships in what is now called Tokyo Bay. The Japanese came to protest and tell him to go around to Nagasaki where he belonged. They sent a boat to the flagship, and Commodore Biddle magnanimously got down into it to go ashore. He was pushed by a Japanese sailor, and, instead of killing the miscreant, Biddle smiled.

Ah, said the Japanese, another effete Westerner. And so Commodore Biddle's mission failed.

Two years later the prisoners were still in jail. Captain James Glynn was sent out in the ship *Preble* to free them. He, too, came into Tokyo Bay. From the Biddle incident, the Japanese thought they knew how to deal with Americans. They sent several junks full of armed samurai and threatened Captain Glynn. But the captain looked them in the eye and kept the guns trained and the shot and powder ready. One false move, he announced, and the junks would be blown out of the water.

This was the sort of talk the Japanese could understand. Masahiro Abe, the minister of the shogunate entrusted with coastal defense, had refused to deal with Biddle. But Abe had dealt with the French after they had bombarded one of his ports, and now Captain Glynn was reminding him of hard times. So Minister Abe reported to the palace, the shogun ordered the American prisoners brought to the *Preble*, and Glynn sailed away triumphantly.

When Captain Glynn reached America, the news of his success was soon broadcast, and it found several welcoming audiences. The business and shipping communities were eager for trade, since they were already sampling the advantages of the China trade. The Protestant missionaries, who had also been meeting with success in China and elsewhere in Asia, were eager to get their tentacles around Japan. The sprouting scientific community was also eager to learn about these hidden islands. The U.S. Navy was just moving into the age of steam and competing for coaling stations in the Pacific with the navies of Britain, France, Germany, and Russia. All America, it seemed, had some stake in the development of Japan. Soon Congress was discussing the idea.

In America in the twentieth century the name of President Millard Fillmore tends to evoke laughter and the thought, What did he ever do? But Professor William E. Griffis, a contemporary who later devoted his career to the study of Japan, ascribes to Fillmore the impetus for the Japan expedition. "Perhaps of all Americans," says Griffis, "Fillmore enjoys the highest share of honor in winning the Japanese to fraternity."

The American concept was that "the sun goddess had sulked in the cave long enough" and that it was now time for the Japanese to become god-fearing Christians and for Japan to be a source of coal and a base for U.S. warships, and a source of raw materials and a market for American manufactures.

One of the major obligations of the Dutch, in order to maintain their most-favored-nation status in Japan, was to report regularly to the shogunate about developments in the West that might affect Japan. So the word went to Edo that the Americans were talking about mounting a major naval expedition to Japan. Commodore Matthew Calbraith Perry would bring a fleet of ships. They were loading up not only shot and shell, but also a railway and a locomotive, telegraph wires and machinery, ploughs, tools, sewing machines, keys, locks, lamps, and a hundred other American products.

The shogun ordered Minister Abe to strengthen his forts, and extra resources were devoted to the development of weaponry to try to produce defense weapons that could repel the Western warships. But by 1853 the Japanese had still not been able to produce guns that could sink ships. This failure did much within the circle of advisors to the shogun to further the American cause. Such men as Lord Hatta saw that Japan would have to learn from the Western world, and learn quickly, if Japan were not to become a vassal to the West as had Asian nations all around it.

When Commodore Perry arrived, he played his diplomatic and military cards well. He kept to his cabin and was soon known as "the high and mighty mysteriousness." He refused to meet or even be seen by any lesser figure than the governor of Uraga, the port city for Edo. The Japanese were even more impressed when Perry let it be known that he had letters from President Fillmore for the ruler of Japan. And so the letters were delivered to the shogun, and it was arranged that Perry would return the following spring for the answers.

The departure of the Americans started a Japanese colloquy. How was this foreign invasion to be met? The shogun's advisors split into two camps. The first camp, joined by the supporters of Hirohito's ancestor, the Emperor Komei at Kyoto, said the foreign invasion must be repelled. The second camp believed that the foreign invasion must be accepted. And within this group were those who wisely cautioned that while accepting foreign overtures, the Japanese must never loosen their control of Japan. They must control the instruments of change. This caution ultimately prevented Japan from going the way of China and India. The forces of change secured a working consensus for the moment, and the Japanese presented a more or less united front to the Westerners.

The Americans came back in February 1854, with nine "black ships," which impressed the Japanese. A treaty of friendship was worked out, but only with much pain. The Japanese were careful with every clause, including such apparently simple matters as control of the movement of the foreigners, who, it was decided, could go inland a distance of seven *ri*, or Japanese miles, which was the distance a man could reach and return to home in a day of walking.

Commodore Perry sailed away, but two years later, on August 21, 1856, Townsend Harris arrived with papers that proclaimed him to be the U.S. Consul General to Japan. He took up residence in an abandoned Shinto temple near Shimoda. A flagstaff was set up in the temple yard, and on September 4, 1856, the U.S. flag was run up the pole to proclaim the U.S. presence. That presence would continue without interruption until December 8, 1941.

Within the year Consul Harris had negotiated a new treaty. Nagasaki was to be opened to U.S. ships. U.S. citizens would have extraterritoriality—would be under the legal control of their own consuls—and a rate of exchange for U.S. and Japanese currency was fixed. Soon Harris was invited to visit the shogun at Edo, and he traveled in great style along the Tokkaido road, past Hakone to Odawara on the other side of the pass. Then it was on to Kanazawa and across the bay to Yokohama. There Harris saw three ships in the harbor. At first, because of the design, he thought they were European ships. And he was right in a sense, because these were three vessels that the Japanese had just bought from the Dutch. The shogun was taking the advice of his moderate ministers; the new ships were the nucleus of a Japanese navy. So as Townsend

Harris came to the shogun's castle in Edo, he was moving in a Japan that had just entered the nineteenth century and was now going to try to catch up with Europe and America.

This was an attitude unprecedented anywhere in Asia, an attitude that would shape Japan and have a profound effect upon the world.

3

Emperor Meiji: A Modern Man

To understand Emperor Hirohito and modern Japan, one must also be familiar with the life of his grandfather, the Emperor Meiji, and the tradition that Meiji established for the Japanese Empire.

In the fifth year of his reign, 1871, the Emperor Meiji undertook the establishment of an entirely new military system. Until this time, the old daimyo-samurai relationships had continued and the strength of the military had remained localized, with the central authority maintaining power by cultivating the warlords. But Meiji wanted to change all that, and his advisors advocated the establishment of a Western-style military system. Looking to Europe, the Japanese were taken by the snap and efficiency of the Prussian army and so decided to model their land forces on the German. For a model for their navy, they turned to England.

Since the 1850s the Japanese empire had been in ferment. The Emperor still lived at Kyoto, but now the imperial forces challenged the shogun, at Edo, and the shogun's government, called the Bakufu. The challenge was assisted by the shogun's internal troubles.

In 1863, angered by a series of attacks on foreigners, the British Far Eastern Fleet had sent a squadron to Tokyo Bay, and seven ships went off on an expedition against the region of Satsuma, where much of the trouble had originated. Satsuma was concentrated around Kagoshima, at the extreme southern end of the island of Kyushu. On August 15 the British attacked Satsuma, which responded with cannon fire. About sixty Englishmen were lost in this battle, and many more Japanese. The British gunfire also caused about a third of Kagoshima to burn. As a result the Satsuma leaders promised good behavior toward foreigners and began to allow direct contact between the people of Satsuma and the British.

By this time, 1863, the Japanese xenophobia had begun to subside. The center of antiforeignism had then devolved to the Choshu clan. In August 1864, the Choshu burned Kyoto, in a factional dispute. The fire lasted for three days and burned up 27,000 houses and 250 temples. During the struggle a shell fell on the grounds of the Imperial Palace, terrifying young Prince Meiji.

This was the period during which the British, French, and Americans were all intervening in Japanese affairs, and the period to which Emperor Hirohito referred in his speech on that fateful August 14, 1945, as he was discussing the good or evil that might come from renewed foreign intervention in Japanese affairs.

The Choshu were put down by a British, French, Dutch, and American coalition at the Battle of Shimonoseki in September 1864. The foreign intervention continued for another few years. The Emperor Komei died from smallpox in January 1867, and the Emperor Meiji was enthroned on February 13, 1867. He was only 14 years old, so obviously the reins of power were actually in other hands.

At Tokyo the last shogun was still in control, although his power was slight and heavily buttressed by foreigners, particularly the French. Shogun Yoshinobu was turning more and more to the West. French instructors came to the area in the spring of 1867 to open a school of infantry, cavalry, and artillery. By the end of that year the Bakufu army numbered 12,000 infantry trained in modern warfare, French style, plus four regiments of artillery and one of cavalry.

In January 1868, all the cross-currents of Japanese politics met at Kyoto, and in the resulting whirlpools a civil war was born. The Emperor's following raised an army. By the end of that month the armies of the imperial government at Kyoto were pursuing the former shogun's forces, and General Takamori Saigo marched to Tokyo and took control. The palace at Tokyo was occupied, and in April the last vestiges of shogunal power were eradicated. But by summer, three of the old lordly domains in the north declared themselves independent of the Meiji government, and the civil war, known as the Boshin War, became intense. In all this period the foreigners took sides and interfered shamelessly in Japanese affairs. In May 1869 power was transferred to Tokyo, and the Emperor Meiji moved there to rule as the war continued.

In 1871 a new imperial army of 10,000 men was created, in a reform program that touched every aspect of government. A new financial policy established as the currency unit, the yen, with a gold content of 1.5 grams, or the equivalent of one U.S. dollar.

These reforms were carried out in the Emperor's name, but he was still only 16 years old, and power was in the hands of his advisory council, a loose coalition of reform-minded nobles who had recognized the need to swallow or be swallowed and were bent on adopting Western ways.

By impressing on the young Emperor Meiji the need to consult his advisors before taking any action, these nobles established the system under which the modern emperors would reign, but not rule. Their representatives were traveling all over the West, taking notes on everything that could be transposed to Japan, and they were preparing the Meiji Constitution, which would assure the control of Japan by their oligarchy. The instrument was to be the Emperor.

Military conscription in Japan began in 1872, and this marked the end of the hereditary professional soldier. In 1873 the Japanese adopted the Western-style calendar. Western-style education also came into effect, with schools of languages, industry, sciences, law, arts, and medicine. The roots of Tokyo Imperial University were planted then.

This year, 1873, was a year of transition. Several of the older ministers resigned in a policy dispute and were replaced by modern young men with an eye on the Western world. Between 1873 and 1878 most of the vestiges of feudalism in Japan were wiped out. One of the unifying factors was the Japanese army expedition against Formosa, led by General Takamori Saigo, in May 1874. From this expedition Japan secured unquestioned control of the Ryukyu Islands (Okinawa). But, back in Japan, Saigo fell out with the other leaders, and in 1876 he led a rebellion that ran like wildfire across Kyushu Island. Ultimately the rebellion was suppressed, and Saigo committed suicide in September 1877. That was the end of any sort of resistance against the Meiji government. The country was truly unified.

Reforms continued year after year. In 1889 what seemed to be a Western-style constitution was promulgated. It had one major difference with liberal Western constitutions, however: the Emperor was head of state, but he was also actively commander in chief of the armed forces, and the military leaders did not have to report to him through government channels. Every general had guaranteed access to the Emperor. This was done to keep control of the defense forces out of the hands of the politicians. Japan was to experiment with political democracy for the first time, and the oligarchy distrusted the process. Therefore several safeguards were built into the constitution.

The legislative branch of government consisted of two houses; the House of Peers, filled with princes, marquises, counts, and barons; and the Chamber of Deputies, which was chosen by electors who paid a tax of 15 yen or more. In the Chamber of Deputies, the Liberal Party (ancestor of the present Democratic-Liberal Party, which rules Japan) obtained 127 of the 300 seats. By the standards of the day the Liberal Party was an opposition party, but together with the Progressive Party, which had won 44 seats, it was able to control the lower house and oppose the government. But no party could bring down the government, because the Emperor was an absolute power. This unique characteristic of Japanese government would persist into the reign of Emperor Hirohito.

The 15-yen tax on voters meant that the poor had no part in Japanese government. Meanwhile the control of Japan's economy had passed from the baronial class into the hands of the old rice merchant families, the Mitsui and Mitsubishi, and other wealthy trading families, for example the Sumitomo and Yasuda. These were forming themselves into the great cartels governing banking, producing, and distributing goods and services, each cartel virtually an empire unto itself, and altogether becoming known as the *zaibatsu*.

Socially, Japan was going through every sort of convulsion. The old samurai robes were exchanged for trousers (sometimes worn underneath the robes), and Western jackets and belts (sometimes worn over the robes). The short and long sword of the samurai persisted up to the end of the life of that class. Boots replaced sandals among the military, but not among the coolies who carried the palanquins and drew the rickshas along the rutted and often muddy roads.

The court ladies loosened their hair and then began to adopt Western clothes. A photograph from 1885 shows two Japanese ladies dressed in the height of fashion. Except for their oriental physiognomies they might have been ladies of London or New York, in their black taffeta evening gowns with white cuffs and collars, high black boots, and perky hats. These ladies represented the craze of Western fashion consciousness that swept across Tokyo. A young Kobe lady of this period was photographed in white silk, with a waist cinched up by whalebone corsets and a great bustle behind. To show even the silhouette of her figure was very unJapanese, but also very stylish. This was a major social dilemma of the period. For in reality, after the festive occasion, the ladies would go home to their wooden houses with the sliding screens and straw floor mats, change into comfortable kimonos, and sit on the floor.

All Japan was changing. Huge mills were going up to turn silk and cotton threads into cloth. The cloth-factory work force was almost entirely female. Men worked in the shipyards that were organized and built to produce vessels for the new Japanese navy, vessels that were themselves undergoing the world transition from sail to steam, with some odd structural changes—carrying both sail and a tall smokestack. Other shipyards were turning out merchant ships, as Japan began building her own fleet.

The Emperor's priorities were clear. The photograph of him that he particularly favored showed him in the uniform of a general, with gold braid, medals, and sashes, holding a ceremonial sword of the Western variety.

In every way the Japanese court of the late nineteenth century was a Westernized court. The new Imperial Palace, in the old shogun's castle behind the moat, was spruced up in Western style. The public rooms were lavish: parquet floors; plush settees, which an ordinary Japanese would have to strain to sit on; enormous chandeliers, Western chairs and tables. The table in the state dining room would seat eighty in Western style. Gas streetlights came to Tokyo and then began to give way to electricity, and in the 1890s the telephone came along. But beneath the Western facade Japan was still Japanese. Workmen stripped down to their loincloths as they worked on the streets with pick and shovel. The ladies on the streets were almost always in kimonos, clopping along on their wooden *geta*, and the men standing on the street corners smoked cigarettes and wore derby hats, but retained their traditional kimonos.

In 1890, a year after the promulgation of the new constitution, a very intelligent Japanese government revised its codes of law to meet the standards of Western nations, thus eliminating any excuse for extraterritoriality. Japan then was the only nation in Asia that could meet the foreigners on their own ground and control their activities inside its borders. This took almost a decade to achieve, but it was done.

The middle of the 1890s was marked by the Sino-Japanese war (1894–95), which was really a struggle for control of Korea, but when Japan won the war, the Treaty of Shimonoseki gave Japan control of Taiwan and the Liaotung Peninsula of China. The big prize was the Chinese agreement to "full independence" for Korea, which made that kingdom ripe for further Japanese expansion. The one problem here was the ambition of the Russians, who desperately wanted a warm-water port below their Siberian line, and had expected to have it on the east coast of Korea. The Russians had been exploiting Korean resources, which the Japanese also coveted. By 1896 the struggle for Korea was reaching a critical stage.

Japan continued to progress. By 1900 fast trains were rushing along the Kanto plain in the shadow of Mount Fuji, and the internal communications system was becoming thoroughly modernized. By 1910 the whole country was crisscrossed by rail lines, the weakest area being the north shore of Honshu Island, which was cut off from the south shore by high mountain ranges. The rivers were being dammed, and an extensive hydroelectric system was being built.

By 1903 Japan had built her modern military and naval machines and was ready to test them. The opportunity came in Korea and Manchuria, where the Russians insisted on trying to take control of resources Japan wanted. The Russo-Japanese war broke out with a lightning unannounced attack by the Japanese fleet on the Russian fleet at Port Arthur. The result of this war was Japan's emergence as the major power in Asia, with control of Korea and a major foothold in Manchuria. The men around the Meiji Emperor had set out to make Japan a Western-type power, and now they had an empire.

For one so active, the Meiji Emperor was most unfortunate in his children. His son, Crown Prince Yoshihito, was not strong, either physically or mentally. But such failings could not be admitted in a kingdom that traced its lineage back nearly six thousand years, and so they were ignored. On May 10, 1900, Prince Yoshihito was married to Princess Sadako, of an affiliated noble line, and just about a year later (April 29, 1901), Prince Hirohito was born, one of three sons born to the Crown Prince and his princess.

4

Hirohito Enters

A photograph of the royal family of Japan taken in 1903 shows a re-markable resemblance between the grandfather, Emperor Meiji, with his long jaw, black Van Dyke beard, and bushy eyebrows, and his son, the Crown Prince and later the Taisho Emperor, sporting a mustache like his father's but no beard. The 2-year-old Prince Hirohito, whose nose even then bore the distinguishing mark of the family line, also had eyebrows that were bushy for a 2-year-old. He was dressed for the occasion in the high-necked court uniform of the day, replete with gold braid, gold buttons, and gold epaulets.

Hirohito's childhood was not like those of most children. He was taken from his mother when he was 3 months old, to protect him from the social contacts of life at the Akasaka Palace, where the Crown Prince kept court and where colds and fevers were common. Hirohito was turned over for his early years to Count Sumiyoshi Kawamura, who was also a vice admiral in the Imperial Navy. In the Kawamura household the new heir was allowed to grow up as normally as possible, and playmates were brought into the household for him.

Neither the count nor the Crown Prince nor the Emperor Meiji had a great deal of time to bestow on the little boy. The Russo-Japanese war came in 1904, and although the Japanese triumphed on land and sea, the cost in lives and resources very nearly bankrupted Japan. The army and navy officers were confident that victory would restore the imperial finances through cash reparations levied on the former enemy, but the U.S. president, Theodore Roosevelt, stepped in at the drafting of the Treaty of Portsmouth and balked the Japanese. That act created a definite anti-American feeling in Japan, and also a dilemma for the Japanese government. How was it to finance its military expansion? The fact was that this could not be done, and therefore the expansion had to slow down.

In 1905 Prince Hirohito and his two younger brothers, Prince Chichibu and Prince Takamatsu, were moved back to the Akasaka Palace, where they were installed in quarters of their own. They seldom saw their father, the Crown Prince, who was enormously busy with his concubines, and they saw their mother only once a week. Theoretically they had play-mates; several children of court officials were brought to their quarters every day, but actually Hirohito was almost never out of the sight of his adult supervisors. The other princes were allowed to do pretty well as they liked, but not Hirohito. If he wanted to play rough games, he was restrained by his guardians.

Hirohito was a slight boy, and although no one knew it at the time, he was extremely nearsighted. Therefore he gained a reputation among the other boys as being unnecessarily timid, though this was really not quite the case. Even as a small boy he was forever being reminded that one day he would be the Emperor, and that he must always comport himself in a seemly fashion. It was a very hard life for a 6-year-old boy, and Hirohito began to learn the art of masking his emotions using *enryo*, the Japanese system of self-restraint, under which a show of emotion of any sort is frowned upon. An Emperor, of course, must be above human emotion, Hirohito was told by his adult guardians.

When Prince Hirohito was 7 years old he was enrolled in the Gaku-shuin, the peers' school, with a dozen other boys, all of them from the Japanese aristocracy. The school was run by Count Maresuke Nogi, a hero of the Bosshin War against the followers of the late Tokugawa shogun. Nogi had enjoyed a distinguished military career (he was the general who had captured Port Arthur in the Russo-Japanese war) and was now retired from military service.

From the Emperor Meiji's point of view, Count Nogi was the epitome of the teacher. He had been raised in the system of bushido, the way of the warrior, and was steeped in reverence for things military. To understand the apparently mild Hirohito, one has to understand his reverence for this particular teacher, who became a father figure to him.

Every morning the boys of the school assembled before Count Nogi. First they bowed toward the Imperial Palace for sixty seconds in reverence to the Emperor Meiji. Then they repeated the Imperial Rescript on Education, which every schoolboy in Japan was forced to commit to memory.

Know ye, our good and faithful subjects: Our Imperial Ancestors have founded our empire on a broad and everlasting basis, and have deeply and firmly implanted virtue in it. Our subjects, ever united in loyalty and filial piety, have from generation to generation illustrated the beauty of it. This is the glory of the basic character of Our Empire, and here lies also the source of our education.

You, our subjects, be faithful to your parents, affectionate to your siblings; as husbands and wives be harmonious; as friends, true; bear yourselves in honesty and moderation; extend your benevolence to all; pursue learning and cultivate the arts; and thereby cultivate also intellectual faculties and perfect moral bearing; furthermore advance the public good and promote the common interests; always respect the Constitution and observe the laws; should emergency arise, courageously offer yourselves to the State, and thus guard and maintain the prosperity of Our Imperial Throne equal to heaven and earth. So shall you not only be our good and faithful subjects, but render illustrious the best traditions of your ancestors. The Way here set forth is the teaching bequeathed by Our Imperial Ancestors to be observed by their descendants and the subjects of the realm, infallible for all ages and true to all places. It is Our wish to lay in your hearts in all reverence in common with you, Our subjects, that we must all thus attain the same virtues.

After that the boys all sang "Kimigayo," the national anthem, then repeated a little litany provided by the count. "What is your dearest ambition?" he would ask.

And the boys would reply in chorus, "To die for the Emperor."

Thus was Hirohito, who one day would be Emperor himself, instructed in the Imperial Way.

In 1912 the Emperor Meiji died. Count Nogi then proved the strength of his convictions. He and his wife sat down on cushions at the low table of their Japanese house. They shared a ceremonial cup of sake, and then the count stabbed his wife to death with a dagger and disemboweled himself with his short samurai sword. Thus did he prove to all the world that he believed what he had been drilling into his young students.

When Prince Hirohito learned the news, he was not particularly surprised, because the evening before, the count had called him to a meeting and for three hours had reviewed all that he had taught the boy, and then had given him a kind of benediction by saying he was not displeased with what Hirohito had learned at his hand. It had been apparent that this was a parting, and so when the news came that the count was dead, Hirohito did not bat an eyelash. The count would have been proud of his restraint.

Hirohito, now the Crown Prince, continued to study at the Gakushuin. He was a good scholar but not much of a talker. He grew lanky and awkward, and this made him shy. Other teachers replaced Count

Nogi. Hirohito saw his father only on ceremonial occasions; he had seen his grandfather practically never. The young prince's whole life was contained in the wing of the Akasaka Palace where the school was kept. He was being groomed for the lonely life of the Emperor.

Hirohito had been 11 years old when his grandfather died and his father Yoshihito became Emperor. It was apparent that Yoshihito, now the Emperor Taisho, would not live a long life. He was subject to fits of melancholy, and to lapses of memory. He preferred the company of his concubines to that of his wife, and spent much of his time sequestered in his apartment. The members of the oligarchy who ran the government behind the scenes began to pay more attention to the grooming of the young Crown Prince.

Two years after the death of the Meiji Emperor, Prince Hirohito moved into his own quarters in a wing of the Akasaka Palace. His father celebrated the change by sending Hirohito one of his personal concubines, but the boy was not interested. Somewhere in the educational process Hirohito had developed a distaste for the ways of his father and grandfather, both mighty drinkers and womanizers. Hirohito preferred a book to a girl.

The palace advisors decided that Hirohito needed toughening, so they appointed as his tutor Admiral Heihachiro Togo, the hero of the Russo-Japanese war. The admiral was disappointed in his pupil, for although he tried to inculcate a deep respect for things military and naval, even he sensed that the Crown Prince was really not interested. But every attempt was made to harden Prince Hirohito. He was roused at 6:00 in the morning and sent to his prayers at the little private shrine. After he had prayed for the health of the Emperor, he ran around the palace grounds, then ate a breakfast of unpolished rice. After that came his lessons, which lasted from 7:30 in the morning until 6:00 in the evening, with only a half-hour break for lunch at noon.

Hirohito studied history, mathematics, ethics, science, geography, and literature, both in Japanese and in the Chinese from which it stemmed. He gained an immense knowledge of poetry and was no mean poet himself, master of an art revered in Japan. He also learned natural history, French, law, and the history of fine art. And above all he had physical training.

Physical culture became one of his major interests, along with science and natural history. Soon enough he abandoned many of the other studies. One day, during his class in Japanese history, he told the tutor that he did not believe in the divinity of the Emperor. The tutor was shocked and reported to the Imperial Palace, where the grand chamberlain told Hirohito's father the story. The Emperor called on one of his most trusted advisors, Prince Kimmochi Saionji, to come to Tokyo and persuade the Crown Prince to follow tradition.

Saionji came and lectured Hirohito, but the prince remained stubborn. He did not believe. So they reached an accommodation. Hirohito promised not to make an issue of his disbelief, and Prince Saionji agreed not to bother him about his beliefs.

Hirohito did not believe he was God, or that becoming occupant of the throne would make him into God. He believed in nature, and he loved wandering around in the hills and collecting various natural specimens, which he brought back to the palace for study. Soon he had a little laboratory of his own at the palace. It was not long before he began the study of marine biology, which fascinated him, particularly when he began to realize how little his countrymen knew about their own marine resources. He sometimes visited his mother, the Empress, whose summer palace was located in Hayama, on Sagami Bay, and he persuaded the Emperor to let him have a little boat there. The imperial advisors agreed that swimming and diving would be good for the Crown Prince, so he got his way. Once a week he went swimming and diving with two pearl divers, who were assigned to help him to collect specimens, and it was not long before he was swimming down for the specimens himself.

Emperor Taisho's era was called the Age of Great Righteousness, but this was a misnomer. The court councillors squabbled over power, and each year the Emperor Taisho showed more signs of the mental illness that would soon make him incapable of public appearances.

Under the system established during the Meiji Era, the Emperor's power was exercised by the Genro, or council of elder statesmen, all of them former prime ministers. As Taisho came to power, the two most important members of the Genro were Prince Aritomo Yamagata of the Choshu clan, a fine soldier, and Prince Saionji, Hirohito's guardian. Saionji was a member of the Satsuma clan. He was also a scholar of the old school, which held that it was a waste of talent to make a good man into a soldier.

The differences between Saionji and Prince Yamagata enabled an ambitious soldier named Prince Taro Katsura, another soldier of the Choshu clan, to come to power as prime minister. Prince Katsura had a specific ambition; he wanted to restore the shogunate, with himself as shogun. With this in view he made a private compact with the expansionist elements of the Imperial Navy, but was frustrated when the princes

Saionji and Yamagata joined forces. Thus was put down the most serious rebellion against the ruling system that had yet appeared in the new Japan.

The Taisho Emperor's official coronation was held in 1915. By this time all the people around the palace knew that the Emperor could not last long. His bouts of drinking and losses of memory were becoming more frequent. He could not be trusted to make the simplest decisions. The attention of the Genro turned more to Hirohito. He was lectured every day on his responsibilities. He exercised constantly to gain strength. He lived a cold-water life, and even in the coldest weather never was allowed to wear anything but thin cotton clothing. Photographs of the period show a boy who was growing to look ever more like his grandfather. He was extremely nearsighted, but no one gave him spectacles. He mentioned the matter, but was told that Emperors do not wear glasses.

After only one year of reign, the Emperor Taisho became completely unfit for public appearances and was retired by the Genro to the summer palace on the beach at Hayama. In the fall of 1916, on the third day of the eleventh month of the fifth year of Taisho, as the Japanese counted, Hirohito was officially installed as Crown Prince. His official picture shows a serious young man in a headpiece resembling a European bishop's miter, in black robes decorated with the imperial chrysanthemum, holding the imperial wand of office. Hirohito was then just over 15 years old. He was tall for a Japanese (five feet, six inches), and at that point, without spectacles, he seemed handsome. But now the Crown Prince rebelled, and although no one from the imperial family had ever appeared in public in eyeglasses, he insisted that he would have spectacles.

The Genro were in a hurry to prepare Hirohito for high office. They did not know how long the Taisho Emperor could live; his periods of lucidity were growing fewer and fewer. Prince Saionji and Prince Yamagata decided that the Crown Prince should be married and begin producing sons, to guarantee the future of Great Japan. And so the talk around the palaces was of marriage, and the search was on for a suitable consort. But suitable to the Genro and suitable to Prince Hirohito were two different matters. The manipulators of the Genro wanted a consort they could manage. Hirohito, however, wanted to choose his own bride, a matter unheard of in Japanese history. Even the Meiji Emperor had taken the woman chosen for him by his advisors.

But not Hirohito. After a good deal of maneuvering, it was announced from the palace that the prince would be betrothed to Princess Nagako, the daughter of Prince Kuniyoshi. The Genro had been outmaneuvered, with the connivance of the prince himself.

It would be a while before Prince Hirohito and Princess Nagako could be married. She must be prepared to assume the responsibilities of Empress. So Nagako was cooped up in her father's palace with seventeen tutors.

Meanwhile, the Genro fought back. They hoped to undo the betrothal and force Hirohito to accept another girl. They planted an article in a magazine that charged that the Kuniyoshi family suffered from color blindness. The implication was clear that there must be other medical evidence against the family. So a long social battle was in the offing, the prize being Imperial power. In this the Crown Prince was an enormous nuisance to the Privy Council, because he had so strong a mind of his own.

Prince Yamagata conceived the idea of sending Hirohito on a long trip abroad. A few months of absence would give the Genro a chance to undo the ties. So Yamagata stirred up another controversy. The Black Dragon Society was an ultranationalist organization, then dedicated to the eradication of the white race in Asia. Its chief officer, Mitsuru Toyama, was a powerful figure in Japan. General Yamagata enlisted his aid, saying that the Kuniyoshi clan would sell out to the whites.

But the Crown Prince would not listen to any of them, and on February 14, 1921, he insisted that the betrothal be announced.

Less than three weeks later, Crown Prince Hirohito sailed from Yokohama on the first foreign trip ever to be made by an heir apparent to the royal family. It had been 75 years since Commodore Perry's Black Ships had sailed up Tokyo Bay, and Japan seemed to be turning ever more outward. So said the editorial writers in the west. But the impression was in large part illusory. At home in Japan, goaded by the Black Dragon Society, a furious controversy raged over the Crown Prince's trip abroad. "Most unseemly" was the verdict of the jingoists.

For the Crown Prince, however, the unique voyage was an opportunity to see the world and to learn, and that, he said, was precisely what he was going to make of it.

5

A Voyage of Discovery

As the Crown Prince went off on his trip to Europe, the controversy still raged about his willfull behavior and his insistence on choosing his own bride. On March 3, 1921, he sailed from Yokohama, on a voyage that would last for six months and take him to five European countries.

On that day, the Crown Prince donned his uniform as admiral of the fleet and boarded the Imperial Navy battleship *Katori* off the coast of Hayama. He was accompanied by several nobles, including his uncle, Prince Naruhiko Higashikuni.

The correspondent of the *London Times* exhibited enthusiasm about the prince's planned trip to England. The reporter looked upon the prince as a symbol of hope and remarked on how much he resembled his grandfather, the Meiji Emperor. Meiji also had adopted rigorous self-restraint as his defense against the courtly world of imperial Japan, unlike the Taisho Emperor, who was known for his temper tantrums (he even beat up his soldiers and attendants from time to time) and his strange lapses from normal behavior. Once when opening the Diet, as was his responsibility, Yoshihito rolled up his imperial speech as if it were a paper telescope and sat peering at the members of the Diet through this instrument. As one wag remarked, the Diet was not much, in terms of rectitude or power, but still. . . .

Nevertheless, Hirohito was not his grandfather, just as the days in which he lived were not his grandfather's days. In the Japan of the nineteenth century, womanizing and drunkenness were considered not only manly but proper. The Meiji Emperor and his Taisho son both kept scores of concubines. When Taisho sent his son that concubine in Hirohito's thirteenth year, the Emperor was only doing for the Crown Prince what his father had done for him. The Meiji Emperor and the Taisho Emperor vied with all around them as drinkers. Hirohito, however, was an ascetic intellectual, who did not find it easy to come out of his shell and mingle with the world. And yet he did so with remarkable aplomb on this European trip, winning the undying loyalty of his servitors.

On the voyage to England, Hirohito spent the mornings studying English and French (which he would have to use on the trip). In the afternoons he played "deck golf" or swam in the open-air swimming pool erected on the battleship's main deck for the royal tour. He was not a great athlete, and he often lost to his companions while playing deck golf, but he always showed a good temper about it, unlike his father, who could not stand to be opposed in anything. In the evenings Hirohito read. To improve his skill he read about the French Revolution in French and about Queen Elizabeth I in English.

The voyage was scarcely a month along when tragedy struck. Aboard the accompanying cruiser *Kashin* one of the boiler tubes blew up, and three stokers were scalded to death. Next day the seamen were buried at sea with honors, and the Crown Prince presided. A few days later the same kind of accident happened aboard the *Katori*, and two more stokers died. Once again the prince did the honors. He told intimates that he was distressed to be, even indirectly, the cause of such trouble to his countrymen. There was none of the public stoicism when he was with his intimates, who on this voyage included several of his cousins.

Those years of spartan life and acceptance of physical hardship now served him well. The Japanese flotilla passed into the Red Sea, and the weather was so hot the ship's bulkheads grew painful to the touch. Most of the party elected to sleep on deck at night, but not Hirohito—he did not even turn on the electric fan in his cabin, and he chose one of the hottest days of the trip to inspect the boiler rooms, where the temperature had reached 130 degrees Fahrenheit.

They came through the Suez Canal and stopped off at Cairo, where Lord Allenby gave a garden party. At Malta Hirohito was met by Prince George (later King George VI) of England, who took him to a performance of *Otello* by an Italian opera company. At Gibraltar he visited the British naval base and went to the horse races.

On May 9, 1921, the royal party arrived in England at Portsmouth Naval Base. Dressed in his admiral's uniform again, and wearing half a dozen medals and a royal sash, Crown Prince Hirohito inspected the crew of a battleship. A fleet review was held for the Crown Prince at Spithead, and it was a magnificent sight, for in the 1920s the Royal Navy sailed the most powerful fleet in the world, and its admirals made sure that Britain put her best foot forward. For indeed, here was the royal prince of Japan, one of Britain's close allies.

In 1902 the British and the Japanese had signed a mutual defense treaty. The treaty had been tested in World War I, when the two countries had combined to assault the German colony of Kiaochao, where the Japanese army forces had actually besieged and then captured the fortress and city of Qingdao. Now, in days of peace, the British and Japanese naval authorities were worrying about fleet problems, and the Washington Naval Conference would soon be called, to produce a treaty that would limit Japan's naval strength to three-fifths that of either Britain or the United States. But Prince Hirohito did not share the concerns of his country's advocates of naval expansionism, and he had a strong feeling of attachment for the British alliance, and for things British in general. This was to be enhanced by his voyage.

The second member of the British royal family to greet Crown Prince Hirohito was Edward, the Prince of Wales, who met him at the gangplank of Hirohito's ship. There was not much talk between them, however, because the Prince of Wales did not speak Japanese and Hirohito was too shy to try out his English on a foreigner.

Hirohito was invited to stay at Buckingham Palace, and his whole group (eighteen people) was put up there. A few mornings after their arrival, King George V, Emperor of India, suddenly appeared in the Japanese prince's quarters dressed in trousers, a shirt, and carpet slippers, his braces showing. Hirohito's people were shocked; no member of the Japanese royal family would ever appear even in the presence of other members unless fully dressed in proper court costume.

And, to complete the culture shock, the king walked up to Crown Prince Hirohito, slapped him smartly on the back, and spoke to him like a Dutch uncle. "I hope, me boy," he said, "that everyone is giving you everything you want while you are here. If there is anything you need, just ask. I'll never forget how your grandfather [Meiji] treated me and me brother when we were in Yokohama [where the two British princes had visited as midshipmen of the Royal Navy on a Royal Navy cruise]. I've always wanted to repay the kindness. No geisha here, though. I'm afraid Her Majesty would never allow it."

That, of course, was the king at rest. A few hours later he and Crown Prince Hirohito were riding in the royal carriage, in full uniform with medals, past the guardsmen in the bearskin hats, who were holding back crowds intent on waving the flag of the rising sun to show their goodwill toward the visitor from so far away.

The Prince of Wales shepherded Hirohito through a whole series of receptions, banquets, and parades. For army ceremonies Hirohito changed from his naval uniform into that of a general of the Imperial Army. For diplomatic receptions he donned morning coat, striped trousers, top hat, and high wing collar. They visited a nightclub. They went to the theater. The Prince of Wales introduced Hirohito to the game of golf, which quite enchanted the Japanese prince (and was responsible for the Japanese taking up the game, with the intensity that is peculiar to Japan). They visited Eton and also the Tower of London, where Hirohito learned something of a British history as bloody as Japan's. Hirohito shook hands with Boy Scouts and went to the Bank of England. He went to the British Museum and looked at the exhibits. He went to Oxford and visited the university. He dressed up in academic gown at Cambridge and received an honorary degree. He met Lloyd George, the prime minister. Throughout he spoke in Japanese, of course, and comported himself with great dignity.

On May 21, 1921, Crown Prince Hirohito and his entourage went to Scotland, where they were met by the Duke of Atholl, who had a bodyguard of 800 kilted Highlanders. They put on a show for the Japanese, marching with the pipes and performing feats of strength and daring that included the throwing of the caber and Scottish dancing. Fifty of the guardsmen, Hirohito was told, had been detached to act as his personal bodyguard. In the evening the pipers played "Kimigayo," the Japanese national anthem, and the duchess played Japanese music on the piano.

Hirohito had already developed a great attachment for the British royal family, and now, as he looked around the country, he saw the sort of democratic government he would like to have in Japan. At Blair Atholl Castle he found more evidence to support his opinion. The duke had brought in many villagers and local people to help with the ceremonies. They danced and sang and showed an intimacy with the ducal family that Hirohito found charming and impressive, although his servitors were shocked by this behavior, which would have been unthinkable in Japan.

All this cemented in Hirohito's mind a new feeling for England, and a desire to create of his Oriental monarchy in Japan a constitutional monarchy of the sort that England enjoyed.

The Japanese tourists visited Manchester and Glasgow, touchy places at the time because of the economic depression that had hit the British Isles in 1921, with high unemployment, many strikes, and much public misery. But all went well. Hirohito shook hands with shipyard workers and toured factories. He had his picture painted by the celebrated portraitist Augustus John.

Then the Japanese entourage boarded their warship tour fleet once more and crossed the channel to France. The warships docked on May

30, and the Japanese tour went to Paris, where Hirohito visited the Louvre. He was taken in tow by Marshal Henri Pétain, who took him on a tour of the Western Front battlefields, where Hirohito had his picture taken sitting astride a great cannon, with Pétain standing owlishly in the background.

President Alexandre Millerand gave a luncheon at the Elysée Palace. The Japanese group also visited the palace at Versailles, and the site of the treaty-making which had caused Japan so much pain in the years since the end of World War I. They went to the opera. They traveled to the Netherlands and visited the Rijksmuseum.

Italy came next, starting with Naples. In Rome they were entertained at the Quirinal Palace by King Victor Emmanuel. The Italians took a siesta after lunch, but Crown Prince Hirohito spent the time writing letters. The Japanese press was publicizing the Crown Prince's voyage every day, and he was receiving thousands of letters from home, many of them from schoolchildren. He answered as many as he could.

The prince had an audience with Pope Benedict XV, and he also saw President Tomáš G. Masaryk of Czechoslovakia, who was visiting Rome just then. Hirohito spent two days visiting tourist spots, the Coliseum, the Forum, St. Peter's, and other popular sights, and then he went to Pompeii, whose ruins had been recently excavated.

Then it was back to Naples and the battleship. The voyage home would take another two months. An American journalist asked him why he had not included the United States in his trip abroad, and the Crown Prince had said that there simply was not time. But, like a statesman, he had come up with the proper words: "I know to what point justice and freedom are valued in America and that no efforts are spared by her people in the cause of humanity. I hope that America and Japan may always be found working hand in hand not only to our mutual benefit, but to ensure lasting peace throughout the world." The Crown Prince was still not really a part of the Japanese government, and this states-manlike speech did not make any particularly important impact. But it was an indication of Hirohito's thinking. Unlike many of his compatriots, he had nothing against Westerners, and nothing against Americans. At that time he hoped to visit the United States, not then knowing of the pressures that would all too soon be brought on him at home.

When the ships of the royal tour returned to Japan, they docked at Yokohama. From there Hirohito went by train to Tokyo's Central Railroad Station, where a welcoming crowd was waiting. Hirohito had left Japan as a little-known prince of the realm, but since his every move had been chronicled in the world press, and had met with overwhelming public approval, he came home a world figure.

6

Violence in Japan

It was inevitable that the more or less peaceful revolution that had altered Japanese society in fifty years would leave scars, and it had. The destruction of the samurai class had left a minority of people who still believed in the old ways of strict bushido, and many of these gravitated to the army and the navy. Still others banded into secret societies, such as Toyama's Black Dragon Society, which was so important that its support had been sought by both sides in the dispute over Hirohito's engagement.

That society had been important in Japanese inner politics, taking sides with the Satsuma clan against the Choshu clan in the struggles of the inner circle around the Emperor. But in the 1920s the Black Dragon Society changed its aims and set itself up against any and all new ideas that would try to undermine the old structure of Japanese society.

By that time the Russian Revolution had succeeded, and Soviet communism, or Bolshevism, had become an important factor in the world. The Soviets had moved their influence into China, which was too close to Japan for comfort, and so the Black Dragon Society declared war on Bolshevism. But the Black Dragon description of "Bolshevism" extended far beyond the Communist International Movement, and it was not long before any liberal ideas were being labeled communist by Toyama and his people.

These people were outright advocates of "thought control," and were pleased to see this idea creeping into Japanese society, where the army and police began to keep track of "dangerous" elements. Dangerous meant free-thinking. The right wing of the army embraced the Black Dragon Society and soon began creating small societies of its own, modeled on the same principle of ultranationalism and unquestioning obedience to the throne—which meant obedience to the Genro, who governed in the name of the throne.

Crown Prince Hirohito came home with many liberal ideas, and these were regarded by many of his elder statesmen as dangerous.

Japan was suffering even more than England from the economic downturn following the enormous production surpluses of World War I. Further, the army was being squeezed, and demands were made by Diet members and the public for reduction in military budgets. The army still claimed that it had to stay strong to support the occupation of Siberia, but this excuse was wearing thin with the public.

The only people who had the vote were well-to-do taxpayers, who tended to believe in the same precepts that attracted the followers of the Black Dragon Society. They favored the growth of empire and dreamed of the day when Japan would dominate Asia, and possibly the world. They worshipped the Emperor. They opposed jazz, cigarette smoking, women's rights, and anything modern or derived from the Western world. They were vastly encouraged by the anti-Oriental attitude of the Americans, who had been mistreating the Chinese for fifty years and more recently had become viciously anti-Japanese, spurred on by the yellow press, which found this attitude a good circulation builder.

In 1921 Britain refused to renew the Anglo-Japanese Alliance, which was a blow to the Japanese. A few months later the U.S. Supreme Court declared that Japanese were ineligible to become U.S. citizens. These insults angered the Japanese people and encouraged the jingoists. By 1921 the secret societies, many of them funded secretly by the army, were making public threats against anyone who did not follow their precepts of "good Japanese citizenship."

All this movement to the right was masked by the right wing under the term "protection of the Constitution," which in Black Dragon terms meant protection of the divine right of the Emperor and opposition to extending the rudiments of democracy to the common people.

A month after the Crown Prince's return from the Western world, the pot boiled over. Prime Minister Takashi Hara was leaving Tokyo for a trip to Kyoto. He was about to board the train at Shimbashi Station when a young man rushed up to him and stabbed him in the back with a dagger. Hara died. The assassin made no attempt to escape, but gave himself up to the police and declared that he had acted from a spirit of the highest patriotism because the prime minister had "betrayed the constitution."

What the prime minister had done, perhaps not quite legally, was to assume the portfolio of the minister of the navy, Admiral Tomasakuro Kato, while the admiral went to Washington for the Washington Naval Conference of 1921. If Hara had not done so, the admiral would have been forced to resign. But the constitution said that the minister of the navy must be a naval officer on active service, and the prime minister was a civilian. This gave the Black Dragon Society an excuse to kill a liberal prime minister who was a thorn in their side.

As noted, Hirohito had returned to Japan with many Western ideas. His particular hero was the Prince of Wales. In London Hirohito had attended one of the Prince of Wales's social affairs, at which "flappers" danced the Charleston in rolled stockings and revealing dresses and young men went around slapping the prince on the back and calling him Edward. This was constitutional monarchy, and a sort of egalitarianism among the aristocracy that Hirohito admired. In his own way he hoped to bring it to Japan.

So he organized a party more or less along Western lines, to be held at Akasaka Palace. The guests were all men—Japanese ladies did not mix with men socially—but there were plenty of geisha to serve them. For the occasion Hirohito brought out a keg of fine malt whiskey given him by the Duke of Atholl. The hard drinkers, and there were plenty of them among his acquaintance, chose that tipple. And before the night was out, Hirohito had his wish; his guests had relaxed—some of them had unraveled—and the evening was the epitome of Western informality, Japanese style.

Two days later Hirohito had a visit from Prince Saionji, who had made a two-hour trip from his winter villa. Saionji had been designated by all the other elder statesmen to talk sense to the Crown Prince. It was not the party that bothered them, or the fact that most of the party-goers had become drunk on the unfamiliar Scotch whiskey—it was the familiarity with which Hirohito had allowed himself to be treated by his guests. (After all, God does not give wild parties and ask people to call him Hirohito, and not Your Royal Highness!)

Hirohito did not try to defend his action. Since childhood he had been taught to accept the advice of the Genro. There would be no more parties, no further attempt to introduce egalitarianism.

The prince's father, the Taisho Emperor, had now moved permanently to the seacoast for his health, and it was apparent that he would not last much longer. So it was all the more important that Hirohito be prepared in every way to accept the crown and its awesome responsibility.

Having expressed his sorrow for violating Japanese tradition with the party, Hirohito felt free to adopt some of the other ideas that had impressed him in England. He caused a nine-hole golf course to be built on the grounds of the Imperial Palace, and although he had not yet moved into the palace, he played golf there. He had bought a gramophone in England, and he played gramophone records, as he had seen the British royal family do. He also adopted some Western eating customs, such as his breakfast of fried eggs and grilled bacon instead of the raw egg, grilled fish, and steamed rice usual in Japan. For the rest of his life Hirohito would indulge himself each morning with an English breakfast.

These Western habits upset the Black Dragon Society. They were an indication of the dreadful changes that might overtake Japan if every avenue were not watched, so the society set out to eradicate Western ideas from Japan. The Prince's advisors, particularly Prince Saionji, the oldest and most respected, also lectured the prince on his duties and on the unseemliness of adopting Western ways.

The political fires continued to smolder, and then began to burn brightly. In March 1922 a young man appeared in front of the Imperial Palace and blew himself up with a bomb. At the time not much was thought about it, but within the month the Prince of Wales visited Japan on a friendship tour. Crown Prince Hirohito met him, appeared with him in public, and behaved very much as the host, as Prince Edward had for him when he had visited England. The Black Dragon Society was incensed. It was an insult to all Japanese and to Japanese tradition for the royal heir to behave in such fashion.

Does God consort with humans? Of course not. Let God retire to his palace and do the things that God does, carry out the equinoxial ceremonies, pray to the older gods, and propitiate the universe on behalf of Japan.

Toyama made a public announcement: the young man who had killed himself was a member of the Black Dragon Society, and he had taken "this unselfish way" of protesting the royal behavior.

And so, persuaded by his advisors that public display of sympathy for Western ideas was unacceptable, Hirohito quelled his spirit and retired to the precincts of the palace. Not for a quarter of a century would he again attempt to mingle with the people or exhibit any Western ways. But inside the palace he built a Western-style library for himself, with a writing desk, chairs, and overstuffed furniture. He had brought back from Europe busts of his heroes, George Washington, Napoleon Bonaparte, and Charles Darwin, and these were kept in the study. He read books in English for information and entertainment, and privately he never lost his admiration for England and English things.

By the time Hirohito had settled in after his European trip, it was known throughout Japan that the Emperor's health was failing and that he no longer really ruled in any way. The Genro met to consider this problem and decided that Hirohito would have to be given the title of regent, because he was being forced to carry out many of the ceremonies that were the responsibility of the Emperor.

So it was done, at a formal ceremony in the palace, and on November 25, 1921, the newspapers were filled with pictures of the Crown Prince, in uniform, indicating his new role in life. His brief period as free soul had ended almost before it began. He was constrained to living his private life in seclusion and to appearing to agree with the ultranationalists by not protesting the truth he knew—that he was not a god but just an ordinary monarch. And so Hirohito reverted to *enryo* and began to conceal his Western inclinations from all but his closest servitors. The crisis passed.

The Crown Prince and Princess Nagako had been engaged for five years, and during most of that time the Genro had been split about the marriage, with the old Satsuma-Choshu quarrel revived. But Hirohito had made it clear that he was not going to change his mind and would not be persuaded to delay the marriage indefinitely. So a date for the wedding was set in 1923.

But on September 1, 1923, the Tokyo area and the whole great Kanto plain, which stretches along the southern side of Honshu Island, were struck by a strong earthquake. Gas mains ruptured, oil tanks spilled, and fires broke out. Yokohama and Tokyo began to burn, and the fires raged for five days. The Emperor Taisho escaped the trouble because the Empress had taken him to Nikko, but Crown Prince Hirohito was eating lunch at Akasaka Palace that day and was in the heart of the earthquake. Fortunately the palace survived.

The Crown Prince was supposed to meet Admiral Gompei Yamamoto that day. A few days earlier the Crown Prince, acting as regent, had appointed Yamamoto to form a new cabinet for Japan, and the admiral had now done so. The ceremony of announcement was to be carried out at the Imperial Palace that afternoon, but the admiral, though unhurt, was trapped in the middle of the area damaged by the earthquake and could not get there. So the ceremony was delayed a full day and finally was held at the Akasaka Palace, because the Imperial Palace was in the center of the wrecked area.

This whole matter of the earthquake was an indication of what had happened to Hirohito since he had come home from Europe. Since he had arrived in Japan the Genro had been criticizing him, and this was particularly true of his most trusted advisor, Prince Saionji. With the earthquake devastating his people, the Crown Prince, now also the Prince

Regent, did not know what to do, and in view of the lectures from Prince Saionji he did nothing. For several days he stayed in the Akasaka Palace, surrounded by servants who would pay no attention to his demands for information. He was like a queen bee in the middle of her hive, deaf and blind, insulated from reality. The courtiers were concerned only for his personal welfare. Prince Saionji, the only one of the Genro who had the good sense to understand what a personal tour of the disaster area by the Prince Regent would have done for Japanese morale, was stranded at his country home, cut off from telephone, telegraph, and rail communication with Tokyo.

The disaster to Japan was even greater than it appeared on the surface. For the army, and the army-controlled police, who had been growing steadily in power, took this opportunity to settle many old scores. The Koreans who had emigrated to Japan since their country had been absorbed in the empire, and who were not titularly Japanese citizens, had been most unpopular, and thousands of them were massacred by the police in the confusion of the earthquake and fires. The police also took it upon themselves to wipe out many leftists. The Kempeitai, the army's special police force, was the worst element. The Kempeitai were known as the military police, but they were not like any other military police force in the world, except perhaps Hitler's brownshirts and Mussolini's blackshirts. The Kempeitai went where they pleased in this time of crisis and murdered hundreds of political opponents of the regime.

Ten days after the earthquake, Hirohito finally persuaded his courtiers that he must go out and see the people. He put on an army officer's uniform and rode out on horseback, which was the only sensible manner of transport just then, with a small escort, to tour the city. On one ride he went to the Ginza, on another to Asakusa, and then to Ueno Park.

The appearance of the Prince Regent, even belatedly, did a great deal to restore morale. Then came the announcement that his wedding, scheduled soon, would be postponed on account of the disaster, and the people felt sure that their ruler cared for them. When he announced that he was contributing the equivalent of $2.5 million to relief, his popularity had never been so high. But there was another aspect to these public appearances which aroused so much cheering; the prince's army officer escort began to worry about his popularity, for it did not fit in with their plans for Japan. What they wanted was a ruler who sat in private splendor in the Imperial Palace and let the army run the country and the world as it saw fit.

Japan was months in recovering from this terrible earthquake disaster. On December 27, 1923, Crown Prince Hirohito drove through the wreckage of Tokyo to the Diet buildings in the center of the city, as it was his responsibility to open the new session of the Diet. In the To-ranomon section, a young man suddenly darted out from the crowd, leveled a gun just outside the window of the prince regent's Daimler limousine, and fired. The bullet missed Hirohito, ricocheted around inside the car, and wounded one of his chamberlains.

The would-be assassin was captured and brought to trial. He said his name was Daisaku Namba, and that is about all the truth they got out of him. The police interrogated and tortured him for eleven months, but who did what and why is not known and never will be, since the records were all burned in the firebombing of Tokyo in 1945. Several things do seem clear. Namba said he was a leftist, but he did not behave like a leftist; he behaved like an ultranationalist, and that was well established. He was known to be a follower of the Choshu clan and of Prince Yamagata, a general of the army, who had been quarreling with Prince Saionji about the control of Japan for several years.

Namba's father was a member of the Diet, liberal by persuasion. When he learned of his son's action, he retired to his home. His son was executed, and the old man died not long afterward.

The police claimed that Namba's last words were "Banzai for the proletariat" and that he was nothing but a communist. Nobody really believed that. The police thrust for power was already under way, and soon new laws, more restrictive year after year, would gradually bring "thought control" to Japan.

Still, at the moment, liberalism seemed to be the way of the country. All the old oligarchs of the original Meiji Genro had died off, and the closest to them was Prince Saionji. The Japanese had come back from the Washington Naval Conference with a number of treaties, and Navy Minister Kato stated that war with the United States was not inevitable, as many Japanese naval and army figures were saying, nor was it desirable. Representative democracy seemed to be gaining strength, but in fact the army was already conspiring to take power.

A new cabinet came to power in 1924, and the chief figure was a general named Jazushige Ugaki, the minister of war. His assigned task was to strengthen the army by cutting out the deadwood, by strengthening the air arm, and by creating a modern armored force. This seemed innocent enough, but underneath it represented a struggle for power between the old Choshu clan faction, which represented the samurai of the past, and the new officer class, which had grown up in the Meiji Era and was largely led by officers who came up through the ranks from the peasantry. At the moment this struggle was all sub rosa.

Japan was beginning to be prosperous again, and on the surface calm had descended. And on January 24, 1924, Crown Prince Hirohito, Regent of Japan, and Princess Nagako Kuniyoshi were married inside the Imperial Palace. Despite all the Crown Prince's protestations of internationalism and liberalism, the marriage was a very Japanese ceremony, attended only by seven hundred noble guests, all of them Japanese. Foreigners were restricted to a reception held later. This was not the way Hirohito wanted to behave, but his acceptance of the strictures was an indication of what had happened to him.

The prince came from the Akasaka Palace and the princess from her home in Shibuya. The Emperor did not come at all, for which the Genro were grateful, because he might have disrupted the ceremony with his insane antics.

The prince and princess retired to the robing rooms inside the Imperial Palace and then emerged in full court costume, he carrying a scepter and she a court fan. The Shinto wedding ceremony was performed by the master of rites. It was followed by a 101-gun salute from the battery on Miyake Hill, from the ships in the harbor, and from the guns of the forts all over Japan. A national holiday was declared.

Then the couple went on their honeymoon, to the palace of Hirohito's uncle, Prince Takamatsu, at Okinajima, and Japan waited for the next great news—the coming of an heir.

7

Emperor

The earthquake and the violence of 1923 gave way to demands for reform in Japan and for a cutback of the armed forces to reduce taxes. Reforms were made, but the cutback in armed forces was not to be realized.

In 1924 Prime Minister Takaaki Kato proposed to increase suffrage to include all men age 25 or older, and Regent Hirohito endorsed the plan. At the same time Kato demanded that the army cut back its ranks severely to save money. The appearance of this was achieved by eliminating four divisions of troops, but in fact, by adroit juggling, War Minister Ugaki merely disbanded those divisions and reassigned the same troops to air and armored corps units. At the end of the year the army was stronger than ever.

Furthermore, the army now moved into the central core of Japanese life. In the Meiji years Japan had imposed universal military training. Now the army established training units at the high schools and prepared to impose military training on every high school student. Furthermore, in 1925 the apparent liberalization of the Japanese political system with universal male suffrage was countered by the first Public Peace Bill, which gave the national police new power to suppress political dissidence. In Japan this was called the Dangerous Thoughts Bill. In the years to come the police would be given even greater power, until by the end of the 1930s no one was immune from police snooping and Japan had become truly a police state.

Princess Nagako became pregnant in 1925. She and Hirohito spent the summer at their new imperial villa at Hayama, where he went fishing every day, collecting shrimp, crabs, and fish and bringing them back for leisurely examination in his laboratory. At the end of September the prince and princess moved back to the Akasaka Palace in Tokyo. The royal baby was expected in November, and the Japanese press adopted a festive air, setting up tents near the palace and manning them twenty-four hours a day. All sorts of speculation raced through the pages of the newspapers, and prizes were offered for children born the same day, the same hour, the same moment as the royal baby. But the royal baby did not appear until December 6, and then was a great disappointment to the press, the public, and the Genro—a girl. Hirohito announced that her name would be Terunomiya, which means Little Sunshine, and that she would bring joy to the hearts of the people.

As Christmas approached (although in Japan Christmas is a celebration without Christ) it became known that the Emperor Taisho was dying of lung cancer. On December 18 he developed a high fever and a very rapid pulse. He had shrunk to skin and bone and was being kept alive on soup and milk. Early on the morning of December 25 he died, Hirohito at his side, in the imperial villa at Hayama.

Afterward, Hirohito, now the Emperor, and Empress Nagako went back to their own villa in the same town. He had become the 124th God Emperor of Japan, tracing his lineage in history and legend back to the heaven-descended ancestor Jimmu, who had lived 2,600 years earlier.

The royal couple passed over a road swept clean by hand and lined with townspeople. In their car was the grand chamberlain, carrying the Sword and the Jewels, two of the three sacred treasures of Japan, to the new Emperor's abode. (The third great treasure, the Mirror, had long reposed at the sacred shrine of Ise.) Hirohito bowed to the people as he passed. A few hours later the newspapers announced that the new Imperial Era would be called Showa, the time of enlightenment and peace.

> Simplicity instead of vain display, originality rather than blind imitation, progress in this period of evolution, improvement to keep pace with the advances of civilization, national harmony in purpose and action, beneficence to all classes of people, and friendship to all the nations of the earth: these are the cardinal aims to which Our most profound and abiding solicitude is directed.

This was the pledge of Showa.

Now Hirohito's life changed enormously. No longer would he be free to wander about the beach and collect his marine specimens. He was Emperor, a bird in the golden cage of the palace. His life would follow a set routine. He would arise at six o'clock in the morning, shave and dress himself, pray to his ancestors, and then go out for a morning stroll. Sometimes he would chop wood for exercise. He would come back in an hour and have breakfast with the Empress, a big English breakfast of cereal, eggs, bacon, toast, and coffee. Then he would retire to his study.

The study was furnished in Western style, with carpet on the tatami matting, a table, chairs, and a sofa on which he sometimes took a nap. The walls were hung with mementos from his European voyage, photographs of himself with Marshal Pétain of France, the Prince of Wales and King George of England, and Crown Prince Leopold of Belgium. The busts of his Western heroes stood on tables in the room. At one end of the room the shoji screen opened onto the private imperial park where had been built the golf course, a covered riding ring, and a bomb-proof underground shelter which housed the Imperial Library.

In the study the Emperor would begin the workday by reading the major Japanese daily newspapers and the English-language newspaper, then the *Japan Advertiser*. An hour later, Lord Privy Seal Nobuaki Makino would come in, and they would discuss the political and military obligations of the day. Soon Count Sutemi Chinda, the grand chamberlain, would come in to discuss the day's religious and social obligations. If, perhaps, one of the army or navy chiefs of staff had exercised his "right to direct access" to the Emperor as guaranteed by the Meiji Constitution, Hirohito would see him and discuss whatever matter seemed so important.

Then from 10:00 until 12:30 Hirohito would receive visitors. Most of these were formal visits, received in the official throne room, the Phoenix Hall. He would greet the guest, accept the report the guest made, and dismiss him. But some of the visitors were cabinet ministers or others with whom Hirohito wanted to discuss affairs. So they would talk, the visitor standing at attention.

Hirohito would break his routine at 12:30 for a light lunch, and then receive again until 2:00, when he would play golf or go riding in the ring.

At 4:00 Hirohito took his bath in a deep wooden Japanese tub, where he soaked for a while. Then, in cotton kimono, he would return to the study and sign papers submitted by the lord privy seal. At 6:00 in the evening he would stop work and retire to the private imperial apartments to dine and spend the evening with Empress Nagako.

This daily schedule varied on Wednesdays, when the Privy Council met to discuss matters of state. The council consisted of princes of the blood, cabinet ministers, and distinguished nobles who had served on the Empire well in the past.

On Saturdays Hirohito liked to devote the morning to his biological studies. He studied disease-causing fungi, and some of his findings were later published. He also studied shellfish and other sea life.

Twenty-seven times a year, on the first day, the eleventh day and the twenty-first day of each month, and on twenty-four national holidays, Hirohito had to preside over religious ceremonies. Most of these were held in the palace grounds. The Shinto priests would intone the services, and Hirohito, in robes of white silk, would make the invocation.

But even as Emperor Hirohito settled into the seat of sublime power in Japan, forces outside the palace were working to upset his hopes for a peaceful and prosperous world, with Japan a friend to all nations.

The United States and Australia were proving difficult for the Japanese to deal with. Australia was afraid of a Japanese population invasion and therefore began to restrict immigration. The United States became even more unkind to the Japanese. New immigration laws made it virtually impossible for any Japanese to move there. The new U.S. laws were accompanied by insulting articles in the American press, which were picked up and answered with insulting articles about Americans in the Japanese press. So the propaganda war began, which in Japan played into the hands of the ultranationalists. One part of the campaign was the demand for living room for Japan, which had a density of 400 people per square mile, as compared then to the American density of 30 per square mile. And in Japanese military circles began to travel the word *kodo*—the Imperial Way.

But this time *kodo* represented a different sort of Imperial Way from the past. The military men shrewdly assessed the national mood, which itself was growing nationalistic, and they brought reverence for the Emperor, who personified Japan, to a new level. To be sure, a Count Nogi might kill himself in the old samurai fashion upon the death of his Emperor, but most Japanese in the 1920s would not. The military men set out to renew the old samurai attitudes and extend them to the whole nation. This was the new Imperial Way.

The Emperor was not yet aware of the implications of this changing pattern. He was trying to live as normal a human life as possible. The Empress gave birth to another child, a second daughter, who was to survive only two years. Hirohito, a proud father, welcomed the new child. He was an affectionate family man and liked to play with his children. Whenever possible they all escaped from the Tokyo palace to the relative freedom of their summer palace at Hayama, built very close to the site of Emperor Taisho's summer palace.

If there was anyone in the world that Hirohito envied, it was his younger brother Prince Chichibu, who lived the sort of life Hirohito had wanted for himself. Chichiku had gone to university at Oxford, he had traveled widely, and his social life was broad and free. But under the

Japanese system of government there was, of course, no way that the Emperor's freedom could be extended.

In the middle of the 1920s, Hirohito's major concerns were the economy and the spirit of the people, which was very low. But by 1927 prosperity seemed to be about to come back. The expansionists said Japan's future lay with development of empire. In February 1928 elections for the Diet were held, accompanied by demonstrations against militarism and thought control. Five thousand people were arrested, and because of the protests, the Peace Preservation (Thought Control) laws were strengthened. The militarists forced further expansion of the Japanese influence in other countries.

In China, Chiang Kai-shek, the Nationalist leader, was marching northward to try to unify his country under his banner. This was a matter of great interest to Japan's ultranationalists, who believed that the only road to Japanese prosperity was expansion. They considered Japan as having been rudely deprived of the fruits of conquest by the Versailles Treaty that ended World War I. The Japanese and British had captured the German colony of Kiaochao on the Shandong Peninsula, and Japan had occupied the port of Qingdao and some towns along the Qingdao-Jinan railroad.

The Japanese had made investments in the area, and many had settled in the cities. The Kwantung forces had come ocasionally in the years since to protect Japanese interests, threatened by fighting among the warlords in the area. In the spring of 1927 there had been some trouble, and Kaku Mori, who was the power behind the Seiyukai Party, had pushed the Japanese prime minister, General Giichi Tanaka, into sending troops. But in 1927 Chiang Kai-shek had begun his campaign to put down these warlords and make them adhere to the Nationalist cause of unification of China. He had begun his march north and was heading toward Shandong.

In the elections of 1928 General Tanaka would be returned as prime minister. The fact that he was a general was not unusual. Since the days of the Meiji reformation the military had taken major roles in government; it was a part of the Japanese pattern, stemming from the shogunate, for of course the shoguns had been generals first and rulers of Japan second.

The real power behind the Seiyukai Party continued to be Mori, a strong nationalist who espoused empire building. With Mori's enthusiastic support, in 1927 General Tanaka embarked on a program designed to lead to annexation of Manchuria by Japan. To further the program Tanaka made a trip to Manchuria and met with the major officials of

the Japanese enterprises there and in Mongolia. His ambition also included Inner Mongolia, which the Japanese army wanted as a buffer
against Russia. Tanaka was very frank with the Japanese in Manchuria,
who of course favored colonization of the area by Japan. He offered an
eight-point program, one point of which stipulated that the Japanese
government would support any Manchurian government that would guarantee Japan's special economic and military position there. He had some
hopes for Marshal Zhang Zoulin, the warlord of Manchuria, but the
difficulty between Tanaka and the Manchurian leader was control of the
military destiny of the area, which Zhang was not willing to give up.

After the meeting General Tanaka was questioned by Major General
Noboyushi Muto, who had attended as a representative of the Kwantung
Peninsula defense force. This force was a relatively small unit, about ten
thousand men, charged mainly with protecting the corridor of the South
Manchurian Railway, which connected most of the major Japanese enterprises. General Muto noted that if the eight-point program of Tanaka's
was carried out it would bring the Japanese government into direct confrontation with the U.S. open door policy, which guaranteed all countries
free trade with China.

Tanaka said he was aware of that, and that Japan was prepared for
war, if necessary, to support its visions of empire.

Tanaka's trip was supposed to be a secret, but a Shanghai newspaper
secured a digest of his eight-point program and printed it, calling it the
Tanaka Memorial. The general denied the whole story vehemently, but
recently published diaries of the period prove that it was true, and a
forecast of events to come.

Shortly after the Tanaka trip to Manchuria, Chiang Kai-Shek's army
arrived. General Tanaka was trying to negotiate with Zhang to carry on
the government in Manchuria and give the Japanese the concessions
that they wanted. By this time Chiang Kai-shek had persuaded the
warlords Feng Yuhsiang and Yen Shishan to join his cause. They were
the sworn enemies of Zhang and threatened his claims to Peking and
other parts of northern China. At that time Zhang was living in Peking,
the old capital of the Chinese empire, still regarded as the capital by
some. With the arrival of Chiang Kai-shek in the spring of 1928, the
Japanese military attache at Jinan called for troops again to be sent to
protect the 19,000 Japanese living in Shandong. Once again on Mori's
insistence, 5,000 troops of the Kwantung force were sent to Shandong.
On May 18, 1928, Chiang Kai-shek was warned not to move to Manchuria to try to take control. But the Japanese attempts to persuade
Marshal Zhang to abandon Peking and concentrate his power in Man-

churia as the servant of the Japanese were unavailing. Zhang said he would rather die than see his home of Peking in the hands of his old enemy Feng.

Since the marshal was proving so difficult, Mori decided that he must be eliminated. On May 20 the Imperial General Staff at Tokyo prepared mobilization. Three columns of troops would march. Zhang would be disarmed, and the Kwantung Army would take power in Manchuria.

The Americans got wind of this move and indicated that they might choose to act militarily if the Japanese moved. Prime Minister Tanaka wavered. On May 22 General Chotaro Muraoka, the commander of the Kwantung Army, came from his headquarters at Port Arthur to Mukden, awaiting Tanaka's order to move. But the next day an emissary from Tokyo announced that General Tanaka had changed his mind and the army would not march. General Muraoka protested to the war minister.

Meanwhile, Chiang Kai-shek had been marching on Peking, and, as he came up, Zhang prepared to retreat into Manchuria. The Manchuria force of Japanese numbered only about 12,000 men, and they were concerned lest Zhang arrive with his huge army and outnumber and outmaneuver them. Colonel Daisaku Komoto of this force decided the time for action had come. He wanted to go to Tokyo and talk to the generals at Imperial Headquarters, but General Muraoka said no. Muraoka wanted to hire an assassin to kill Marshal Zhang. Colonel Komoto protested that to do this would be to risk the Japanese being identified as the perpetrators. Instead Komoto had a plan of his own, which, he now put into effect without consulting anyone.

He sent an emissary to Peking to get the details of the marshal's travel plans and then schemed to blow up the marshal's train. The place would be Huangkutan, where the tracks of the South Manchuria Railroad passed over those of the Peking-Mukden Railroad. They would blow up the railroad as the train passed. The plan was put into effect; Marshal Zhang was blown up at that spot at 5:20 A.M. on June 4, 1928. Three dissident Manchurians had been hired to lurk by the side of the line, and if the marshal did not die in the explosion they were to rush into the car and kill him. But the marshal did die, and the three Manchurians now represented a threat and were to be killed themselves. But one of them escaped the Japanese and, furious at having been betrayed, took his story straight to Zhang Xueliang, the marshal's son, who now took over the command of the troops of Manchuria.

In Tokyo General Tanaka learned that the Kwantung Army had murdered Zhang Zoulin, and Tanaka sent an investigator to Mukden to find out the facts. The stories had seeped into the Imperial Household, and

Prince Saionji, the imperial advisor, had a good idea of what had happened. But the enthronement of the Emperor was near at hand, and so for the moment everyone agreed to hush the growing scandal. But before the coronation Saionji insisted that General Tanaka inform the Emperor. The general stalled. The army wanted General Muraoka and Colonel Komoto to be put quietly on the retirement list.

Finally the war minister did respond to some questioning by the Emperor by telling part of the story, and General Tanaka followed with the truth that the Kwantung Army had been responsible for the killing, and no other. Hirohito was furious. He told General Tanaka that the guilty must be brought to justice and punished. Tanaka agreed, but when he went back to his cabinet, the other members said that to do this would be to jeopardize the whole government. The army did not want the guilty punished, but wanted to handle the matter "administratively," without scandal. There was no real evidence of any army part in the murder, said the generals. Muraoka and Komoto had been found guilty of failing to guard the marshal's rail route properly—that was all.

General Tanaka took this story to the palace and tried to persuade the Emperor that it was the true version. The Emperor reminded him that he and his war minister could not keep their stories straight, and that Tanaka himself had already told the Emperor of the guilt of Muraoka and Komoto. Hirohito was virtually beside himself with anger.

Tanaka said he could explain.

"No" said the Emperor, "Don't explain. Just leave your resignation as you go."

Tanaka left the audience room sweating. He asked Grand Chamberlain Kantaro Suzuki for another audience and Suzuki made the request, but the Emperor refused.

And so, on July 1, 1928, General Tanaka resigned in disgrace and all his ministers resigned with him. The Emperor for the first time had used his power to force the resignation of a prime minister who had displeased him. Tanaka was abject and his spirit was broken. Not long afterward he died.

But with the army steadfastly denying that there had been wrongdoing. Emperor Hirohito had no way to force the punishment of the crimes of General Muraoka and Colonel Komoto, and they got off scot-free. Worse than that, the Kodo Ha, or Imperial Way, faction of the army had scored a great triumph. The Kwantung Army felt that it was nearing its goal of taking over Manchuria. There was no way the Emperor could bring the army to heel.

Little by little, through Saionji and others, some of the details of this scandal leaked out over the years. But the whole story was not known until after Hirohito's death, when Count Makino published part of his diary, a first-person story by someone who had participated in the mess. This diary showed the many machinations of the Kwantung Army and the growing suspicions within the Imperial Household, as well as the attempts of the military to deceive Emperor Hirohito to attain its own ends. It gave the reason for the depth of the Emperor's feeling that his army was really disloyal to him—a belief he never lost until the end, when he defied his generals and surrendered the nation.

That same year, 1928, Hirohito was enthroned. Hirohito put aside his anger about the incident in China and traveled to Kyoto, where on November 10, 1928, he changed into robes of orange, the color of the rising sun, and mounted his grandfather's throne. He prayed and made offerings through the night to his ancestors, and in the morning the ceremony was completed. For three days Kyoto celebrated. The royal carriage clattered along the streets, which were lined by thousands of eager citizens, clamoring for a look at their sovereign. And then came parades, with floats of wood and paper and flowers, and thousands of troops marching in columns.

When the celebration ended, Emperor Hirohito returned to Tokyo and the problems of state. The most serious of the moment was still the murder of Zhang Zoulin, which Prime Minister Tanaka had traced to elements of the army, but which had been concealed in the end.

The Emperor and the civilians worried lest the army pursue its course of empire building and seize control of the government, and they wanted full disclosure of Japanese army responsibility. In line with this, the opposition Minseito Party led the demand for a new investigation and exposure of the army's interference in Manchuria. But the army closed ranks and the right-wing civilians joined, so that the Minseito demand for an open investigation was denied in the Diet and the Manchurian affair was hushed up.

The situation remained through 1929 and 1930 at virtual impasse. The world economic crisis, triggered by the New York and London stock market crashes, diverted attention from Manchuria for a while.

In Japan at this time the Emperor was turned from political affairs to a more personal problem: his failure to produce an heir. Empress Nagako gave birth to two more daughters. Within the palace the pressure began to grow. The Genro wanted Hirohito to take a concubine, but he would not. He was a different sort of person, this Hirohito, and not one the palace elders found easy to control. This was not just a personal issue, but a political one, with the expansionists insisting that the Emperor was serving the country badly by not producing a son.

In 1930 the political pot boiled over again, on an issue that involved the ultranationalists and the direction of Japan. A group of ardent nationalists, in league with the big Japanese industrial combines, which were now known as the *zaibatsu*, formed themselves into the Nikkyo, or All-Japan Patriots' Society, and tried to reform the government. Their policy was called Kodo Ha, after the army clique of that name, and they also invented the term *hakko ichiu*, all the world under one roof, which to them meant benevolence on the part of the government, but to the army meant something entirely different—Japanese control of Asia and then perhaps the world.

Prime Minister Yuko Hamaguchi, who had succeeded General Tanaka, was just the sort of government leader that Hirohito wanted. His program called for a cutback in military expenses and for reforms that would increase civilian control. But Hamaguchi was hampered by the world depression, and by the continued growth of militarism within the army and navy. The London Naval Disarmament Conference of 1930 reaffirmed the 5–5–3 navy ratio, that is, five American and five British ships to three Japanese, and infuriated the "fleet" faction of the navy, which was secretly plotting an enormous naval growth.

The prime minister sought an audience with the Emperor, who told him to fight for Japanese acceptance of the naval treaty no matter what the hotheads of the navy said. So the treaty was accepted. But this affair marked the last action of orderly government in Japan, because on November 14, while getting aboard a train at Tokyo Station, Prime Minister Hamaguchi was shot by a would-be assassin, a member of one of the ultrapatriotic, right-wing societies which had been encouraged by the army. He did not die until the following summer, but he was so badly disabled that from that point on he was effectively out of politics, and the politicians were warned: to go against the army and the navy was to risk assassination.

Japan's years of peaceful change had ended, and Emperor Hirohito's command of the government had suddenly been seriously compromised. Some students of Japan have suggested that if the Emperor had seized control at this point, he might have stopped the army's march to power. This seems most doubtful, however, given the whole of the evidence. In the first place, such a move would have been revolutionary, and Hirohito was not of that mind. He wanted to live within the Japanese constitution, not outside it. And second, the army had organized itself into a cabal. In the affair of the Zhang Zoulin murder the army had already shown its unity and its strength, and its ability to frustrate the civilian authorities. Further proof of the army's intentions and its strength would emerge in the next few months.

8

The Rape of Manchuria

In the spring of 1931, while Prime Minister Hamaguchi was in the hospital trying to regain his strength after the assassination attempt, his cabinet persisted in office under a caretaker regime. The Emperor sanctioned this unusual arrangement because he knew that this moderate cabinet was Japan's best chance to maintain civilian control of the government.

Hirohito was aware of the political currents that swirled around him. He had shown his disapproval of the army's interference in China, but in spite of the imperial disapproval, the army had enlarged its force in Manchuria. The headquarters of this force were at Dalian, but its major force was at Mukden (or Shenyang, as the Chinese called it). The force altogether was not large, about twelve thousand men, or the size of a reinforced division, but it was too large to be explained easily. The army told the Emperor that so large a force was necessary to guard the South Manchurian Railway and protect Japanese interests. Hirohito did not believe it, but there was nothing he could do. He also knew that senior army and navy officers ambitious for control and expansion were drawing to them many of the junior officers of both services. He knew that at least one element within the army was plotting to seize power.

The officers, in turn, knew that the Emperor disapproved of their activities in China, but they were determined to go ahead. Their aim now was to isolate the Emperor, and they could see that under the Japanese constitution this was not too difficult a job. All they need do was emasculate the civilian leaders around the throne. Cooped up inside the Imperial Palace, the Emperor was virtually a prisoner of the system, and it would take a major effort and an enormous gamble for him to move against the military if they once took power.

The center of the new plot against the civilian government was Mukden, the transportation center of Southern Manchuria. After the assassination of Zhang Zoulin, the Japanese had expected that it would be easy to control his son and heir, Zhang Xueliang, because the younger Zhang was an opium addict, and such are not noted for their clarity of thought or willingness to take strong action. But Zhang was a tough young man and a Chinese nationalist. In 1929 he declared his allegiance to Chiang Kai-shek's Kuomintang regime.

The Japanese scheming in Manchuria was evident to anyone who wanted to look. Foreign reporters wrote that it would not be long before the Kwantung Army made a move to seize Manchuria and North China. Miles W. Vaughan, the far eastern manager of the United Press Associations, said it was only a matter of time, that the Kwantung Army could move whenever it wished.

How right Vaughan was! The coup was planned by several young Kwantung Army officers—Colonel Seishiro Itagaki, Lieutenant Colonel Kanji Ishihara, and Major Kenji Doihara. Colonel Itagaki was commander of the 33rd Infantry Regiment, stationed at Mukden, and he had replaced Colonel Komoto, who was responsible for the assassination of Zhang Zoulin, as senior staff officer of the Kwantung Army. Colonel Komoto had been sacrificed to the Emperor: he had shouldered the blame for bombing Zhang Zoulin's train. Lieutenant Colonel Ishihara, who was regarded in army circles in Tokyo as a budding genius, had made himself an expert on Chinese affairs. His father was a priest of the militant and ultrapatriotic Nichiren Buddhist sect, and from that connection Ishihara had a large following. Major Doihara was one of the army's China experts and head of the army's special intelligence bureau in Manchuria.

In 1930 Zhang Xueliang made an outright challenge to Japan's supremacy in South Manchuria by building new railroads parallel to the South Manchurian Railroad, in an attempt to diminish Japanese power in the region. If the Chinese could not ship on the South Manchurian Railroad, they could use the other roads, and this hurt the Japanese considerably. The Kwantung Army leaders decided they must move soon, before Zhang and Chiang Kai-shek could build up the defenses of the area.

The militarists in Tokyo were also moving. In September the army intelligence service drew up a paper, in the guise of an Inspection of General Circumstances, the traditional appraisal of Japan's defense posture in the world. This new appraisal called for a "perfection of the national structure." What was needed, said the army paper, was removal of the influence of the corrupt politicians and the cartels and establishment of a Showa restoration, which meant a new, militarized Japan. The army then set up a debating society, the Sakurakai, or Cherry Society, which was really formed to propagandize for military takeover.

So as of 1930 the army was united in its ambitions toward China and prepared to move. Just at this time, Emperor Hirohito's attention was distracted by the navy. In the naval maneuvers of that year, the Emperor boarded the battleship *Haruna* to review the fleet, which was simulating war games against the United States.

The games that October were held in the Inland Sea, and there the naval air arm produced some surprises. That arm of the fleet was headed by Admiral Isoroku Yamamoto, one of the advocates of naval air power, and he had been training his pilots very hard to show that the carrier was the wave of the future. In these maneuvers he certainly proved his point. His White Fleet decisively defeated the Blue Fleet by the use of carrier-based planes. Emperor Hirohito was impressed, and so were the other admirals in their ostrich-plumed hats, in spite of their personal proclivity for the battleship, a proclivity then shared by the admirals of every fleet in the world. After this performance it was agreed that the force of four Japanese carriers had to be vastly increased.

In the ensuing focus of interest on the affairs of the navy, the army movements in the north were overlooked. In league with conspirators in the army headquarters in Tokyo, the leaders of the Kwantung Army moved steadily toward seizure of power.

The Kodo Ha group was ready to stage a coup. Lieutenant Colonel Kingoro Hashimoto, a prominent leader of the Sakurakai, conspired with several civilians to set up the plot. It was to begin with a demonstration outside the National Diet building on March 20, 1931. The demonstrators were to be provided with two hundred practice grenades, which they were to explode, to create confusion and the semblance of a violent uprising. Thereupon, Hashimoto and a number of other officers would arrive with troops, take over in the name of law and order, invade the Diet, and declare a military government. War Minister Ugaki would become prime minister. He would declare that *kodo*, the Imperial Way, had been established, and the invasion of Manchuria would begin.

But the plot fizzled out at the last moment, when General Ugaki decided it was too risky for him.

That summer Prime Minister Hamaguchi finally died, as a result of the wound he had received at the train station, and Reijiro Wakatsuki took over as prime minister. He had been a trusted minister under Hamaguchi, and the Emperor and Prince Saionji hoped that Wakatsuki would follow the Hamaguchi road.

But the army had other ideas.

On August 1, 1931, General Shigeru Honjo was appointed commander of the Kwantung Army in Manchuria. He took command just as the young officers of the command were plotting their coup. As General Honjo traveled to Dalian, Major General Yoshitsugu Tatekawa was presenting a document to the army general staff called "General Principles Regarding Solution to the Manchurian and Mongolian Problem," which advocated Japanese occupation of both areas.

In the aftermath there was some confusion regarding General Honjo's role in the Manchurian affair, but publication of his diary in 1967 made it clear that he did not himself originate the plot. In June the Kwantung staff sent Major Tadashi Hanaya back to Tokyo to obtain the army leaders' approval for action in Manchuria in the fall. And on August 3, just as General Honjo was getting ready to leave his headquarters for Mukden, his officers revealed to him the plan for takeover of Manchuria.

The officers at Tokyo headquarters who were involved in the plot were General Senjuro Hayashi, commander of Japanese Korea; General Honjo; General Jinzaburo Mazaki, chief of forces on Taiwan; Vice Chief of Staff General Harushige Ninomiya; General Hajime Sugiyama, vice war minister; General Kuniaki Koiso, chief of the military affairs bureau; General Tetsuzan Nagata; and General Tatekawa, head of the military strategy department.

In the next few hours government officials heard of the plan, and they asked the army to send a high-ranking officer to Mukden to prevent the army from taking any action. The army officials picked General Tatekawa, who, as we have seen, had originally drawn the plans for the Manchurian takeover.

When the conspirators in Mukden learned that Tatekawa was coming and the nature of his mission, Colonel Itagaki laid on a party at a geisha house. The general was whisked there from his train and, while the conspirators acted, he was entertained all through the night by several officers and many geisha. Meanwhile, on the night of September 18, 1931, the conspirators blew up a section of the South Manchurian Railway and blamed the Chinese for the deed. That gave them an excuse to act.

General Honjo may have been convinced by his subordinates that the Chinese really were responsible. For until the end of his life (he committed suicide in 1945 after the Japanese surrender) he insisted that the Japanese actions had been purely defensive and that the Chinese had blown up the railroad. In any event, he called out the troops and they went into action. The reason, he said, was that the Kwantung Army force numbered only 12,000 and the Manchurian soldiers at least 150,000. Only by swift action could the Japanese retain control of the railway.

Within three days, General Hayashi, commander of the troops in Korea, also knew all about the plans for the Manchurian Incident.

None of this had been done with the knowledge or compliance of the Emperor. When he heard the news he erupted in anger and demanded that the army stop immediately. The Kwantung Army had precipitated a constitutional crisis; unless the cabinet took strong action, power would pass into the hands of the army.

Hirohito's advisors cornered Prime Minister Wakatsuki and made this fact quite clear to him. They told him that the Emperor had ordered this rebellion quelled. Wakatsuki agreed, and the advisors went their own ways. In fact, most of them went into hiding, because they were very much afraid of assassination. This left Wakatsuki to solve the problem without support, and this he was unable to do.

Within a matter of hours the army had moved to strengthen its position. Wakatsuki called on Prince Saionji for help, but Saionji was out of town. And at this point, Wakatsuki's cabinet deserted him. They told him they were convinced that the army needed support, not control, and that they supported the war minister's demand for more funds to be made available immediately.

This was really the end of the line. The army saw that there was no one around Hirohito who could help him stave off the bid for control. The army's most important ally in Manchuria, Yosuke Matsuoka, a U.S.-educated civilian of the ultrapatriot group, controlled the South Manchurian Railway. He turned it over to the army for movement of troops and supplies.

As the fighting continued and the Japanese took more territory, the Chinese protested to the League of Nations, to which both countries belonged. When the league eventually found in China's favor, the power of the Japanese army leaders was such that Japan withdrew from the League of Nations.

In the next few weeks the army paid no attention to the Diet, no attention to the cabinet, no attention to the Genro, and no attention to the Emperor's wishes. General Honjo announced publicly that he was going to move against Zhang Xueliang, and no one dared criticize. The three most important generals, Kanaya, Muto, and Minami, issued a dictum to the cabinet: to settle the Manchurian issue, the government must legalize the army's seizure of the area.

Once more the extreme right wing of the army plotted to seize outright control of the government, and once more Lieutenant Colonel Hashimoto was in the forefront. This plot was to be executed on October 24. The Wakatsuki cabinet would all be wiped out by a bomb placed in the prime minister's official residence, and then army troops would seize the government offices. Meanwhile other troops would run through the streets in armored vehicles and fly airplanes over Tokyo to show unified army support of the revolution. But Hashimoto talked too much; he got drunk too often; he spent too much money trying to suborn the younger officers, and he alienated many of those whose support would be needed. One day Hashimoto told Vice War Minister Sugiyama that he must support the rebellion or else. The plot included action against the Emperor. He was to be told that he must support the rebellion, or the officers would put him aboard a warship and send him out to sea.

General Ugaki was offered the leadership of this rebellion. He was noncommittal. War Minister General Sadao Araki was approached for support at a geisha party and was alternately cajoled and threatened. Araki decided this matter had gone too far, and so he called on generals Minami and Kanaya. They held an all-night meeting, the outcome of which was the arrest of Hashimoto and the other major conspirators.

Under the Japanese constitution all of the plotters were guilty of treason and could have been put to death. But none of them was even scratched. Hashimoto had the most severe punishment: twenty days' confinement, which he served in a geisha house.

The Emperor was very angry with the army, but aside from acquiescence he had only one alternative, which was pointed out to him by his younger brother Prince Chichibu, who was himself an army officer. The generals, said Prince Chichibu, had proved themselves disloyal to the government. Hirohito should take the reins of power into his own hands, dismiss the generals, and reform the army into one that was responsive to the imperial will.

So counseled the prince, but Hirohito hesitated. It was true that the actions of the generals threatened the constitution, which stipulated a sharing of power by the civil and military authorities. But for Hirohito to take power into his own hands would be a violation of the spirit of the constitution, which also stipulated that the Emperor should make no move unless endorsed by at least one minister of state. Of course, it would be possible to appoint a minister of state who would endorse anything Hirohito did, but this was not Hirohito's way. As he recalled years later in his conversations with Hidenari Terasaki, he decided to reject that course, full knowing that without it he would be putting himself in the hands of the military. The Emperor declined to interfere because he did not want to be the one to damage the constitution.

Before the month of October 1931 was out, another plot was discovered, this one designed to put General Araki at the forefront and secure the adherence of the Emperor by hook or by crook. This plot was serious in a different way—it involved troops as well as ambitious officers. A whole regiment of the imperial guard, the Emperor's personal soldiers, had been taken into the plot. By this time the civilian government of Japan was in shards. No civilian official dared do anything that would antagonize the army.

Two months later the conquest of Manchuria was complete, and Colonel Itagaki put into action the next part of the Kwantung Army plan. He went to Tianjin and brought back Henry Pu Yi, the last of the Qing dynasty, who had abdicated as Emperor of China in favor of the Chinese Republic. Pu Yi was to be restored to a throne; he was to become the Emperor of Manchukuo, which would be a vassal state to Japan. And if Colonel Itagaki's complete plan succeeded, Emperor Pu Yi would return to the Celestial Throne in the Forbidden City of Peking, ruling all China for his masters, the Japanese, who would have achieved a large part of *hakko ichiu*—their own corner of the world, at least, would now be under one roof.

That was how the world looked to the Japanese army at the beginning of 1932.

9

Against the Emperor's Will

With Manchuria wrested from China, the appetite of the Kwantung Army was only whetted. However, the extension of the army's campaign into North China was stopped for a while, because Foreign Minister Kijuro Shidehara came to Manchuria and convinced General Honjo that to keep going just then would be to court military action by the United States and Britain.

But the army soon saw that the threat was illusory, because Britain and the United States were preoccupied with internal financial problems. In a few weeks the Japanese were again moving. General Honjo himself did not favor the establishment of a true puppet government in Manchuria. He wanted a government that was Manchu in nature, friendly to Japan, and in no way inimical to Japanese interests, but not a puppet. Of course, this was impossible. The young staff officers of the Kwantung Army, drunk with power, rejected it outright and established their puppet government.

It seems hard to believe that a group of young staff officers, none of them higher in grade than colonel and most of them lieutenant colonels, could control a whole army, and thus a whole government. But the Japanese military systems gave the staff officers almost unlimited authority and responsibility; often the titular commanders did not even know what was going on. This was certainly true of the Kwantung Army, where Colonel Itagaki and his young officers paid virtually no attention to Honjo except to give him lip service.

Henry Pu Yi, the last Emperor, was taken out of Tianjin at the end of 1931, and in March 1932 the old city of Changchun was rechristened Xinqing and made the capital of Manchukuo. Shanhaiguan was captured by the Japanese to "protect" the gateway into North China. But even before the new state was proclaimed, trouble had arisen in Central China.

At this point the army was really beyond control. The men around Hirohito realized it, but they hoped against hope that something could be done to prevent the army from seizing total power. Hirohito saw now that Wakatsuki had been the wrong man for the prime ministry, but it was too late. By the end of 1931 the imperial household was definitely on the defensive. The army was laying plans to "reform" the imperial household itself, which meant removing any possible initiative from the Emperor. Hirohito spoke to Prince Fumimaro Konoye and Marquis Koichi Kido about this, and they told Imperial Household Minister Ichiki to watch out for attempts by the army to infiltrate the imperial household.

And the fact was that the Japanese public found this conquest exciting. It appealed to the spirit of a "New Japan, a Great Japan" which would assume the leadership of Asia and wipe out the Japanese feelings of inferiority to white foreigners.

As the year began, the Emperor faced a major crisis. For the first time his advisors counseled him to give in to the army. The Marquis Kido, Prince Saionji, and Prince Konoye all told him that it was his responsibility to submerge his feelings and accept the trend of his government.

And there was a more important matter to which the Emperor must address himself, said Prince Saionji. It was time for Hirohito to take a concubine and produce sons.

The Emperor refused, but he was weakening. The palace gossips reported that Hirohito began appearing in the afternoons at the pavilion of the Empress's ladies in waiting and chatting with the prettiest of them. Four daughters and no sons—it was a real problem. The courtiers contrived to have pictures taken of three of the prettiest girls and to present these to the Emperor along with their full pedigrees. He could not help but notice that all three were the daughters of Choshu clan generals; the Choshu clan dominated the army. That would certainly be one way to resolve the growing rift between the Imperial Palace and the army.

But Hirohito, though tempted, did not act. His mind was elsewhere. He was still hoping to change Japan's course. In December 1931 Prime Minister Wakatsuki resigned. The Emperor was glad to see him go. The Emperor and Prince Saionji agreed that the only civilian politician who might be able to control the army was Tsuyoshi Inukai, whose Seiyukai Party had triumphed in the most recent elections. Inukai had some strong military connections, but it was known that he was an advocate of civilian control of the government.

The Emperor had a talk with Inukai and made his wishes known. He was satisfied, and appointed Inukai to select a cabinet. Very shortly afterwards, the new prime minister sent a secret emissary to Chiang Kai-shek in China, suggesting that they exchange representatives to find a formula to bring peace between China and Japan. But by this time the army's ears were everywhere, and they had rumors of the move, and rumors that the Emperor was behind it.

So 1932 began with the army and the expansionist elements of the navy on the one side, opposed by the civil government, the Emperor, and the conservative element of the navy on the other side.

On January 8 the army received help from an unlikely source. A Korean patriot made an attempt to assassinate Emperor Hirohito when the Emperor was attending a military review in North Tokyo. The Korean, I Pong-chang, read in the newspapers about the coming review and the Emperor's route to the place. He went there with a grenade in each pocket and found a place on the line of march. As the Emperor's cortege passed, he threw a grenade. It exploded, but not under the Emperor's carriage; instead it damaged the carriage occupied by the imperial household minister. The Korean was quickly captured. When told the identity of the attempted assassin, Hirohito smiled thinly.

"It would be a Korean, wouldn't it?" he said.

The day after the assassination attempt the cabinet resigned, but Hirohito refused to accept the resignations. The army pointed to this incident as an example of the necessity for military rule to restore law and order in Japan. Also in the name of law and order, the Koreans came in for a new round of persecution.

Meanwhile, the army was busy provoking an incident in Shanghai. Japanese agents gave money to Chinese laborers in the Japanese-owned Three Friends cotton towel factory. They also hired a street gang to help cause trouble.

On January 18 three Nichiren Buddhist priests and two disciples came along the street toward the factory banging drums and chanting prayers. They had been organized by Colonel Itagaki, who had strong ties to the Nichiren community. The Chinese towel factory workers and the street gang beat up the Buddhists. In retaliation the Japanese community sent thirty members of the Japanese Young Men's One Purpose Society into the quarter to attack the towel factory, and the next morning they set fire to it. While the fires were burning the Chinese police arrived, and the Japanese fought them. Two policemen were killed and two were wounded, and one Japanese was killed.

That morning the Japanese community of Shanghai held a mass meeting and urged the Japanese community mayor to ask Tokyo for soldiers. The mayor of Shanghai, Wu Tieh-ching, apologized to the Japanese community on behalf of the rowdies of the towel factory, and promised

compensation to the Nichiren provocateurs. But the Japanese also demanded that the mayor force the Chinese community to love the Japanese, and this, the mayor said, he was unfortunately unable to do. For
the next few days young Japanese toughs wandered about the street
picking fights with Chinese.

Now came a really complicated maneuver, in which the Japanese and
Chiang Kai-shek joined hands. Prime Minister Inukai was trying to reach
an accomodation with Chiang, as noted. They had come to the point
of agreeing that by making Manchukuo a state independent of both China
and Japan, the problems might be resolved. Japan would help Chiang
eliminate the Chinese communists, and would then in return be given
trade and industrial concessions. By this agreement Japan would also
destroy the Chinese 19th Route Army, which Chiang wanted out of the
way because it was independent and its generals contested his absolute
rule.

The Emperor liked this plan. He had been worried for several years
about communist inroads in China. This accommodation would serve
the dual purpose of wiping out the communists and creating amity with
China.

With imperial approval a Japanese cruiser and four destroyers arrived
at Shanghai on January 23. On January 24 two aircraft carriers arrived.
Shanghai called for help from Chiang Kai-shek, but he did not send it.
He wanted the 19th Route Army destroyed.

For the next two days the unrest in Shanghai increased. Mayor Wu
told the Japanese he would comply with any requests they made, but the
Japanese admiral told a newspaperman that he had orders to send his
troops into the Chapei district of Shanghai "to protect Japanese lives
and property."

The Japanese landed as promised, but the Chinese 78th Division was
waiting in ambush, and hundreds of Japanese troops were killed before
they could withdraw. The next morning the Chinese threatened to break
through into the Japanese settlement, and the admiral sent his carrier
planes to bomb. The planes burned down several buildings.

Chiang Kai-shek said that he would send troops to Shanghai, but he
did not. The Japanese sent more troops, and the navy asked for help
from the army. In Tokyo Emperor Hirohito became concerned lest the
incident expand further. He asked the army leaders to move very carefully
and to withdraw at the earliest possible moment. He also appointed his
wife's cousin, Prince Fushimi, to be chief of the navy general staff,
another move to keep an eye on the navy.

Early in March, twenty thousand Japanese army troops arrived in

Shanghai, bringing the Japanese force up to about three times that of the 19th Route Army. The Chinese retreated. So the Japanese controlled Shanghai, and the "Shanghai incident" came to an end.

Meanwhile, back in Japan, several assassinations strengthened the hand of the army and the right wing. These assassinations were directed at industrialists who were also politicians, with the joint purpose of eliminating old enemies and frightening the zaibatsu into submission.

The next step for the militants was to secure a prime minister who was not a politician, but first the conspirators had to get rid of Prime Minister Inukai. This they did on May 15, 1932. A group of young officers invaded the prime minister's official residence and shot Inukai. He died a few hours later.

The Emperor tried again to avoid army takeover, this time by appointing a navy man, Admiral Viscount Makoto Saito, to be prime minister.

But Admiral Saito was 81 years old, and the war minister, chosen by the army, was the same General Araki who had sided with the rebels in the last three abortive army attempts to seize power. The Emperor did not dare order that Araki be replaced. If he did so, the army could refuse to supply another war minister, and the cabinet would fall under the constitutional provisions. So the government of "national unity" was formed.

But, this government did not control the drift toward outright army control of Japan, and the drift toward total fascism gained momentum. The Emperor knew what was happening, but he seemed powerless to stop it. Each time he appointed a new prime minister, that minister either was murdered or joined forces with the army.

In Manchuria and in Shanghai the military ran amok. Foreign diplomats were abused by army officers. Chinese citizens were slapped, beaten, and sometimes killed on the streets. Japanese soldiers forced Chinese civilians to bow to them. Why? Because the Japanese were the master race. Bits of information about these excesses reached the palace. One diplomat resigned his post in China and wrote Hirohito that he had been so humiliated by the army's arrogance that he was coming home.

But now the problem had been expanded beyond arrogance. Matsuoka, who had started as an official of the South Manchurian Railroad and thus was more familiar with Manchuria than any other civilian, was sent to Geneva as Japanese delegate to the League of Nations, to argue against the sanctions against Japan demanded by league members. Once the

sanctions were approved, it was Matsuoka who supervised Japan's withdrawal from the league in the quarrel over Japanese aggression in Manchuria.

Emperor Hirohito did what he could to prevent Japan's withdrawal,
because he believed in the principles of the league. When it came time
for the government to announce its withdrawal from the league, he asked
that two points be made. First, it was unfortunate that Japan should have
been placed in the position of withdrawing. Second, Japan would continue to cooperate with other nations in a search for world peace.

The army did not like these two points. General Araki commented
unfavorably on them. And within the army came a new movement, this
time a movement designed to destroy Hirohito himself. The organization
was called Shimpeitai, and its raison d'être was defense of the Imperial
Way, the army concept of Emperor worship.

In the guise of serving the country, General Araki had served the
army well. In the past two years he had stamped onto Japan this concept
of the Imperial Way. "The principle of the Imperial Way is that the
Emperor and the people, the land and morality, are one and indivisible."
Araki was reactivating the old samurai concept of bushido, and the
soldier's obligation to die for his master. To die for the Emperor, he said,
was the wish of every Japanese. It was not true, of course, but no one
dared gainsay the general. "Whether I float as a corpse under the water,
or sink beneath the grasses of the mountainside, I willingly die for the
Emperor," says the old proverb.

This was the philosophy beaten into the soldiers and the people. Araki
was the one who made of Hirohito "our living God," in fact as well as
in fable. For years the Japanese had been saying these things; now the
people began being forced to believe them. The propaganda campaign
was endless. Schoolchildren were taught the Imperial Way from the time
they learned their first lessons. In spite of Hirohito's objections, the
Imperial Way again became Japan's way of life; all the hopes for a be-
nevolent reign were being replaced by demands for imperial rule, by
which was meant a military dictatorship.

At this point Hirohito might have stopped the process by a public
objection to the new concept. But the people were embracing it eagerly,
and he lacked the imagination to see that the army's moves were still
tentative, and the strength to act. Prince Saionji and the other advisors
also objected in private to the army leaders, but the recent spate of
murders had made Hirohito's advisors careful about what they said in
public, and their silence to the nation indicated compliance with the
demands of the army. The army was forcing expansion of the armed

services and a return to the trappings of the samurai. In 1932 the samurai sword was suddenly reintroduced in Japan by Araki.

Each year the military budget soared. No man below the rank of minister of one of the services had ever discussed political matters before, but under the new army regime, generals spoke openly to newspaper correspondents and on the radio.

But defense of the Imperial Way did not mean defense of Emperor Hirohito. Quite to the contrary, the Shimpeitai wanted to get rid of him:

> The soldiers of the Gods aim at the annihilation of the leaders of the financial groups [zaibatsu], the leaders of the political parties, the villains of the Imperial entourage, and their watchdogs who are obstructing the progress of the Empire. They shall thereby establish the Imperial Restoration and proclaim the Imperial Rule throughout the world.

In the spring of 1933, Count Makino told the Emperor he wanted to resign his post as lord keeper of the privy seal. He said the reason was his health, and in a sense he was being quite honest: he was afraid of death by assassination. The Shimpeitai now proposed the elimination of Hirohito, who they said had tried to stop the army's march to glory in Manchuria and in China. He would be killed and his name blackened, and he would be replaced by his brother Prince Chichibu, who was expected to be more malleable, particularly under a new government led by Prince Higashikuni, Chichibu's and Hirohito's uncle, who was a general through and through.

One of the Shimpeitai's arguments against Hirohito was his failure to provide an heir to the throne. They began to move more openly and more noisily, until July 1933, when they finally aroused so much resentment in the palace that the cabinet ordered the police to round up the major figures. They were charged with plotting the assassination of many high officials. No mention was made of Hirohito, lest the idea of assassination take hold with other right-wing groups, But the Shimpeitai was wiped out. Hirohito knew all about the plot and about the attitude of General Araki, who had been known to make comments about the Emperor's failure to produce an heir.

But then, on December 22, 1933, Empress Nagako gave birth to another child, and this child was a boy. The public indicated overwhelming approval of the imperial family, and, since there was no eating the unkind words General Araki had spoken about the Emperor, Araki lost no time in resigning as war minister. The army had overstepped, and had received its first setback since Manchuria.

10

The Struggle for Power

1934. The son of Enlightened Peace blossomed in the palace nursery, but the sun of Enlightened Peace was sinking low on the horizon as the army continued to drive for dictatorship. One by one the Emperor's hopes for a long and peaceful reign were being diminished.

Bergamini's *Japan's Imperial Conspiracy*, published in 1971, was a detailed attempt to throw onto Hirohito's frail shoulders the responsibility for the Japanese drive to war and empire in the 1930s and 1940s. The book details each event accurately, and then in each case indicates that the instructions to act came straight from the throne. For example, discussing the plans of the Mukden cabal to seize Manchuria, Bergamini writes, "Since receiving Hirohito's go ahead in early June, 1931, Ishiwara had worked with a fanatic's zeal to prepare for his scheme of inside out conquest."

But one might ask, what go-ahead, and how was it delivered? The Emperor was not in the habit of granting audiences to colonels.

This technique appears throughout the book: accurate discussion of events, and then, almost as an afterthought, each conspiracy, each action, large or small, is attached to a coat made for Hirohito. But the coat does not fit; the book does not have the ring of truth, perhaps because the attempt to indict is so intense and so hammering.

Had Hirohito's grandfather been in his place, the coat might have fit quite well. Physically Hirohito bore a considerable resemblance to his grandfather the Meiji Emperor, although it was diminished by his spectacles and his refusal to wear a beard. In temperament, however, he was very little like his grandfather. Hirohito was a modern man of the twentieth century, a scholar and a moderate. Unlike his forebears, he neither drank nor smoked. When he came to power he had dismissed his father's forty-eight concubines, and he had not replaced them.

To be sure, he had been tempted in that trying period when the

Empress was producing daughters but no sons. The photographs of the three beauties remained on his desk for many weeks, and he did go to the pavilion of the ladies in waiting, and did chat with many of the eager young women.

But by the early weeks of 1934, all this was behind the Emperor. The Empress, who had been upset by the rumors she heard from the pavilion of the ladies in waiting, settled down, and the rumors in the palace ceased. The gaiety of the ladies' pavilion was notably hushed, as it appeared that there would be no chance for a royal concubine.

On New Year's Day, 1934, the Emperor turned his attention to one of his favorite occupations, the management of the Imperial Poetry Contest. Ten prizes were awarded, for haiku (seventeen syllables, three lines) and for tanka (five lines, thirty-one syllables), and the lucky winners were told that they would be coming to the palace to have their poems read before the all-highest himself.

What would his grandfather have done at such a time? Haiku contest, yes—the Meiji Emperor was a notable poet, and Hirohito often quoted his works. But in the conflict with the army, what would Meiji have done? From the record of Meiji's two wars, it is apparent that there would have been no conflict with the army, for the Emperor would have been solidly behind the military expansion and the broadening of empire.

Hirohito was treading a new path, however, opposing the army which had been established by his grandfather. That army's officers had always believed in empire.

The men around Hirohito were loyal to him, and were doing their best to prevent the army takeover of government. Prince Saionji remained the major advisor to the Emperor, but in 1934 he was 85 years old and growing physically feeble, so he liked to spend his time at his country estate.

Therefore most of the duties of political advisor fell upon the Lord Privy Seal, who at that time was Nobuaki Makino. Makino had held the post since the Emperor was still regent of the Empire. He was an intelligent man and a friend of the West. He had accompanied his father on the Iwakura Mission to the United States and Europe in 1871, when the Meiji government was searching for Western ideas, and had stayed behind in the United States until 1874 to go to school. He had served in the Japanese foreign service in England, Italy, and Austria. Makino was a liberal, a constitutional monarchist, who believed that Japan must maintain friendly ties with the United States and Britain. Because of this attitude toward the West, Makino was regarded by the army militants as a prime enemy, and had already been the target of several failed assassination attempts.

The next important official of the palace guard was Grand Chamberlain Kantaro Suzuki. He was a navy admiral, and he had been chosen for the job in 1929 to offset the army influence around the throne. Suzuki was an advocate of the London Naval Treaty, written in 1930, which was coming up for new discussions in 1934. Those in the "fleet" faction of the navy, still determined to build the most powerful navy in the Pacific, found themselves stymied by Admiral Suzuki, and increasingly they turned toward the army extremists. Suzuki was also on the army black-list, because he had opposed the Manchurian takeover, particularly the use of the troops stationed in Korea, quite without orders, by General Hayashi.

The next important official was Kurahei Yuasa, the imperial household minster, who had, among other jobs, served as head of the security bureau of the Home Ministry. This meant he had been Japan's chief policeman and knew a great deal about the activities of the police force. It was through his influence that the Shimpeitai had been brought down. But because he had opposed the "dangerous thoughts" legislation, which was already turning Japan into a police state, he was high on the right wing's list for removal.

The young lions of the Kwantung Army had decided as early as 1932 that General Honjo was not militant enough, and they managed through their Tokyo connections to have him sent back to the capital.

Honjo was given a seat on the Supreme War Council, a sop to his long and faithful service, and on April 6, 1933, he was appointed to be chief military aide to Emperor Hirohito. This, the army leaders believed, was a brilliant stroke. They expected Honjo, as a part of the Manchuria conspiracy, to continue to act in their interests. His predecessor, General Takuhara Nara, had always made it a point to tell the Emperor only what the army wanted Hirohito to hear, and to conceal as much as possible.

Indeed, Honjo had been selected for the post of chief aide-de-camp by General Araki, that hawk of hawks. It was understood that Hondo's major role was to keep Araki informed of developments at the palace, and not the other way around. But by 1934 General Araki had been forced into resignation, so Honjo no longer had that special relationship with the war minister.

Honjo's responsibility was considerable. Under him were eight other aides, five from the army and three from the navy.

When Honjo was appointed, Hirohito was not pleased. He told Prince

Saionji that he was not sure he could trust the general. Saionji agreed, but said there really was no choice at the moment.

General Honjo was hardly comfortable in his new position, and he was critical of the Emperor, because he did not believe Hirohito had the best interests of the army at heart. But Minister Yuasa pointed out to Honjo that Hirohito had two roles to play: he was chief of the armed services, and he was also chief of the civil government. Yuasa also told how Hirohito had stood out in a pouring rain to review the troops one day that winter, although he was just recovering from a cold.

In a short time Honjo underwent a total conversion and became loyal to his Emperor. Or perhaps it might be put another way: he had always been loyal to the throne, but he had been first an army officer. Now, given the post of imperial military aide, he took his duties seriously and kept Hirohito informed of every army move, and of his own feelings, too, which was sometimes more valuable.

Prince Saionji's secretary, who did not believe in telling the Emperor anything embarrassing about national affairs, complained about Honjo. "He passes on directly to the Emperor what the army officers are saying. He does not measure up to the former chief aide, Nara, who had the good sense to be discriminating about the information transmitted between the Emperor and the army." So by the beginning of 1934 the relationship between military aide and Emperor was very good, better than it had ever been with another aide.

The prime minister of Japan in the winter of 1934 was still Admiral Saito, but his new war minister was General Hayashi, Grand Chamberlain Suzuki's bitter enemy. Saito endorsed the London Naval Treaty, but of course Hayashi did not; it was a matter of army faith to oppose any sort of arms limitation.

Equally important was the general movement of the government against liberal thought, a movement backed increasingly by press and public. Professor Hajime Kawakami had been dismissed from the Imperial University of Kyoto in 1933 for his Marxist views, just a few months after Professor Yukitoko Takigawa was dismissed for "liberal" views. The net of thought control was tightening.

Matters were not helped at all by the bad weather and crop failures of the preceding two years. Farmers were selling their daughters to geisha houses and brothels to preserve the rest of their families. In such circumstances, the militants' promise that expansionism was the only road to prosperity fell on receptive ears. One reason for this receptivity was that there had been a shift in the balance of the officer corps; by the middle of the 1930s the preponderance of young officers came from peasant families. When their parents wrote to these officers that their little sisters had been sold to the brothels, one need not exercise much imagination to understand how they felt.

The army, that winter, was undergoing some paroxysms of its own. Following the fall of General Araki, General Nagata became chief of the military affairs bureau of the army, the bureau that really controlled personnel and policy, with General Hayashi as war minister. Nagata's first step was to purge from office all the followers of General Araki and replace them with men of the "control" faction of the army. This group believed in centralized direction by army headquarters. So as far as the public was concerned, it was a case of one form of military control or another; it made little difference which.

At the court the problem was somewhat different. Prince Saionji had always believed that Hirohito ought to comport himself as a constitutional monarch, of the sort that George V of England was. But behind Saionji's belief, modern though it was, there lurked another belief, far more Japanese. This was the theory of *taisei ni shitagau*—follow the trend, or, in colloquial terms, "go with the flow"—and if the flow happened to be inimical, then *yamu o enai*—it can't be helped. On several occasions in the past, Hirohito had wanted to intervene in military affairs. The first occasion had been the Mukden Incident, when the Kwantung Army took over Manchuria. As noted, Emperor Hirohito had issued a statement that he heartily approved of the Wakatsuki government's efforts to contain the incident. The army had been furious at this statement, and the generals had blamed the men around Hirohito. All these men were blessed with a fine sense of personal survival, and thereafter they did their best to insulate Emperor Hirohito from the government and the world, because of their own interest in staying in power.

In 1933, when General Hideki Tojo of the Kwantung Army had launched an offensive into Jehol Province of China to cut Inner Mongolia off from China proper so the army could exploit that area, Hirohito had offered to convene an imperial conference and order the army to desist. Prince Saionji objected. If the Emperor did this and the army refused to obey orders, then the Emperor's power would be badly eroded.

Hirohito then made a critical error. He took Saionji's advice, thus losing a major opportunity to curb the army. He might have wondered: what good was power so slender that if it was used the rod might break? His acceptance of Saionji's bad advice indicated the vacillation that would bedevil Hirohito for the next eleven years. It was not that the Emperor was weak; he would prove his strength of character at least twice during this period. He could be strong, but he was also shy, even timid, and more than that he was misguided by self-serving advisors. Too often he allowed them to persuade him to the course of *taisei ni shitagau.*

As Saionji aged, he grew more conservative. He wanted to avoid trouble. Once when Hirohito was about to confront Foreign Minister Shidehara with charges of mismanagement of a delicate issue, Saionji privately told Shidehara, "It is not proper to lie, but tell him things that will ease his mind."

By 1934 the right wing of the army was pouring hundreds of thousands of yen into a propaganda campaign against civilian government. Several newspapers had been bribed with secret army funds. Hirohito learned of this campaign and told General Honjo to inform General Hayashi that he would have to assert control over the army.

That spring of 1934 Hirohito inquired frequently into the attitude of the army units, and he frequently questioned the other members of the royal family, including his brother Chichibu. He was particularly interested in the opinions of the young officers. At the end of March, War Minister Hayashi reported to the Emperor that the young officers were "much more tranquil" than in the past. But, he added, the young officers were watching everything Hayashi did and everything the government did. "Consequently if the government accomplishes nothing, and if bad policies follow one after another, I cannot say with confidence that difficulties will not again arise."

That same day the Emperor discussed this conversation with General Honjo. He lamented the aggressive attitude of the young officers. It was not possible to move the way they wanted, he said. After all, he had acceded to the army's demands for reform when the cabinet removed from the civil service lists the inspector general of police, the chief of the home ministry security police, and the secretaries of the two houses of the Diet.

Reforms? These were hardly reforms. They were openings for the army to take over these all-important appointments.

A few days later Hirohito dined with his supreme war council and the division commanders, who had all come to Tokyo, as they did once a year, to report formally on the condition of the army. During the dinner his uncle, Prince Higashikuni, who was commander of the second division, invited the Emperor to come down to the division headquarters and go hunting at the Koshigaya hunting grounds, famous for their wildlife. "I can't," said Hirohito gloomily. "Security. I can't go anywhere."

11

The First Crisis

It had been Hirohito's practice to go every spring for a holiday at the villa in Hayama, where for a few weeks he could go diving and collect marine specimens to his heart's content. Hayama, although only a few hours from Tokyo, was secluded (no train service), and the Emperor's palace, on the shore, was fenced and guarded on three sides. But in 1934, Pu Yi's coronation and Admiral Heihachiro Togo's death delayed this visit until the end of May. Upon his arrival the Emperor caught cold, his nose ran, and he could not go diving at all. So the holiday was a total failure.

This was the year of the second London Naval Conference, and the navy was badly split on the question of future naval power. The conservative element was willing to accept the 5–5–3 ratio of ships, with Japan having only three-fifths of the naval power of either the United States or Britain, but the more radical element was not. Navy Minister Osumi came to see Emperor Hirohito and reported that the delegates (led by Admiral Isoroku Yamamoto) had been told to exercise their own judgment, and that the navy favored disarmament, not armament.

"Good," said Hirohito. That was just what he wanted. But privately the navy chief of staff, Prince Fushimi, a member of the imperial family, told the Emperor the navy must have equality with the big powers or navy morale would disintegrate. Thus controversy began once more, and it would last through the London Naval Conference. The conference would fail, and Japan would begin an unrestricted naval building program, against the wishes of the Emperor.

That summer of 1934, the imperial family went off to another summer palace, at Nasu, for the month of August, and even this simple move created a controversy, stemming from the Imperial Way philosophy, which had now permeated virtually all of official Japan.

For years Hirohito had taken his children with him whenever the royal family moved from one palace to another. But this year the royal chamberlain suggested that only the Crown Prince, Akihito, travel with the Emperor and Empress, and that all the other children travel separately. "The crown prince, being the heir to the throne, is a descendant of the Sun Goddess, so he should be segregated from the other princes and princesses in order to enhance his majesty and dignity from early in his life."

And Hirohito allowed himself to be pummeled into doing what the royal stewards wanted.

Back in Tokyo in mid-September, Hirohito was still troubled by Prince Fushimi's attitude toward naval parity. The Emperor asked questions. Why did the navy insist that it must have absolute parity or else it would jettison the naval treaty? The latter course would enable America and Britain to build enormous navies.

That was true, said Prince Fushimi, but... And there he stopped. Because what he could not say was that he was under the influence of the "fleet" faction of the navy, which was determined to junk the London treaty and build an enormous navy at any cost, and ultimately to use that navy to fight a war against the United States.

For the next few days, on the eve of the dispatch of the delegation to London, the matter was discussed at the palace. But it was apparent that the two factions were solidified, and no compromise was reached. As chief military aide, General Honjo stated the military position as follows:

> Because all the powers are confronting serious economic difficulties, there is little danger that war will break out even if the powers concerned fail to conclude a naval arms limitation agreement. If Japan were forced to accept less than parity with Great Britain and the United States, it will not again be able to hold its head up high. From the standpoint of national defense, failure to reach an agreement would be better than acquiescing to an unfavorable one.

One of the most voluble advocates of the "fleet" faction of the navy was Admiral Masanobu Suetsugu, who had recently been making inflammatory speeches on the subject. At a meeting Hirohito told Prince Fushimi to get Suetsugu under control, and he also emphatically told Prince Kanin of the army that the army and navy officers must live up to their oaths of office. When the report of this meeting was transcribed, General Honjo knew that the radical army and navy leaders would object, so he asked that those remarks be deleted. Instead of standing firm and bringing about the crisis while he could still control it, the Emperor allowed General Honjo to delete his remarks. Years later he would admit that his fear of the army was rising at that time.

It was now two years since the establishment of Manchukuo, and liberal elements in the cabinet were demanding a relaxation of Japanese control. The Emperor agreed and said so. When, he asked, was civilian control going to be returned to Manchukuo?

The army made conciliatory statements, but General Honjo explained that nothing could be done "until peace is restored." By peace, the army meant: until the last vestiges of Chinese opposition and guerilla warfare were eliminated (and this, of course, never did happen).

Hirohito did not give up on the issue just then. A few days later he had General Honjo in conference again, asking more embarrassing questions.

"Why should the commander of the Kwantung Army be in charge of the internal political affairs of Manchuria? Why shouldn't civilians run the government?"

"Of course they should," said General Honjo, "but...." And what the "but" meant was that the Kwantung Army had not the slightest intention of giving up its iron control of the state of Manchukuo. So in December 1934 new regulations which made the army control even tighter were issued. Even Emperor Pu Yi's personal guard of Manchus was disarmed. Emperor Hirohito, who probably was not aware of that last insult, was reduced to remarking that the tightening was all very well, since it was only "temporary," as General Honjo had insisted, but that for the long run, civil control was best.

The army assented, and proceeded to do precisely as it chose.

Emperor Pu Yi of Manchukuo was scheduled to come to Tokyo in April 1935 for a state visit, and to review selected elements of the Japanese Imperial Army. The Emperor announced that he planned to attend.

But the army complained. He must not attend, said the generals. "The Japanese army's reverence for the Japanese Emperor makes it incapable of saluting a foreign emperor and not the Japanese Emperor when he is also present."

However, Imperial Household Minister Yuasa told General Honjo that it would be a grave violation of protocol and hospitality if the Emperor did not attend the review. He insisted that the Emperor attend.

War Minister Hayashi then said that if Emperor Hirohito came, the army would refuse to dip its banners to the Manchurian Emperor. Furthermore, said Hayashi, it would demean God if, when he met Emperor Pu Yi at Tokyo Railway Station, at any point his Majesty were to walk behind the Manchurian emperor in view of the troops.

But Hirohito and the imperial household would not accept these dicta. They insisted that Emperor was going to attend and that the army was going to behave itself. As for the meeting at the station, the Emperor was particularly contemptuous of the army's demands and refused to discuss the matter.

In this instance the army backed down. The army would make a great show when the Emperor of Japan arrived and left, however, and he agreed to arrive late and leave early. So the Emperor won a modest victory, for a change.

But the generals never gave up. Next came the issue of the "Emperor organ" theory of government, begun by a college professor, who had written a magazine article claiming that the Emperor ruled under the constitution. An examination of the Meiji Constitution makes that very clear, but the army held that "the military worships his majesty as divinity incarnate, and if his majesty were to be treated just like any other person in accordance with the organ theory, it would create grave difficulties in the areas of military education and the supreme command."

There was the problem. In the eyes of the army Emperor Hirohito was supposed to exist for the purposes of the military, and for those alone. The military wanted him to stand above affairs of state, with his wishes forever to be carried out by his subordinates. The idea was to seclude the Emperor, to keep him from making appearances because he was too lofty.

"But I am not a god," said Hirohito. "I am an ordinary human being. See: I have arms and legs and also," he pointed to his midriff, "intestines, just like anyone else. This whole 'Emperor divine' theory is nonsense," he said. "Ridiculous. The Emperor is an organ of the state, just like the Diet."

The Emperor remained inimical to the whole idea of being a divine puppet. Several times he complained bitterly about this to General Honjo.

"His remarks filled me with a deep sense of sorrow," wrote Honjo. But the general's sorrow was not so great as to persuade him to try to change the situation.

Prince Saionji was forever advising the Emperor to stay out of controversy. The reason was to prevent him—and themselves —from being criticized.

Don't call any Imperial Conferences, said Saionji.

If you do call an Imperial Conference, then don't say anything.
And if you do say anything, for goodness sake don't talk politics.

Even knowing how the Emperor felt about "divinity," the generals
continued the Emperor Organ theory controversy. The rub, as Hirohito
noted, was that if the army were to have its way, the Meiji Constitution
would have to be abrogated.

General Mazaki, now the inspector general of military education,
issued a directive saying that the Emperor was God and that was all there
was to it.

The Emperor objected. "I too would gladly adopt the theory of imperial
sovereignty if it did not lead to the bane of despotism, if it did not result
in disapproval by foreign nations, and if it did not conflict with our
national policy and history. Unfortunately I have yet to encounter an
explanation of this theory that is worthy of respect." And he told General
Honjo to inform the war minister that the practice of issuing special
pamphlets had to cease.

General Honjo summed up the army case:

> After the great European war, politicians began to oppress and attack the
> military. The number of men aspiring to enter the military service declined
> sharply. Military budgets were reduced stringently. The cut in resources
> for national defense brought a deep frustration to the military. Precisely
> at this point came the Manchurian Incident. At the same time democratic
> and liberal thought declined, while the theory of national policy based
> on the Imperial Way began to rise, and spiritual rejuvenation followed.

In the course of preparing for the visit from the Manchurian delegation,
the war minister came up with a request that Hirohito tell Pu Yi that
he, Hirohito, had absolute confidence in the commanding general of the
Kwantung Army.

What a strange request! But there was a reason for it.

The Japanese military in Manchuria were comporting themselves with
such arrogance that the Manchurians were becoming infuriated, and
even the leaders of the Kwantung Army were afraid they had gone too
far.

Hirohito listened to the army request, framed through General Honjo,
and was noncommittal. But then he consulted with his civilian minister
of the household and called Honjo in again.

"I will grant the army's request," he said. "But in return you must
have the commanding general of the Kwantung Army make certain that

the Japanese officials, as well as other Japanese residents in Manchuria, do not mindlessly harbor an attitude of superiority over the people of Manchuria and oppress them. Otherwise my words about having the full confidence in the commanding general will turn out to be meaningless."

In June 1935, trouble broke out again in North China, trouble fomented by the Kwantung Army and the Tientsin Japanese garrison. The army behaved with its usual arrogance, and the Chinese ultimately gave way. The army made many statements about its rights and the rectitude of its position in China, but Hirohito knew the truth.

That month a new·Chinese ambassador, Tso Ping, presented himself at the Japanese court. In greeting the new ambassador, Emperor Hirohito went far beyond the call of duty and lamented the recent troubles in North China, expressing his gratitude that the particular difficulty had been settled. "I am aware that that was made possible largely by the efforts of their excellencies, Chiang Kai-shek and Wang Ching-wei. I would like the ambassador to convey my appreciation to these two excellencies."

The army was furious. To have their Emperor tell the Chinese now that their leaders had been responsible for bringing peace was an intolerable insult—the fact that the Emperor's statement was true just made matters worse. At this point General Honjo was so upset that he asked the grand chamberlain of the court that the report of the Emperor's conversation be kept from the rank and file of the army, "because it is already being bruited about that the imperial court is the center of the weak-kneed foreign policy" (that policy being Foreign Minister Koki Hirota's attempts to seek an accommodation with the Chinese).

But the Emperor was not moved. On July 13, when Prime Minister Keisuke Okada came to an audience, Hirohito remarked to him that the cabinet really ought to be on guard against being led by the nose by the military forces stationed overseas.

As a result, General Mazaki was ousted from his job as inspector general of military education and was kicked upstairs to the Supreme War Council, where he could not do much harm. This change, made over the objections of army leaders, including General Honjo, represented a real victory for Hirohito.

12

Four Days That Shook Japan

The term was *gekokuju oe*, "the tail wags the dog," and it referred to the alarming tendency of the young officers to beard their superiors and give them orders.

One of the key figures in creating this problem was General Mazaki, who had been cashiered after his open attempt to create a military dictatorship. But Mazaki had ardent followers, one of whom was Lieutenant Colonel Saburo Aizawa. On August 12, 1935, Aizawa walked into the office of General Tetsuzan Nagata, Mazaki's successor, and killed him with a samurai sword. Aizawa's reason: Mazaki had convinced him that Nagata had been responsible for Mazaki's downfall. His only regret, Aizawa told the arresting officers, was that he had done a sloppy job (not with one blow but with half a dozen), which embarrassed him because he was a fencing master.

One immediate result of the murder of General Nagata was the resignation of War Minister Hayashi, who was caught in the middle of the controversy about responsibility for the action. That resignation served to polarize the two elements of the army even further, and the new war minister, General Yoshiyuki Kawashima, came to the palace to promise that he would use a benign rather than coercive policy in dealing with personnel. The fact that he felt this was necessary indicated how far discipline had slipped within the army.

The Emperor's dilemma continued. How was he to deal with the growing signs of rebellion within the ranks? Occasionally some event came up that gave Emperor Hirohito an occasion to express his own sentiments. In mid-September 1935 came one such, the arrival of Sir Frederick Leith-Ross, a special representative of King George V of England, who had been sent to study the Chinese situation. King George was using his official position and his friendship with young Emperor Hirohito to try to defuse the tense situation in China.

The message brought by Leith-Ross was that King George was very much concerned about the trend of events in China and that he was aware of Japan's strong economic interests there, as well as Britain's own economic interests. It was important, he said, that England and Japan should cooperate fully in dealing with Chinese affairs.

Hirohito seized upon this message to let his own government know how he felt about the army's continued incursions into China. He told the grand chamberlain and the lord privy seal that those who drafted the reply should consult with the foreign office. And when they did, he wanted to make sure that they knew that the King of England's sentiments were in complete harmony with his own. He also gave this information to his military aide, General Honjo, to pass along to the war minister.

That winter, Hirohito learned that General Araki, who had gone on the reserve list after his disgrace of the year before, was manipulating the Military Reserve Association to keep alive his Imperial Way concept. The association demanded from the government a statement to the effect that "the Emperor is the principal entity who possesses sovereignty."

On hearing of this, Hirohito exploded. He could see behind the facade: if that statement were made, Araki and his friends would stretch it to mean that the Emperor was divine. But once again, from around Hirohito came the counsel of patience. Let him approve such a statement; it was essentially innocuous and true, his advisors said.

So the Emperor was swayed.

Would such a statement cause the military to cease its pressure for the Imperial Way? If so, he said, he was willing to give his approval to the idea.

Saionji assured him solemnly that this statement would end the matter, and Hirohito approved it. But after the prime minister and the cabinet drafted a statement, the war minister refused to approve it because it was not strong enough. So the fight continued.

Next step: the army demanded the removal of Tokujiro Kanamori, the chief of the cabinet legislative bureau, because he was a known advocate of the Emperor Organ theory of government, an enemy of the Imperial Way.

Finally the tension became so great that Hirohito dissolved the Diet and called for new elections. Parliamentary elections were held on February 20, 1936, and the election results bonded together the army's rebellious factions. The right wing had campaigned on a pro-fascist and pro–Imperial Way platform and had lost ground; this was a warning to the Araki-Mazaki faction that its days were numbered unless it undertook quick action. So the activist faction in the army decided on a military coup.

Hirohito had noted that the "Manchuria virus" was widespread in the Tianjin garrison in North China. He decided to order some changes, and told General Honjo it was time to take some divisions out of Manchuria and bring in fresh blood. So the 1st Division of the Imperial Japanese Army was selected to go to Manchuria.

Now the almost total politicization of the army became apparent. By and large, the young officers of the First Division were followers of General Araki. They decided that they were being moved to get them out of Tokyo and politics, and also that they must stage a rebellion to overthrow the government and prevent a return to liberalism.

On the night of February 25, 1936, they wrote a manifesto listing their complaints and arranged for its delivery to the major Tokyo morning newspapers. Their manifesto claimed that:

1. Only through the Imperial Way could the national glory be spread throughout the world and all men live happy and productive lives.
2. Only by the elimination of the power brokers of Japan could the nation be saved, since the power brokers had infringed upon the prerogatives of the imperial line and impaired the empire.

And who were these villains? The elder statesmen (*genro*), the financial magnates (*zaibatsu*), the government officials, and the political parties. What was to be done?

It is clearer than light that our country is on the verge of war with Russia, China, Britain, and America, who wish to crush our ancestral land. Now Japan is faced by a crisis. Unless we now rise and annihilate the unrighteous and disloyal creatures who surround the imperial throne and obstruct the course of true reform, the imperial prestige will be destroyed.

Therefore it is our duty to take proper steps to safeguard our fatherland by killing those responsible.

On the eve of our departure for Manchuria, we have risen in revolt to obtain our aims by direct action. We believe it is our duty to remove the villains who surround the throne. We, the children of our dear land of the gods, act with pure sincerity of heart. May the spirit of our imperial ancestors assist us in our endeavors. . . .

The distribution to *Asahi*, *Mainichi*, and other big newspapers was hard going, because a blizzard swept through Tokyo that night, lasting until midnight and leaving the streets covered with powdery snow.

Even as the sleepy night editors were reading the manifesto in the early hours of the morning, the mutineers were about their grisly self-appointed task of murder. At 2 A.M. the First and Third Regiments of the division were aroused by their young officers. First the officers harangued them about the need for action, while others, who opposed the mutiny, warned the soldiers against it. By 3 A.M. some 1,350 soldiers had elected to act, under the orders of Captain Nonaka and Captain Teruzo Ando, both of the Third Infantry Regiment. Another conspirator was Captain Yamaguchi, the son-in-law of General Honjo.

By 4 A.M. the soldiers were assembling in the streets outside their barracks. They were joined there by the Seventh Company of the Third Regiment of the Imperial Guard, who did not know (except for the lieutenant, Motoaki Nakahashi) that they were being pulled into a rebellion.

The rebels then began to march, and by 4:30 A.M. they had surrounded the nerve center of Tokyo, wherein lay the Imperial Palace, the Diet, the war ministry, police headquarters, the army general staff offices, and the official residences of most of the ministers of the government.

By 5 A.M. the rebels had established headquarters at the Sanno Hotel. They had invaded the war minister's house and were parlaying with War Minister Kawashima.

At the offices of the imperial general staff there was a flurry of excitement, also at 5 A.M. Colonel Kanji Ishiwara, who had led the Kwantung Army in the Mukden Incident, had been promoted to operations chief of the general staff. He had heard of the uprising the night before and had come to stop it. Learning that the rebels had surrounded the war office, he stormed out, shooting dead a rebel guard who tried to bar his way. He got into his car and drove off to seek outside help. He found it at Kempeitai headquarters, where he established a government of martial law.

Meanwhile, three hundred soldiers, led by five officers, had headed for the house of Prime Minister Okada. First they attacked and killed the four policemen who guarded the house, and then they began searching the many rooms for the bedroom of the prime minister.

But Okada's brother-in-law, Colonel Matsuo Denzo, found him first. The prime minister was sleeping off a drunken evening, and the colonel and several maids got him up and hustled him into the servants' quarters, where they locked him in a toilet. The colonel went dashing into the courtyard shouting, "Tenno heika Banzai!" ("May the Emperor live ten thousand years!")

The victim's head was nearly blown off by a hail of machine-gun fire, which so disfigured his face that no one could identify his body. But by checking photos of the prime minister, the soldiers decided they had gotten the right man.

Meanwhile, at 4:30, a sleepy reporter on night duty at the *Mainichi Shimbun* had received a telephone call in which a voice shrieked, "The prime minister's house is being raided! Our own army is attacking us!" and then the line went dead.

Another reporter was sent out in his car to find out what was happening. But he was stopped just past Hibiya Park by one of the rebel soldiers.

"I'm from *Mainichi*," said the reporter.

The soldier looked at him grimly and leveled his rifle. "Who cares about the press. Turn back," was the order. And the gun came up.

So the *Mainichi* reporter went back to his office without learning what was going on.

Just after 5 A.M., Lieutenant Nakahashi of the Imperial Guards division surrounded the house of Finance Minister Korekiyo Takahashi with a hundred soldiers. A policeman was on guard outside. Nakahashi shot the policeman down and burst into the house. The 81-year-old Takahashi was sound asleep when Nakahashi swept into his bedroom and ripped the quilt off the old man on his futon.

"Tenchu!" the lieutenant shouted. "Divine punishment!"

The lieutenant had a gun in one hand and a short samurai sword in the other. The finance minister opened his eyes sleepily, and at the sign of recognition, the lieutenant shot him three times, and then stabbed him twice. The minister died.

A unit of two hundred soldiers with four officers surrounded the house of Admiral Saito, the former prime minister, who had replaced Count Makino as lord privy seal a few weeks earlier. Makino, fearing he would be assassinated, had pleaded ill health and resigned.

Hearing the young officers charging through the house, Saito's wife got up and locked the bedroom door, but in a few moments the door was forced. By this time Saito had gotten up from the futon and was standing behind his wife, wearing his *yukata*, or cotton sleeping kimono. Three of the officers shot him at the same time. Saito fell, and his wife fell on his body and clung to it. The hysterical young officers tried to drag her off but could not, so they thrust their weapons underneath her and fired more shots. Altogether they fired forty-seven bullets into the body, and wounded the viscountess three times as well. Then they turned, shouting, "Banzai, Banzai, Banzai!" and rushed out of the house.

Captain Ando led an attack at about that time on the house of Grand

Chamberlain Suzuki. There, an alert policeman on guard challenged the soldiers, and when they would not stop he began shooting. The policeman delayed them for ten minutes, but Ando then wounded him and the troops surged by.

They found the grand chamberlain in his bedroom with his wife. He and Captain Ando then began to discuss the political events of recent days. After ten minutes Ando tired of the argument and fired three shots into the chamberlain. He leaned down.

"I can still feel a pulse," he said to the Baroness Suzuki. "Now I shall kill him with my sword."

The baroness looked at him contemptuously. "If you feel it necessary to assault a dying man, then why don't you let me do it?" she asked.

Captain Ando was shamed to be spoken to thus by a woman before his men. He slunk out of the room.

Suzuki eventually recovered from his wounds.

Some of the men who had murdered Admiral Saito now went to the house of General Jotaro Watanabe, who had replaced General Mazaki as inspector general of the army's military education program. They blew the lock off the front door with machine gun fire and then swarmed into the house. Watanabe's wife confronted them. They brushed past her and into the next room, where they found the general. He shouted, "Halt!" but by the time the words were out of his mouth the lieutenant leading the men had shot the general down. He was hit scores of times by more bullets. A lieutenant then completed the job by cutting the throat of the dead general with his samurai sword.

The rebellion was not confined to Tokyo; outside the capital it was organized by the Reserve Officer's Association, which was loyal to General Araki.

A group of soldiers and reservists appeared at Okitsu to assassinate Prince Saionji, but they were met and dispersed by a larger number of policemen.

At Yugiwara Hot Springs, Makino, the former lord privy seal, was hiding out with his 20-year-old granddaughter Kazuko. At 5:40 that morning Captain Hisashi Kono led a squad of soldiers to the inn, and they set up a machine gun outside. They found the innkeeper and demanded that he produce Makino. Instead, Makino's bodyguard appeared, firing a submachine gun. He wounded Captain Kono but was shot down by the machine gun. The gunfire sprayed through the wooden house and wounded several people, but Makino and his granddaughter escaped out the back door of the inn and climbed the hill behind.

As the murderers swarmed through Chiyoda-ku, the government district of Tokyo, other rebels seized the offices of the big daily newspapers. They wrecked the presses of the *Asahi Shimbun*, which had been the most critical of the army. By 7 A.M. the rebels were in control of the whole government district. Their rebellion seemed to have been a success.

But the rebels had underestimated Hirohito and the imperial will. Just after 5 A.M. General Honjo had been awakened in his house in northwest Tokyo by an emissary from his son-in-law, Captain Yamaguchi, who told him that five hundred officers and men of the First Regiment had left their barracks. Honjo told the emissary to hurry back and tell Captain Yamaguchi to stop the rebellion. But the lieutenant shook his head. It was too late, he said.

Honjo telephoned the commander in chief of the secret police, who was on duty at the Imperial Palace. Then he called a car and set out for the palace. Near the British embassy he encountered a group of soldiers, but he did not stop to talk to them. Instead he drove straight to the palace.

The Emperor was already up and at work at his desk. He was dressed unusually early, in an army general's uniform. He already knew of the rebellion. "Put an end to this business now, and we may turn disaster to our advantage," he said.

The general, thinking of his son-in-law, put in a good word for the rebels. "The young officers only. . . . "

But Hirohito was not listening. He was angry, particularly because the rebellion involved his own Imperial Guards.

At 7 A.M. War Minister Kawashima began to talk to the officers of the rebel group, who presented these demands:

1. The government must announce a full restoration of the Emperor to power (which, conversely, meant the government must deprive the Emperor of all his power).
2. The army must rid itself of factionalism (by destroying the control faction).
3. The "archtraitors," generals Minami, Koiso, Tatekawa, and Ugaki (of the control faction), must be arrested. Other officers (also control faction) must be dismissed.
4. General Araki must be made commander of the Kwantung Army.
5. General Mazaki must be brought back into the counsels of the Emperor.

At 8 A.M. Prince Fushimi, chief of the navy general staff, arrived at the palace. He told Hirohito that fleet units had already sailed from

Yokosuka Naval Base into Tokyo Bay and would soon be ready to shell the rebel positions if the Emperor so ordered. He also advised Hirohito to form a new cabinet and to compromise with the rebels.

Hirohito turned a steely eye on the prince and dismissed him from the royal presence.

At 8:15 A.M. the war ministry issued its first bulletin. It assumed that Prime Minister Okada was dead (not true) and noted that Admiral Saito and General Watanabe had been murdered and that Admiral Suzuki and Finance Minister Takahashi were wounded (actually Takahashi was dead).

At 9 A.M. War Minister Kawashima arrived at the palace. He produced the rebel demands and read them to the Emperor.

> After humble reflection as children of the land of the gods we submit these grievances to the one eternal god, the Emperor, under whose high command we serve. . . .

Then came many sentences of tortured prose.

> Insofar as we can, we and our kindred spirits must make it our responsibility to break down the inner doors and strike off the heads of the treacherous army traitors in the palace. Though mere retainers, we now take a positive road as if we were the trusted lieutenants of the throne. Even if our actions cost us our lives and our honor, vacillation now has no meaning for us.

When the war minister had finished, Hirohito looked at him coldly and demanded that he suppress the rebellion.

The war minister withdrew to think over his course of action, and Hirohito began interviewing individually the members of the supreme war council, who had assembled at the palace. He told each that the army must take the full responsibility for this treacherous action and that the army must clean its own nest. And if the army failed, then he would call in the navy to do it. Or he would lead the Imperial Guards out to do it himself.

At War Minister Kawashima's house, the leaders of the rebellion waited for Kawashima to return. During this time Major Tadashi Katakura, a nephew of General Inami, who was one of the generals on the death list, came to the house on a routine mission and was greeted with a shot in the head, which Katakura survived. This incident illustrates the degree of hysteria that had seized the rebels by midmorning.

At noon the last war councillor was interviewed by the Emperor. War

Minister Kawashima conferred with the Emperor again, and then sent Major General Tomoyuke Yamashita back to Kawashima's house to inform the rebel leaders that the Emperor knew of their intentions, and that the Supreme War Council had met and decided to act.

When the rebels received that message, they knew they had lost, since the supreme war council could not be committed to putting down the rebellion without the Emperor's approval. But the rebels were determined to die fighting, and they so told General Yamashita, who telephoned the Imperial Palace and was assured that reinforcements would come. Soon he was joined by two other officers to try to negotiate with the rebels, while Hirohito called the privy council into session. The cabinet also met, though without Prime Minister Okada, who was still thought to be dead. The supreme war council went back into session.

The afternoon waned. Emperor Hirohito refused to appoint a new prime minister. To do so would be to make the young rebels believe that their demands for "reform" had been heeded. The Emperor would make no concessions, nor would he allow the supreme war council to make any concessions to the rebels.

Late in the afternoon the council issued orders to the mutineers to return to their posts. The army imposed martial law. The First Division soldiers took up defense positions around the palace. General Yamashita came back, and three of the rebel officers tried to follow him into the palace. They were stopped by the palace guard.

That night seven generals went to the rebel headquarters, including Mazaki and Araki. The rebels repeated their demands and said they must not be called traitors. Nothing was resolved.

The cabinet members all resigned, but Hirohito refused to form a new cabinet until the rebellion was put down. The lamps burned late at the palace that night, but finally, at around 2 A.M., Hirohito went to bed.

On February 27 the capital of Japan was under martial law. Various officials and relatives of the Emperor kept pressing him to form a new cabinet, but he still refused. Not until the rebellion was finished, he said.

Again General Honjo came to the Imperial study to plead for the rebels, to argue that the young rebels were sincere.

"They killed my most trusted advisors," replied the Emperor. "There is no excuse for their behavior. I don't care what they thought. When they killed my people they were trying to kill me."

Honjo persisted, but Hirohito was unmoved. He was furious with the army leaders for not putting down the rebellion, and he threatened to take command of the Konoye Guards and crush the insurgents himself.

On this second day, Emperor Hirohito kept demanding of Honjo word that the army had crushed the rebellion. But Araki and Mazaki and several other generals were holding out for the rebels, and so Honjo could give the Emperor no good news. The Imperial Guards took up positions facing the northwest edge of the rebel line, and the loyal units of the First Division did the same along the southwestern and southeastern edges. Along the northeastern edge ran the moat of the Imperial Palace.

That night the princes of the royal blood met in family council, hoping to persuade Hirohito to treat with the rebels. Prince Chichibu, the Emperor's younger brother, who was a general on active service, was known to be friendly to some of the rebel leaders. Just after 5 P.M. Chichibu had arrived in a train at Ueno Station and was met by a police escort and driven swiftly to the palace. The various princes at the council offered several arguments, but Hirohito met them all. This was open rebellion; if it succeeded there would be no controlling the rebels. He would not yield. In the end the princes all agreed to stand behind Hirohito. Prince Chichibu wrote a letter to his friend Captain Nonaka, asking him to withdraw.

That night generals Mazaki, Abe, and Nishi told the rebel leaders that they had failed and must submit themselves to the imperial will. The rebels seemed to agree, but afterward they returned to their original positions. The night ended with no change in sight.

On the third day, February 28, General Honjo learned that the rebels had refused to give up. This was disastrous news for General Honjo; his son-in-law was deeply implicated, and Honjo was disgraced.

At 11 A.M. Captain Yamaguchi, the Honjo son-in-law, appeared at martial law headquarters in the secret police building near the Imperial Palace, where he argued the rebel cause eloquently. The generals seemed to be listening sympathetically. But then Colonel Ishiwara got up. He had not forgotten those first hours of the rebellion, when he had been stopped by a rebel at the war ministry and had shot the man dead. He announced an immediate attack.

The forces loyal to the Emperor were ready to attack, but the generals wanted to avoid bloodshed, so they stalled. Prince Chichibu's message was delivered to Captain Nonaka. General Yamashita and General Kawashima came to the palace to propose to General Honjo that a chamberlain be sent out to the rebels, whereupon he would witness all the officers committing suicide.

But the Emperor was adamant. "If they want to commit suicide let them do it. To send an Imperial witness to honor such men is unthinkable."

General Honjo said the First Division was not happy about fighting its former comrades. Hirohito told him coldly that if the commander of the First Division could not control his troops he ought to quit. Honjo had never seen the Emperor so angry.

The army leaders had not believed Hirohito had such strength of character. They were stunned by his outright rejection of the easy way. Captain Yamaguchi called his father-in-law and pleaded with him. Honjo told him it was useless, that the Emperor's mind was made up, and he hung up the phone.

General Sugiyama, the vice chief of staff, tried once more to get Hirohito to ameliorate his position. The young officers, he said, did not expect a witness at their suicides. They only wanted the Emperor to know, and so it would be fine if a steward looked at the bodies afterward.

But Hirohito would not be budged. To him these men were lower than dirt; they had lost all right to respect. He refused to have anything to do with them. Sugiyama was so upset that he lay down in the doorway and asked the Emperor to trample on him. Hirohito stepped over the supine body and walked into another room.

Sugiyama and the other generals did nothing. They said it was too late to attack that day. The attack would be carried out first thing next morning. Hirohito accused them of stalling to make the incident seem more important to the people and the world.

Honjo appealed to the Emperor once more, saying that the army was misunderstood.

Hirohito paused for a moment. Then he spoke.

> You appealed to me on the grounds that unjust criticisms are being directed against the army, and you did so with tears. But I say to you that if this incident is not resolved quickly a critical situation will follow. Three days have passed and the seat of government has not yet been recovered from the rebels. Foreign exchange has almost stopped, and there may be a run on the banks. Unrest is spreading outside the capital, and there is danger of rebellion. The loyal elements of the First Division might join their comrades who killed my best friends. Don't talk to me. Talk to the supreme war council if you like.

And that was dismissal—the Emperor had just told his military aide that he had no further use for his services.

The generals dithered for the rest of the day, trying to find some way out of their dilemma: they did not want to open fire on the rebels. Prince Kanin arrived, and they asked him to intercede with the Emperor. He refused.

And then generals Araki, Hayashi, and Sugiyama all went to the martial law headquarters, where they met with the staff. "We must at all costs avoid an open clash that will destroy army morale," they said.

Colonel Ishiwara looked at them coldly. His orders had been held up since noon by the generals. He spoke to Araki. "This is a violation of the Emperor's supreme command. Please state your name and rank, Sir."

"You know that I am General Araki," said the general. "I would advise you to hold your tongue."

"I cannot," said Ishiwara. "It is impermissible for soldiers to use the arms of the throne against the throne."

So General Araki and the other generals went angrily out of the room, and the attack was scheduled for the morning. All night long, sound trucks and radios broadcast demands to the rebels to surrender without fighting. Planes flew over and dropped leaflets.

Captain Nonaka made one last gesture: he sent a young lieutenant to cross the moat, enter the Imperial Palace, and make an impassioned appeal to the Emperor to recognize the rebels. The lieutenant set out and was passed through the lines of the Imperial Guards regiment, which was in collusion with the rebels. He was to find the Emperor, read him the message, and ask for imperial approval. If the Emperor did not approve, the young lieutenant was to murder the Emperor. After that, the Nonaka theory went, Prince Chichibu, Nonaka's friend, would ascend the throne of Heaven.

It was reported that the lieutenant did cross the moat, did get into the Imperial Palace, did find the Emperor. He burst into the Emperor's study.

The Emperor rose from his desk and stared at him, every inch the army general in his uniform. "How dare you come in here? Do you not know that I am your Emperor?"

And the young officer, overwhelmed at what he had done, dropped to the floor, kowtowed, and backed out on hands and knees. Then he ran back across the moat, returned to the rebel lines, and committed ritual suicide for his crime.

That night many things happened. Captain Yamaguchi was arrested by the Kempeitai for high treason. Small groups of noncommissioned officers and soldiers began to drift back toward their barracks, buoyed by the announcements that only officers would be punished for the rebellion.

The attack against the rebels began at 8:30 A.M. on February 29, 1936.

Units of the First Division moved ahead in a skirmish line, and the rebels drew back to the buildings they had occupied. By 10 A.M. the rebel soldiers were drifting off in twos and threes and giving themselves up. At noon Captain Nonaka read Prince Chichibu's letter once more and then killed himself. By two o'clock the revolution was all over.

That afternoon Hirohito said he was ready to authorize a new cabinet, but March 1 was a Sunday, so the work was put off a day. On March 2 the selection process began, and finally Foreign Minister Koki Hirota was chosen to be prime minister. Hirota was the man who had tried to reach an accommodation with China, without success because of the blockage by the army.

On March 4 Hirohito presided over the privy council and elicited from them a decision that all the rebel leaders would be tried by court martial in secret, that they would have no right of appeal of their sentences, and that the sentences would be carried out immediately.

All the army generals resigned to show their regret over the incident. Hirohito accepted the resignations, with three exceptions: General Terauchi, General Nishi, and General Ueda. On this triangular rock the army would be rebuilt. The other generals to be kept on were Prince Kanin, Prince Asaka, and Prince Higashikuni, all members of the royal family. All this while, to show his anger and remind all concerned of his authority, Emperor Hirohito dressed daily in the uniform of an army general.

The ruthless cleanup of the army began under the Emperor's personal supervision. As war minister in the Hirota cabinet, General Terauchi led the way, consulting with the Emperor frequently on appointments. In the next six months a quarter of the commissioned army officers were weeded out, and the average age of general officers dropped by more than ten years.

General Honjo resigned, his spirit broken by his son-in-law's treason. Within five months the courts handed out seventeen death sentences, including one to Captain Yamaguchi. All were killed by firing squads in secret.

The rebellion went down in Japanese history as the *ni niju roku san ju roku jiken* (the 2–26–36 Incident) and is still known today to every school child studying history. A week after the rebellion had collapsed, a *Mainichi* correspondent summed up the American reaction:

> Americans sympathetic toward Japan are finding it impossible to explain or excuse the recent Tokyo atrocities, which they had thought possible only in semi-civilized countries. Americans are now convinced that

whoever organizes the next cabinet, Japan's policy will become more pronounced to satisfy nationalistic clamors.

That was a good guess, although for the moment Emperor Hirohito had managed to seize the initiative and had brought the army under control.

All the same, emotional elements remained. The young officers were quelled for the time being, but their ideas were unchanged. What remained to be seen in the summer of 1936 was whether Emperor Hirohito could maintain control of the military machine.

One element, sometimes overstated, was a difference within the army as to who was the enemy of Japan. The Araki faction (to which General Hideki Tojo then belonged) believed that the Soviet Union was the enemy, while most members of the control faction, which had emerged from the 1936 rebellion in control of the army, favored an attack south to secure natural resources for the war against China. These are referred to by historians as the "strike north" and "strike south" factions. But it was never was as simple as that; it was a matter of priorities. For by 1936 the entire army was permeated by the desire for conquest and the building of the Dai Nippon Empire—Great Japanese Empire—which was to rule the whole of Asia, and perhaps even the world.

So far had Hirohito's dream of "enlightened peace" and constitutional rule been twisted by 1936.

13

The China War

Emperor Hirohito was gulled into believing that the strong action he had taken in February 1936 had put down the unrest within the army and restored the political balance of Japan. But sadly this was not true.

The expansionist elements within the army had been balked in their effort to seize power by force. There was another road to power, however, one established in the Meiji Constitution. That constitution, as already noted, had been written for Hirohito's grandfather, with a dichotomy of civil and military functions. Hirohito was head of the civil government, and separately chief of the military. One clause said that ministers of the army and navy must be military men. In the past, the prime minister–elect had been given almost complete latitude in meeting this requirement. He could even pick an officer from the reserve corps if he chose. In recent years this had been one way in which prime ministers had avoided dealing with the two militant factions within the army.

But after the 2–26–36 Incident the army insisted that the minister of war should be an active-duty officer. Since General Terauchi had undertaken the housecleaning demanded by Emperor Hirohito, and had finished up by ousting almost half the generals and 20 percent of the younger officers, Hirohito was inclined to accept that stricture, particularly since Terauchi explained that it would be useful in keeping such men as Mazaki and Araki out of office.

Therefore, in the Hirota cabinet the new precedent was established, and by the simple means of accepting or withholding approval of the appointment of a war minister, the army suddenly had the power to make or break a cabinet. It was a brilliant stroke, and Hirohito remained unaware of it until it was too late to argue.

In the beginning the Hirota government seemed to move smoothly. Hirota appointed Admiral Zengo Yoshida as navy minister. Since Yoshida was a liberal, who favored the naval treaties and opposed adventurism, the liberals in Japan and abroad felt they might have something to cheer about. Although the war minister, General Terauchi, was an important figure in the Tosei Ha, or control, faction of the army, just now he was being most circumspect.

Two circumstances prepared Japan for the takeover by the militarists. The first was the elimination of factionalism in the army. The second was the expiration of the naval treaties, which left Japan free to build as large a fleet as she wished. In fact, the naval hawks had started enlarging the fleet before the army rebellion.

In the guise of "security" against more rebellions, the police and military tightened strictures on freedom of speech, thought, and action. This was enforced through neighborhood associations, in which neighbor spied on neighbor, and the granting of almost judicial power to the police, who maintained *koban*, or police boxes, in every neighborhood. Here the citizens came to receive information, pay fines, and report on any changes in their households.

To foreigners this tightening was most noticeable in the police concern over their movements and in their use of cameras. But the foreigners, who in 1936 began to use the word "police state" to describe Japan, saw only the tip of the iceberg. The military were laying the groundwork for seizure of control.

Hirohito knew absolutely nothing about these changes, so completely insulated was he from Japanese society. Most of his functions were performed inside the imperial castle. If he traveled it was by motorcade, accompanied by a powerful army escort, or by train to one of the many shrines at which he must occasionally worship. From time to time, for a change, he visited one or another of the lesser palaces. His favorite was always Hayama, where he could read newspapers and nap on the beach, build sand castles with the children, and go out into the bay in his little boat to dive and collect marine specimens. He never seemed to notice that just outside diving range stood a pair of police boats. He had become inured to the life of *tenno*—of being constitutionally "sacred and inviolable."

A number of historians have blamed Prime Minister Hirota for the development of the police state, and they may be right. The war crimes prosecutors certainly thought so when they presented the evidence that sent Hirota to the gallows after the Pacific war. The prime minister seemed only too willing to lend himself as a tool to the army. He was, after all, a member of the Black Dragon Society, and the nationalistic purposes of the society, the building of Dai Nippon, coincided with the ambitions of the generals.

Under the Hirota government, the army and navy built and stockpiled furiously, running up the budget and adding six new divisions to the army. Hirohito was aware of the increased expenses, but as the months went on his command of affairs became ever more muzzy. The army was doing its best to keep him in ignorance. The failed rebellion had deprived the Emperor of seven of his most trusted advisors. General Honjo, his military eyes and ears, had resigned, and Honjo's successors told the Emperor only what they wanted him to hear. Prince Saionji was growing frail, and found his interest in government was waning. Saionji's secretary, Baron Kumao Harada, did not believe in telling the Emperor anything that might upset his digestion. The Marquis Kido, secretary to the lord keeper of the privy seal, resigned his post in fear of assassination. Steadily the old advisors were leaving the palace as having too dangerous an ambience.

The Hirota government began to have its troubles. Soon Admiral Yoshida resigned in an argument over policy, and was replaced as navy minister by Osami Nagano, who was dedicated to the buildup of the fleet.

The Hirota cabinet finally collapsed in a quarrel between civilian and military elements. The liberals in the Diet opposed the enormous expenditure of funds for military purposes. In an angry exchange on the floor of the lower house, Speaker Kunimatsu Hamada accused the army of using corrupt means, including bribery of newspapers and other public-oriented groups, to attempt to overthrow civilian government. He addressed these remarks to General Terauchi, who remained silent. The speaker then allowed his emotions to get the best of him and attacked again. He accused the army of planning to seize power and create a dictatorship in the pattern of Germany. Rising to a height of emotional oratory, Hamada offered to commit ritual suicide if anyone could prove that the remarks were untrue. Then he suggested that if his remarks were true, General Terauchi ought to be the one to commit seppuku.

The following day General Terauchi resigned as war minister and advised Prime Minister Hirota that he might as well quit, because he was not going to get another war minister from the army. Soon enough Hirota discovered that this was true, and the whole cabinet resigned.

Emperor Hirohito chose General Ugaki to succeed Hirota, because Ugaki was known as a moderate who opposed further military adventures in China. However, Ugaki was unable to form a cabinet, because no general would serve as his war minister. Hirohito then selected General Hayashi to form a cabinet. Hayashi seemed moderate enough, but then one day he announced that in the future the Imperial Way—the army's Imperial Way—would thereafter be the way of Japan, and that ordinary political life would have to be suspended.

The Diet then became so riddled with factionalism, most of it involving military matters, that on March 31, 1937, Hirohito dissolved the legislature and called for new elections. These were held in April and resulted in a resounding defeat for the army faction. The two civilian-oriented parties, both committed to opposing the Imperial Way, polled 98 percent of the vote. Despite the public cheering for the military and military adventures, the majority of the people did not want purely military control of their government.

Had one of the two parties been able to achieve a real majority at this point, events might have followed a different track. But all the defeat did was convince the army leaders that they had to seize control of the government, since they could not deal successfully with the civilians in any other way.

At this point Hirohito scarcely knew where to turn. There was one man who might do: Prince Konoye, a longtime friend and companion and the former leader of the House of Peers. He was a man about town, a traveler and bon vivant, who knew everybody who counted. He had many friends in the military and in business and civil government. He was the obvious choice to try to smooth over the growing differences.

In June 1937 Prince Konoye formed a cabinet. Hirohito suggested that he make a radio broadcast and promise an era of reconciliation among the army, the political parties, and the public.

For several years Prince Konoye had been nursing a dream of a nonpolitical society. This was to be achieved by the formation of a single political unit which would replace parties altogether. Thus was born the concept that would later be the basis of the Imperial Rule Assistance Association, which was virtually the same as the single-party systems of Soviet Russia, Germany, and Italy. When it came into being it would mean the creation of a monolithic state.

But when Konoye came to office, he was not yet ready to make such changes. He saw as his first task the unification of Japan, so he appointed a council of advisors which included representatives of all factions. Pressed by the army and the navy, he also established another agency, a fuel board, to control Japan's most delicate commodity, oil for the lamps and automobiles, but also for the tanks and battleships. The military, thinking about future war, announced that Japan had less than a year's supply of precious fuel. And not a drop had yet been used in conflict.

14

Incident or War?

1937. The isolation of Emperor Hirohito was complete. The Marquis Kido joined the Konoye cabinet, but he did not come to the palace to report on its doings. Kido's successor as palace advisor, Lord Yuasa, was almost completely ineffectual. Instead of addressing himself to the major issues of the day, Yuasa spent his time worrying about the Emperor's public and religious relations.

Was Hirohito spending too much time on marine biology and not enough on propitiating the gods? The army found the Emperor's scientific efforts peculiar; he should be worrying about high strategy, and not playing with fish. Yuasa persuaded Hirohito to keep his marine biology activities secret, as not befitting a god. Thereafter Hirohito practiced a sort of clandestine science, with his friend and former biology teacher, Professor Hirotaro Hattori, coming to the palace in the dead of night and leaving before dawn. By such attention to niggling detail, the palace officials comforted themselves that they were doing their job, and were able to look the Emperor in the face even as they betrayed the confidence he had placed in them.

In the army a new figure emerged: Lieutenant General Hideki Tojo, commander of the Kwantung Army. Tojo was an example of the type of officers arising from the democratization of the Japanese army by Emperor Meiji. He came from a poor Kyushu family, and he had made his way up through the ranks, aided by a faculty the army prized: he always paid careful attention to detail. This general was no newcomer to the army's inner politics, and was an ambitious if not particularly gifted man.

He had made himself an expert on Russia in the belief that ultimately Japan would fight the Soviets. He had studied and worked in Germany. He had also held the important post of chief of the Kempeitai in Manchuria, and he knew a great deal about the personal lives of those of his associates who were looking to northern China for further Japanese exploitation. He had achieved a reputation for personal toughness, by leading a military expedition in subzero weather across the marshes of Inner Mongolia to cut off Jehol Province from China. The expedition, however, had been called back in a general agreement with the Chinese.

In that spring of 1937, Tojo's attention was focused on the Soviet Union. He had persuaded himself that the Soviets were about to launch an attack along the northern border of the Japanese colonies, and he proposed a preemptive strike. When the Emperor got wind of this thinking he counseled caution, and Tojo backed off.

To ascertain what was going on, Hirohito now turned to members of the family. In the spring of 1937 he sent Prince Nashimoto, his wife's uncle, to Manchukuo for a look around. While there, Nashimoto inspected garrisons in Korea and Manchuria. Hirohito's uncle, Prince Higashikuni, went to Taiwan. Prince Chichibu went to London, hoping to resurrect the British-Japanese treaty, but failed. Prince Mikasa, his youngest brother, went to Yokohama to keep tabs on the navy.

For five years, Japanese soldiers had been bullying China, and clashing with Chinese troops. The one condition Hirohito had levied on Prince Konoye as prime minister was to do something to stop the aggression. Konoye found this task impossible because, no matter what his war minister promised, the Kwantung Army and the Tianjin garrison did as they pleased.

Most of the clashes at this period were with the Chinese communists, who were eager to fight the invaders and had made the "anti-Japanese struggle" a part of their policy. Having established a post in some northern Chinese town, the Japanese would send out a column for training, and it would be ambushed by guerillas and the Communist Eighth Route Army. The furious Japanese would send more troops, but after inflicting casualties the communists would disappear into the hills. The young officers of the Tianjin garrison, frustrated in the extreme, were clamoring for a cleanup operation.

The world was expecting fireworks in China. Foreign correspondents wrote about "the tinder box." Britain, the United States, France, and Italy, which had all had troops stationed in China since the Boxer Rebellion at the turn of the century, were stepping carefully to avoid getting involved, because, over the Emperor's objection, Konoye had been persuaded to authorize reinforcement of the Tianjin garrison to ten thousand men. Twice the Emperor had complained, but War Minister Sugiyama had been reading General Tojo's dispatches from Manchukuo and replied that the troops were necessary to guard against incursions in northern China by the Soviets and the Chinese communists. In that last, Sugiyama found Hirohito receptive, because the Emperor was strongly opposed to communism.

The incident everyone expected occurred on the night of July 7, 1937, at Lukouchiao, site of the bridge known to Westerners as the Marco Polo Bridge. Japanese soldiers were training in this area, and so were Chinese soldiers. A Japanese and a Chinese column were passing each other going in opposite directions, and someone fired a shot. A shootout resulted, which escalated to a confrontation.

The Tianjin garrison demanded reinforcement. Troops were sent, but so was a representative from army headquarters, ordered by Konoye to settle things down. It might have worked. The Japanese commander of the Tianjin garrison was a reasonable man, but he died of a heart attack, and his woolly staff officers then ordered the shelling of the Chinese garrison at Wanping. The Chinese fought back bravely and caused many Japanese casualties, which further infuriated the staff officers. By the time the new commander of the garrison arrived, the war was general. The Chinese, badly armed and often badly trained, recognized their one great weapon—unlimited manpower—and were willing to sacrifice men for time.

A few Japanese officers, like Colonel Itagaki, the architect of the Mukden Incident, who was commander of the Eleventh Division, recognized the futility of this war and began counseling withdrawal. But these voices went unheard in Tokyo. So did that of another of the Mukden conspirators, Lieutenant General Ishihara. He, too, warned that the war in China would become a quagmire.

Japanese newspaper correspondents covered the affair with enthusiasm, and Tokyo crowds, some of them obviously laid on by the army, demonstrated in favor of supporting the troops. It seemed that the Japanese public was ready for war.

Hirohito summoned General Sugiyama to the palace for an explanation. The suave general replied that the China situation was under control and that in a few days all would be quiet. Hirohito repeated his order to stop the fighting, and he also summoned Prince Konoye and demanded his personal attention to ending the war.

The Emperor also worked directly with Foreign Minister Hirota, the former prime minister. Japanese and Chinese officials in Nanking arranged for a cease-fire, which provided for withdrawal of most Japanese troops from China. The army got wind of the cease-fire and determined to stop the peace effort. It became a race: the army dispatched three more divisions to China, and Foreign Minister Hirota sent a special envoy to speed the settlement in Nanking. Chiang Kai-shek was eagerly awaiting this settlement so that he might turn his full attention to his self-appointed task of extirpating the communists in China.

The army got there first. On August 2, 1937, a Japanese army air force officer driving to Hung Kon Airfield refused to stop for a Chinese gate guard. When threatened by a rifle, the officer pulled out a pistol and killed the guard, and then in turn was killed by other Chinese soldiers. The Japanese army reinforcements rushed in to attack Shanghai, and the Marco Polo Bridge Incident became the China war.

Hirohito's last chance was to go to the people and demand peace. But he did not recognize the possibility, and did not move swiftly enough. The army, on the other hand, moved so swiftly it was apparent that the plans had been well laid. General Iwane Matsui was sent to command the "China expedition force," and he set sail for Shanghai. More divisions of troops were organized. Tanks, planes, more guns were sent to China. Warships of the navy moved into the Yangtze River. Tianjin, captured in midsummer, was thoroughly Japanized. All the major rail centers of northern China were in the hands of the Japanese. General Matsui promised Prime Minister Konoye that the trouble would be over in a few weeks. He would march on Nanjing, capture the Kuomintang capital, and end the war with a flourish.

The Emperor developed insomnia. It grew worse as the days passed, because he knew what horror Japan was visiting upon the world. Virtually every day Emperor Hirohito asked his military aide, "What is happening in China?" But the aide always temporized. Hirohito called in General Sugiyama, but all he received was a tissue of alibis, misrepresentations, and outright lies.

One August day, the angry Hirohito told General Sugiyama he did not believe the representations. If the Emperor would just wait a month, Sugiyama said, the army would end the China Incident and there would be peace.

But in a month matters worsened. The Chinese army retreated, and the Japanese marched up the Yangtze River to begin the drive on Nanking. The drive produced one result so negative that it shocked even the military: in the attack on Nanking, navy planes sank the U.S. gunboat *Panay* and army shore batteries attacked three British gunboats. The incident was so serious that U.S. President Franklin D. Roosevelt sent a special message to Hirohito asking him to stop the rampage of the Japanese army. The Emperor never received that message. It was probably stopped by the wall of silence around him, which kept him from learning of any of the events of this China campaign. In Tokyo the apologies were profuse, and from the navy, sincere. But a few days later Nanking fell and was subject to a campaign of attrition so violent that it has gone down in history as the Rape of Nanking. Hundreds of thousands of Chinese were killed needlessly.

The die was now cast for conquest. Hirohito objected, but Prince Konoye said the best way to end the war was to persuade the Chinese to abandon Chiang Kai-shek. So Konoye declared a policy of nonrecognition of the Republic of China and set up a government in Nanking under Wang Ching-wei, a longtime associate of Chiang in the nationalist movement.

With Japanese soldiers sacrificing their lives in China, Hirohito could hardly come out openly against the war. That last chance to prevent protracted war in China had been lost.

General Tojo, who had followed orders to restrain the Kwantung Army's anti-Soviet ambitions, was rewarded by being made vice war minister. The army, drunk with its power, contemplated Tojo's plan of attack on the Soviet Union. Hirohito said no, but in Tokyo, Army Vice Chief of Staff Hayao Tada conspired with the commander of the Korea garrison to stage an incident that should provoke the desired war with Russia. On July 3, 1938, Soviet troops at Lake Khasan, where the Siberia, Manchuria, and Korea borders meet, saw Japanese soldiers taking up field positions on the far side of the hill overlooking the lake. The Soviet forces moved up on their side and dug in. On July 13 the Korea garrison's commander reported to Tokyo that Russian soldiers were acting offensively (saying nothing about the Japanese soldiers) and asked permission to take military action.

Tojo put tongue in cheek and counseled diplomatic action, but said that if that failed, then the commander should "push them back by force." So the Japanese Nineteenth Division moved up to Lake Khasan. War was very near.

Hirohito knew nothing about it. He was summering at Hayama, and it was five days before he heard that he had troops on the Soviet border in great force. When he did hear, the messenger arrived late and delayed for two hours the Emperor's trip out on the bay to hunt specimens. So the imperial temper was up even at the beginning of the meeting. Hirohito took steps to stop the incident. He called War Minister Itagaki to the summer villa and spoke sharply. In the future not one more soldier was to be moved anywhere without the Emperor's permission. And the Nineteenth Division was to be brought back before there was trouble.

But on July 29, despite receipt of direct orders from the war minister, the commander of the Nineteenth Division started an attack on the Soviet positions.

The Japanese had bitten off more than they could chew. The Soviets were waiting and responded with tanks, guns, and an air attack, and since the attack was unauthorized, the Nineteenth Division could not call for help. From July 29 to August 10 the division took a terrible beating. To stop the fighting, General Tojo sent up two trustworthy colonels to command the fighting regiments, and told them to make a cease-fire. In Moscow, negotiations finally did bring about an end to the fighting, but only after the Nineteenth Division had been decimated.

The army had once again overstepped itself, and it had paid a heavy price, in loss of men and loss of confidence of the Emperor. Quietly a number of officers were transferred. But equally quietly, the "strike north" faction of the army determined that it would try again.

As for the campaign in China, virtually nothing about it was known at the Imperial Palace. Hirohito did observe to Army Chief of Staff Sugiyama that his month had long since come and gone and the fighting was still going on. Sugiyama blenched, but said nothing.

Abroad, the Rape of Nanking started a major campaign of sympathy for the Chinese, but in Japan neither Hirohito nor any one else outside the army knew anything about the matter. Even foreign publications were thoroughly censored before being allowed into Japan, and in those days the United States was not using radio to bypass the news blocks, as it later would with the Voice of America. The Japanese had no way of getting information the government did not wish them to have.

And neither did Hirohito.

15

The Strike to the North

War or peace, the Emperor had many duties other than those that concerned his role as commander of the armed forces. He was the chief priest of the Shinto religion, and as such he arose before dawn on New Year's Day and went to the Shinkade Shrine on the palace grounds, and there prayed to the four directions, to his imperial ancestors, and to the gods in heaven for the peace and security of Japan. He would also worship there on January 3 and on the anniversaries of all his forebears, the anniversary of his enthronement, that of the passing of the Emperor Jimmu, on Hirohito's own birthday (April 29), the spring and fall equinoxes, Thanksgiving, and several other occasions. For the government, he opened Parliament, dissolved the House of Representatives when the time came for new elections, awarded honors, and issued rescripts which dealt with affairs of the day. But from the days of the Emperor Meiji, far more was done in the Emperor's name than was ever done by the Emperor, and the army of Hirohito's day knew exactly how to manipulate this system.

In short, ever since the days of Meiji the Emperor was supposed to have enormous power, but it was understood that he would not employ this. Neither Meiji nor his son Taisho ever had. By 1932 Hirohito had already made more use of power than either of the other two.

It was a measure of the Western misunderstanding of the Japanese imperial system that foreign diplomats would expect the Emperor to act unilaterally, as Franklin D. Roosevelt had requested in the lost letter of 1937. Foreign governments looked to the Emperor as responsible for the Japanese government's actions. This was as unrealistic as if the U.S. president were to call upon King George VI to justify the actions of the British parliament.

In 1938 one reason the Emperor was out of touch with events was the state of his health. For two years, as the international situation worsened, he had been suffering from insomnia, and his constitution was so weak that he was frequently ill with upper respiratory infections. In the summer of 1938 he took the family for a long stay at the summer villa in Hayama, where he lived an almost normal life. Fewer and fewer affairs of state were brought to his attention.

The war in China proceeded. By 1939 the Japanese had pressed Chiang Kai-shek's forces back into Szechwan Province in the west and were consolidating their hold on the eastern seaboard. They held all the major cities of northern and central China. What the army did not admit, of course, was that its communications were tenuous because the towns and villages between the cities were controlled by the Chinese. The Japanese were stuck in the quagmire mentioned by General Ishihara, but the general staff refused to recognize the problem. Just a few more weeks, said the war minister, and China would be pacified.

Because of this apparent success, the "strike north" faction decided that the time had come to beard the Russian bear. To begin with the Soviet border was crossed by a band of Mongolian horsemen under Japanese control. The incident occurred five hundred miles northwest of Mukden. Soviet troops met the Mongolians and drove them back, and noticed that they were accompanied by Japanese advisors from the Twenty-third Division.

The Japanese-controlled Mongols came back and laid waste a small Soviet log fort, which was also bombed by Japanese planes. This violence was enough for the Soviets, and on May 22 they sent out a reconnaissance force to cross the border. A clash occurred at the Khalka River in the Nomonhan area.

It was not long before the Japanese had committed three divisions—sixty thousand men—to the battle. The Soviets sent Lieutenant General Georgi Zhukov with eighty thousand men, five hundred tanks, five hundred armored cars, and five hundred planes. Zhukov launched an offensive on August 19 and in ten days had driven the Japanese back to the border, with twenty thousand of the Japanese troops dead. Before the action ended, more than fifty thousand Japanese men were dead, wounded, or missing.

The Kwantung Army planned a new offensive, prepared to throw another fifty thousand troops into the battle, but within a few days Hirohito sent his former military aide, Lieutenant General Tetsuzo Nakajima, to Nomonhon with orders that the battle must stop. He also told the war minister to sack the commander of the Kwantung Army. The Japanese field commander at Nomonhan, Lieutenant Komatsubara Michitaro, committed suicide, and so did a number of his officers. The "strike north" faction of the army was dead, and it would not rise again during World War II.

During this interval the Emperor was badly let down by Prince Konoye, who had found the machinations of the army too much and had resigned in January 1939. He was replaced by Kiichiro Hiranuma, who turned out to be an unmitigated disaster—a toady to the army. Hiranuma resigned in August. But, as already noted, it was Emperor Hirohito who had finally put an end to the incident. When he learned what the army was doing in Manchuria, he was furious, and he called in the army minister.

"This is not my army," the Emperor said. "This army is out of control. I hate what they do. They never listen to orders. They do as they please." He proceeded to relate a bill of particulars, mentioning the murder of Zhang Zoulin in Manchuria, the Mukden Incident, the Marco Polo Bridge affair and its expansion by the Tianjin garrison into a full-scale war, and now this unwarranted incursion into Manchuria. "In the future," he said, "not one soldier will be moved without my express permission." And, as he told Terasaki later, he dismissed the general to go and report the imperial decision to the army.

The army generals in Tokyo were already in a penitent mood. The Nomonhan Incident had been a disaster for them, showing how unready Japan was for a military struggle with a modern war machine. Twenty-five thousand Japanese men had been killed and a great number wounded, and the Japanese army had been disgraced and embarrassed in the field. Now the Emperor was so furious, the war minister noted, that he might do anything.

So for once the generals were like penitent children, willing to do anything the Emperor asked. General Ueda, commander of the Kwantung Army, was sent back to Japan and retired in disgrace. General Isogai, who had actually issued the orders to fight, was also retired. General Umezu, commander of the First Army, was sent to Manchuria to take over the Kwantung Army and bring some discipline to it. His first order was that no troops would attack or counterattack without his specific approval. Also, by Hirohito's order, the ill-defined Manchukuo-Siberian border was to be left alone—no more incidents.

In this climate, with the fall of the Hiranuma cabinet, the Emperor selected General Noboyuke Abe to be prime minister, hoping that he could control the army. But Abe so angered the civilian Diet that his cabinet lasted only four months. In that period he had presided over the preparation of the Rome-Berlin-Tokyo treaty that the army wanted. When the cabinet fell, in order to try to avoid the treaty, which he did not want signed, Emperor Hirohito appointed Admiral Mitsumasa Yonai to form a cabinet. Admiral Yonai was well known as an advocate of peace, particularly peace with the United States and Britain.

The Yonai selection was made with full knowledge of the pressure being exerted by the army for an alliance with Nazi Germany and fascist Italy. The alliance was the brainchild of the army generals and Yosuke Matsuoka, the anti-American industrial leader who was president of the South Manchurian Railroad, the biggest expansion factor in Manchuria.

Sure enough, Admiral Yonai tabled the Tripartite Pact, but largely because of that fact he ran afoul of the army. General Shunroku Hata, who had been war minister in the Abe and Yonai cabinets, was ordered by the army to resign, which automatically caused the fall of the Yonai cabinet, since no cabinet could function under the constitution without both a war minister and a navy minister.

As Hirohito told Terasaki, this was a low point for him. It was very difficult to find anyone to assume the post of prime minister who would be acceptable to the army, and the army junta had made it plain that anyone unacceptable to them would not get a war minister.

The field had now grown so narrow that there was only one civilian acceptable to the army—again, it was Prince Konoye.

Back into power in July 1940 came the great vacillator. As war minister he chose Hideki Tojo, which did indeed placate the army.

That summer the world seemed to belong to the Axis powers. France fell, and Britain struggled on alone against Hitler. In the collapse of France the Japanese army saw a way to begin its march. By moving into Indochina, Japan would bottle up Chiang Kai-shek's beleaguered government in Chungking. Who was to stop Japan? The French were defeated, and their Asian colony lay like a ripe tomato on a vine, fit for picking. And so the Japanese army moved southeast, although warned by the United States that there would be retaliation. Despite the setback at Nomonhon (about which the army in China knew nothing) the Japanese military men's heads were swollen with success. America was known to be divided on the subject of forceful action. The Japanese army and elements of the navy now believed they could defeat the Western powers.

The Dutch East Indies lay glittering, a prize that would yield precious oil. That jewel of Asia, Hong Kong, lay waiting; so did Malaya with its tin and rubber, and Singapore, with a British naval base that was the pride of Southeast Asia. Further, through Thailand lay access to Burma and India. All this appealed enormously to the Japanese army, which was dedicated to driving the white man from Asia. This element found the ear of Tojo, who became ever more adamant. Urged on by Hitler, the Japanese army began to talk about capturing Singapore.

The Emperor had been relegated to his ceremonial role. The army told him nothing about its plans. Imperial conferences were often held without the imperial presence, but now Hirohito began to appear at them, and these days he always asked questions. From the answers, he could tell that the drift toward war was gaining speed.

Also in the summer of 1940, the court was told that the 2600th anniversary of the founding of Japan would be coming in the fall. So that November, like good little puppets, the imperial family came forth from the palace, across the moat into Hibiya Park, to participate in the festivities. Some fifty thousand persons of note were there by invitation. Army and navy bands played the "Twenty-sixth Century March." The common people on the outskirts shouted "banzai!" on cue. And everyone settled down to a box lunch, including their imperial majesties.

It was a grand party. Next morning the national newspapers announced with awe that the imperial family had eaten precisely the same food as the commoners. Imagine that, the Gods coming down from Olympus!

Now, said the army, the Emperor was truly fulfilling his function in life, exhorting the people by example, showing the way.

Hirohito issued an Imperial Rescript to mark the occasion. "It is our earnest hope that peace will be restored soon and that we may share with all countries happiness and prosperity, even though the world is now in the midst of great turmoil." These words were about as far from those of the Japanese jingoes as one could get, and, had they come from any other source, the person would undoubtedly have been arrested under the new laws against improper thoughts. As it was, no one in the power of government paid the slightest attention to the words of the Emperor.

The Tripartite Treaty was drawn up by Matsuoka, who with the army influence on Konoye had become foreign minister in the cabinet. It was manifestly a treaty made against the United States, and Matsuoka so boasted. The Emperor did not like it. He brought in Admirals Yonai, Inoue, and Yamamoto for consultation, and they all agreed that it was a bad treaty and would ultimately be harmful to Japan.

The Emperor did all he could to sidetrack the treaty, but the cabinet voted for it anyway. As Hirohito told Terasaki years afterward, it was his belief that the signing of that treaty caused the war with the United States. At that time the United States was the sole source of Japanese oil supplies, and it was well known that the United States was siding with the British in the European war. Hirohito believed that when the United States cut off oil to Japan a few months later, it was really at least partly because of American concern lest the Japanese supply Germany with oil from their American source.

The Emperor also held that Ambassador Oshima, who represented Japan in Germany, was overestimating the power of Nazi Germany and so persuading Matsuoka and the army. The army leaders all overestimated German power and underestimated that of their own country, and thus led Japan astray, into the arms of the fascists.

16

War!

1941. The Emperor was sunk deep in gloom. After Japan had moved into Indochina he had told advisor Tsuneo Matsudaira that Japan had behaved like a thief at a fire, taking advantage of France to steal some of her overseas territory.

This dishonorable behavior had gone against the imperial grain. The Emperor was also gloomy about his own role in the events of the preceding months. He might have intervened to stop the signing of the tripartite pact with Germany and Italy. He had opposed the pact, but had been too irresolute to take the strong position.

The Emperor's gloom was deepened by his feeling of entrapment. He saw the nation moving steadily toward a war he did not want. His attitude was almost exactly like that of his favorite admiral, Yamamoto, who had steadfastly opposed war with the Western powers for twenty years but was now preparing the preemptive strike on Pearl Harbor. At an imperial conference that spring, Hirohito acceded to a statement that for self-defense Japan should continue negotiation with the nations over Southeast Asia, but also that Japan should not avoid war with Britain or the United States.

On the advice of Prince Konoye, the politicians, with a great show of patriotism, had disbanded their party structures and formed the League to Fight through the Sacred War. At that moment they meant the war with China, which the Japanese consistently claimed was an attempt to rescue their giant neighbor from depravity and the clutches of the Western world. Soon the league would become the Imperial Rule Assistance Association, and the Diet a rubber stamp for the Japanese cabinet under Konoye.

General Tojo, in his capacity as war minister, had issued a pamphlet "to improve the moral quotient" of the army. Its prescription was the ultimate in bushido, the Japanese code of the fighting man. It said, in effect:

1. Fight to the death. Never surrender.
2. Do not dishonor your name. Strong are those who know shame. You must always be aware of the honor of your kinfolk and strive not to betray their expectations. Do not stay alive in dishonor. Do not die in such a way as to leave a bad name behind you.

The Emperor was well aware of this fierce new doctrine; in fact, the draft had been submitted for his approval. But what was he to do? Should he say no? In the bellicose atmosphere of 1941, that would have been impossible. How could he deny what was just a moral concept?

The cabinet was now talking about American-British–Chinese–Dutch (ABCD) Encirclement. The press and public also were referring to this defense alignment. The big question mark was the United States. What would it do?

Admiral Yamamoto summed it up. "I can run wild for the first six months," he said, "but after that. . . . " And, he added, "considering the character of Admiral Kimmel [the commander of the U.S. Pacific Fleet] the enemy will not necessarily adhere to the classic idea of a battleships-to-battleships showdown."

All this was depressing to Hirohito, reinforcing his feeling that Japan was heading for disaster. Early in August, Hirohito sent the Marquis Kido to persuade Prince Konoye that the war preparations should stop, because it would be impossible to win a war against the United States.

The meeting was inconclusive. Konoye took the matter to the war minister and the navy minister, and they said the problem of natural resources was severe, which of course it was. The China war was eating up Japan's reserves of every vital material. Japan's only oil resource was a tiny pocket in Honshu Island, and Japan was consuming oil at the rate of 28,000 gallons a day in China. If the army did not get oil, the China adventure would have to be abandoned. The army was dead set against that.

Admiral Yamamoto presented his plan for the Pearl Harbor attack, and within hours the Emperor was also shown plans for attacks on the Philippines, the Dutch East Indies, and Malaya.

Early in September Prince Konoye sought an audience with Hirohito to tell him that if no agreements could be reached with the United States, the war with the Western powers would begin soon. The deadline was very near—just over a month.

When Konoye said that, Hirohito unleashed a flood of questions, and every question implied that a war with the United States would be foolhardy.

When Konoye had left that day, Hirohito called in the chiefs of the army and navy general staffs and asked them what they thought were their chances of success. The chiefs answered that they could win a war in three months.

The Emperor said he did not believe it, and he ordered them to turn to negotiation.

The army and navy chiefs bit their lips and left the imperial presence nervously, but they had made up their minds for war.

The Emperor asked the Department of National Planning for a report, and learned that the stockpile of light oil was enough for only ten days of operations. Kerosine supplies would last one month. There was crude oil to run the industrial plants for forty-five days. The supply of nickel would make weapons for two months. Heavy machine oil, to keep the tanks going, would last only three months. For five years the navy had been stockpiling aviation gas and ship fuel, but there was only enough to last about a year.

All these signs pointed to a grim future.

In September the war seemed inevitable. In compliance with the Emperor's wishes, the cabinet had sent emissaries to Washington to negotiate, but both sides remained unyielding on the fate of China. Hirohito called another imperial conference; this was a mark of his concern, because usually these conferences were called by the prime minister.

At such conferences the Emperor rarely spoke or gave any indication of his feelings, but this time, a few minutes before the meeting began he told the Marquis Kido that he intended to do some talking. He had a list of questions.

Kido was aghast. It would never do. Such a breach of precedent would lower the status of the Emperor. Kido said he had already arranged for the president of the Privy Council to ask a series of probing questions, just the ones Kido and the Emperor had been discussing privately.

The Emperor pursed his lips and said nothing, and retreated once more behind the veil of his godship.

The meeting was held in the east wing of the Imperial Palace, in a spacious library room. The table was horseshoe shaped. The Emperor sat at one end on a slightly raised dais, befitting his position. The others sat in a double line around the tables. All the military men were in dress uniform, and the civilians wore formal clothes. The navy chief of staff,

Nagano, spoke first, because if war came the navy would suddenly be thrust into the forefront. But Nagano spoke in platitudes.

The army chief of staff, Sugiyama, spoke next. But he had nothing to say except that the army was getting ready for military action.

Several others also had their say. All of the speakers spoke of war as inevitable, and their discussions concerned logistics and other practicalities. None of them faced the real issue: war or peace?

General Tojo asked the conference to agree that if the negotiations in Washington produced nothing, then by the early part of October Japan should be ready for war.

Suddenly the Emperor rose. Everyone stopped and stared. Hirohito's face was flushed with such emotion that he had to wipe his steamy spectacles. He glared at the navy chief of staff and then at the army chief of staff. Contemptuously he asked them why they had not stated their honest opinions instead of hiding behind a mountain of statistics.

Hirohito read a poem written by his grandfather, the Meiji emperor, in which the peaceful sea surrounded the earth, and the author asked why strife was disrupting the peace among nations. The Emperor said this poem was one of his favorites, because it expressed his grandfather's great love of peace and Hirohito's own love of peace. Then the Emperor sat down and said no more.

And what was the result?

Lip service, and no more, was paid by the high government officials to Hirohito's search for peace. They expressed pious hopes that the Japanese mission to Washington would achieve peace—and they prepared for war. Why not? As everyone really knew, the positions of the United States and Japan relative to China had become inimical.

Further conferences covered the same ground, beneath the skeptical eye of the Emperor. He summoned General Sugiyama several times for explanations, and then reminded him that there had already been three years of broken promises, beginning with the one to end the China Incident in thirty days. He also called on Admiral Nagano to explain why so many Japanese ships had been "sunk" by the "enemy" in the recent maneuvers. What did that mean for the future?

As the imperial conference continued, the military men became nervous and impatient. They did not like the negative prodding of their Emperor.

Prime Minister Konoye, finding the sledding difficult, resigned. He did not wish to be blamed for starting the war. At this point no civilian was acceptable to the army, so Hirohito bowed to force majeure and chose General Tojo, the war minister, to be the new prime minister.

He had a vague hope that this slow, plodding officer would prove more amenable than any of the others and that there still might be a chance for peace. But Hirohito did not know his man well enough. Tojo had already decided that the United States was the enemy, and that the United States could be defeated by Japan.

The Emperor held out one proviso when he appointed Tojo: the prime minister–designate must agree to retract the decision for war, made on September 6 over the Emperor's objections.

By this time Hirohito was definitely decided against war and wondering what he could do in the face of the military machine, which had seized power and rejected his every express wish to turn from war to peace. "It was apparent to me now," he told Hidenari Terasaki years later, "that if I invoked a veto power on their ability to make war, chaos would result. I might be killed, the whole Imperial system might be disrupted; certainly the polity of Japan would be destroyed. So I did not do what I wished to do."

As promised, the Tojo cabinet restudied the question of war or peace, but the ultimate conclusion was the same. The army was bent on war, and really there was no force in Japan powerful enough to stop the military junta.

At the end of November Hirohito made one last effort to stop the war, as he later told his confidant, Minister Terasaki. The Emperor's ultimate effort was to stop the course of events already decided upon. He wanted to summon the Jushin, the association of former prime ministers, to meet with the cabinet.

Hirohito asked the Marquis Kido to try to arrange such a meeting through Prime Minister Tojo, but Tojo refused. Then the Emperor called a meeting of the Jushin himself and questioned each of the former prime ministers on the subject.

Should it be war or should it be peace? Each of the Jushin was posed that direct question, so embarrassing for a Japanese to face directly and alone. But there was no gainsaying the Emperor. Years later, Hirohito recalled what their answers had been.

Prince Konoye: "Konoye spoke loftily about the importance of preserving peace . . . but . . . it was all very abstract and nothing practical was offered."

Baron Hiranuma: "Peace was highly to be preferred to war . . . again abstract and no suggestions of a course of action."

Admiral Yonai: "He spoke of our need for oil and the grave difficulties of securing it, but he spoke of peaceful means as far preferable to others. He went around in circles."

Admiral Okada: "He said he agreed with Yonai. More going around in circles."

Koki Hirota, the only "common man" in the Jushin, the only former prime minister with neither the pedigree of nobility nor that of military service: "Because he was a diplomat he seemed to be on both sides simultaneously. He spoke a lot of nonsense."

General Abe: "At this point there was no road of return. Japan was committed to war."

General Senjuro Hayashi: "He too was very clearly for war."

"So I was faced with two sets of opinions," continued the Emperor. "Those who wanted peace were rambling and indefinite about what was to be done. They really had no program, nor any helpful suggestions. Those who wanted war were positive and very strong."

"But," said Terasaki, "you wanted peace. Why didn't you stop them?"

"Because I was afraid of a coup d'etat. I was afraid of the power of the army."

Therefore the last possible date to preserve peace and call back the striking force that had already set sail from the Kuril Islands, December 1, passed and nothing was done, although the Jushin and the Tojo cabinet were well aware of the Emperor's wish that the peace be preserved.

At this point the Emperor felt he had no recourse but to support his subjects, his countrymen who would fight and die in the war—all in his name.

Also, through its secretary of state, Cordell Hull, the United States had demanded the complete withdrawal of Japanese troops from China and Indochina and the scrapping of the Berlin-Rome-Tokyo axis. To accept those terms would be to lose face, which was impossible. On December 7, 1941 (December 8 in the eastern hemisphere), simultaneous attacks were made on Pearl Harbor, the Philippines, and Malaya. A few hours later the Emperor issued his first imperial rescript of the war:

> Patiently have We waited and long have We endured in the hope that Our government might retrieve the situation in peace, but Our adversaries, showing not the least spirit of conciliation, have unduly delayed a settlement. In the meantime they have intensified the economic and political pressure, thereby to compel Our Empire to submission. We have therefore resolved to declare war on the United States and Britain for the sake of the self-preservation and self-defense of the Empire and for the establishment of enduring peace in East Asia.

Did the Emperor really believe this statement? Certainly it was not hard for him to believe. From the Japanese point of view, the demands of the Americans were impossible to accept without destroying the Japanese empire as it existed. It is hard to escape the feeling that the U.S. Department of State knew exactly what it was doing when it made the Hull proposal. Perhaps by that time there was no room for compromise.

Emperor Meiji and his consort, Empress Shōken

Emperor Taishō and his consort, Empress Teimei

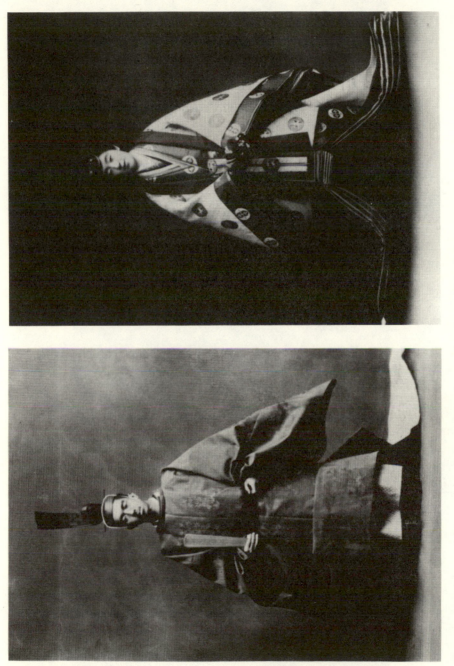

Emperor Hirohito and his consort, Empress Nagako, at the time of his enthronement

Emperor Hirohito and General MacArthur

Emperor Hirohito officiating at the opening of the Tokyo Olympic Games in 1964

Emperor Hirohito and Empress Nagako on their European tour in 1971

17

Days of Victory

In the last days of negotiations, President Roosevelt addressed a personal message to Emperor Hirohito.

> I address myself to Your Majesty at this moment in the fervent hope that you may, as I am doing, give thought in this definite emergency to ways of dispelling the dark clouds. I am confident that both of us, for the sake of the people, not only of our own countries, but for the sake of humanity in neighboring territories, have a sacred duty to restore traditional amity and prevent further death and destruction in the world.

That message reached the Emperor and General Tojo after the Japanese attack had been launched. If it had arrived in time, would it have made any difference? After the war, former Japanese Ambassador Saburu Kurusu wrote:

> I was told upon my return to Tokyo in August 1942, by General Tojo himself, that if the personal message from President Roosevelt to our Emperor had arrived just a few days earlier and if the American note of November 26 [by Hull] had been somewhat more conciliatory, it would have been impossible for Japan to have gone to war.

A few hours after the multipronged attack began, Radio Tokyo broadcast the first imperial rescript of the war:

> The Hallowed Spirits of Our Imperial Ancestors guarding Us from above, We rely upon the loyalty and courage of Our subjects in Our confident expectation that the task bequeathed by Our forefathers will be carried forward and that the source of evil will be speedily eradicated and an enduring peace established in East Asia, preserving, thereby the glory of Our Empire.

And this enthusiasm was shared throughout Japan because of the intensive program of progaganda and the tight controls of the government on the civil population. Enormous rallies were staged at Korakuen Stadium and Hibiya Park. "Let us march on, 100 million of us," was the theme.

Dissenters, and there were some, had no choices. They were badgered at the meetings of the neighborhood associations, the governmental units closest to the people. When a meeting was called, they dared not fail to appear.

Asahi reported on one such meeting:

The residents of Kojimachi Ichiban-cho gathered at the second-floor room of the Nakazawa Confectionery. Mr. Nakazawa's voice was extremely moving. He said, "I presume that every one of you fully understands what the radio announcement means. Now, every one of my neighbours, let us join hands and march on."

Asahi, its presses once destroyed by army militants, had fallen into line behind the militarists months earlier. "Every home is a battleground now," the paper editorialized. "We are all comrades in arms. We must fight through to the end."

Under these circumstances, the Emperor had no choice but to support his subjects. He had to turn all thoughts of peace from his mind.

To maintain the war spirit, every day for the next three and a half years, the imperial rescript on the Pacific war appeared at the top of the front page of every newspaper in Japan.

From the first day of the war, the Japanese won victories with ridiculous ease. Pearl Harbor was a tremendous Japanese victory. Only a few people, notably Admiral Yamamoto, knew that in terms of the potential destruction, the Pearl Harbor attack had been less than satisfactory. The Japanese people were told that 18 U.S. naval vessels, including four battleships, had been sunk and 231 planes destroyed. They were not told that the carrier force, most important to Yamamoto, had escaped, largely because Admiral Chuichi Nagumo, commander of the strike force, was too nervous and too impatient to remain in the area to make a second strike.

Hirohito did not know a great deal more than his subjects; he was aware only of the basic outline, and, as one victory was piled atop another, he issued imperial rescripts to commemorate the events and to spur his soldiers and sailors on to greater effort. He definitely knew nothing about the atrocities perpetrated in his name on prisoners and enemy civilians.

A few hours after Pearl Harbor came the electrifying news that the British capital ships *Repulse* and *Prince of Wales* had been sunk off the Malayan coast—by land-based Japanese naval bombers. That was a real surprise to the Allied naval officers.

These victories came so quickly that all Japan quite lost its sense of perspective. Even in a free country like the United States, once the nation was committed to war, anyone who failed to support the effort was liable to be treated with the deepest suspicion and animosity. Nevertheless, after the war *Mainichi* lamented its own unquestioning journalistic acceptance of government statements it knew to be untrue.

> Looking back at the behaviour of the opinion makers during the war, one tends to believe that the Japanese have had an incurable liking all along for totalitarianism. When our nation was going one way, very many of us were hostile to those who suggested going the other way. Dissenting voices were hurriedly hushed. The Japanese once liked, and may in the future like to bask, in a blissful sense of national oneness. When 'ichioku ichigan' [100 million people as one bullet] was a catchword, few Japanese dared to deviate from the official path.

This also applied to Hirohito. From the beginning of the war, as if it had been necessary, the Marquis Kido reminded Hirohito that it was his constitutional responsibility to support the war effort, no matter where it led. "Once the government decides on a national polity, the Emperor should trust the administration," said Kido. There was no turning back, and from Hirohito no recrimination.

Since the end of the war historians have come full circle in their appraisal of Emperor Hirohito's role in the war. First came the conventional wisdom that the Emperor, following the dictates of the Meiji Constitution and the established practices of Japan, had relinquished all control once the decision for war was made by the cabinet.

But a few years later came a new appraisal, which indicated that had the Emperor stood fast for peace at any price, the Japanese government would have followed his lead. Specifically the followers of that school believe that General Tojo would have done anything the Emperor ordered him to do. Perhaps.

But as the circle has been completed, it becomes apparent that Hirohito, with his particular personality and training, and with the advisors around him, was not likely to issue a flat order except under exceptional circumstances. As Edwin O. Reischauer, ambassador to Japan in the 1960s, put it, Hirohito did not have any room for maneuver at the time.

The army had already shown on at least two occasions that it was prepared to force the Emperor's abdication, or to murder him and install in his place Hirohito's younger brother Prince Chichibu, who was a soldier himself.

What were the war aims of Japan at the outset of the struggle in the Pacific?

From postwar study of staff papers it is easy for an outsider to form the wrong impression, accepting as real planning some farfetched programs outlined by staff officers. One element sought control of all Asia and the world. Occupation currency was printed for Hawaii and Australia, under orders from the navy, because staff officers had a plan for invasion of each. The establishment of a new nation of Alaska was envisioned. It was to include the provinces of Alberta and British Columbia and the state of Washington. Seizing on these half-baked plans, authors have devoted whole books to the subjects.

The real aims were much less exotic. The army wanted tin, rubber, and oil; therefore Southeast Asia was its prime target. The army also wanted to finish the job and control China; therefore the preponderance of Japan's military strength remained in China and Manchuria. The navy wanted to control the western Pacific; that meant defeating the U.S. Pacific Fleet, and that was always the navy's goal.

The furthest the expansionists got was a landing in the Aleutian Islands, with the hope that the beachhead might be expanded. But it never was, and soon the idea was lost altogether as the tide of war changed.

In answer to a question by Hirohito in one of the imperial conferences, General Sugiyama suggested that Singapore might be captured in five months, but that the struggle was going to be a hard one. But to the contrary, the Japanese seemed to walk through the enemy. Hong Kong fell with scarcely a tremor. The Japanese moved steadily down the coast of Malaya, taking one town after another.

Hirohito began to show a lively interest in the progress of the war. Early in February 1942 he sent a military aide to tour the battle areas and report back to him. The aide arrived just in time to see the surrender of Singapore on February 15 by General A. E. Percival of Great Britain, to a vastly inferior force commanded by General Yamashita.

For a while it seemed that Japan's armies and navy were invincible. Early in March Hirohito summoned the Marquis Kido to the Imperial Library for a talk. Kido described the meeting in his diary:

The Emperor was beaming like a child. The fruits of war, he said, "are tumbling into our mouths almost too quickly. The enemy at Bandung on

the Java front announced their surrender on the 7th and now our army
is negotiating for the surrender of all forces in the Dutch East Indies. The
enemy has surrendered at Surabaya and also on the Burma front, has given
up Rangoon."

He was so pleased that I hardly knew how to give him a congratulatory
answer.

Poet Takamura Kotara caught the national mood of self-satisfaction.

Remember December the eighth.
This day world history began anew.
On this day western domination was shattered.
World history began all through Asia's land and sea.
Japan with the help of the gods
Bravely faces white supremacy.

All Japan's soldiers now
Are ready to fight
Until the enemy correct their ways.
World history has begun anew.
Remember December the eighth.

Hirohito was himself caught up in the euphoria of the moment. He sent
congratulatory messages to Imperial General Headquarters, to Admiral
Yamamoto, and to General Terauchi, now commander of all the troops
in the south.

At a parliamentary meeting on the budget, a member courageously
demanded from Foreign Minister Shigenori Togo a statement on the
ministry's official attitude toward peace. Minister Togo said it was as
necessary to end war as it was to begin it, and that he was ready at any
time to work to that end. Members of the house began a noisy protest.
They wanted to drive on toward Washington. The world was their oyster.
In the end the foreign minister's remarks were stricken from the record.

All through the early months of 1942 the spectacular string of successes
continued. Bataan fell, and the Americans in the Philippines were confined to the bastion of Corregidor in Manila Bay. The occupation of
various countries was achieved so quickly that the army could not keep
up with events and sent frantic appeals back to Tokyo for troops and
supplies to hold the conquered territories.

But the Emperor soon realized that the war was a great burden and
should be ended, since Japan had achieved its aim—which he believed
to be legitimate—of securing its oil supply and freeing several areas of
Asia from colonial oppression. He asked Marquis Kido, his lord keeper
of the privy seal, to speak to Tojo on this subject and persuade him to

end the war. Later he noted this in his conversations with Terasaki, and his indirect advice was repeated by Kido in his diary.

Hirohito continued to be haunted by the reports coming from the fronts of the war he did not want. He mused on the past, all those years when Japan and Britain had been allies, not enemies, and he wondered how he might take an initiative for peace. This would be difficult because of the string of victories run up by the Japanese military. But the Emperor continued to worry, even though he showed pride in the accomplishments of his people in the field. When he went to the shrine at Issei on December 10, 1942, he did not pray for victory in the war; he prayed for peace, and he made sure that fact was released to the newspapers, so that thinking Japanese would know just what he meant. (Unfortunately, so great was the impact of jingoism and thought control that very few Japanese people understood the message of the Emperor.)

In the spring of 1942 the Japanese, having paused at the East Indies, then moved into Rabaul and made that their southern bastion. Where could they not go? They considered Fiji, Samoa, Australia, New Zealand. One year after the beginning of the war, along with the compulsory front-page imperial rescript on the war, the *Japan Times* carried an editorial.

> From the icy rocks of the Aleutians, across the vast expanse of the Pacific, and among its countless islands, down the littoral of the Asiatic continent, through the fabled land of the Indies to the very gates of the Antipodes, and then around into the Indian Ocean, the undisputed power of Japan has been established. The sting of Japan's lash has been felt as far afield as the mainland of America, in the harbors of Australia, off the coast of Africa, even in the Atlantic. Over tens of thousands of miles from the Arctic to the tropics, over the seven seas and the five continents, the land has rumbled to the tread of Japan's legions, and the skies have thundered to the roar of Japan's winged knights of the air.

Japan had indeed accomplished the unbelievable: exposed the fatal weakness of the colonial powers. But as the Japanese gloated, the forces of their destruction were at work. The Japanese fleet was halted at the battle of the Coral Sea. As a result of this it failed to take Port Moresby, its spring objective in the southern offensive. At Midway it lost four of the precious aircraft carriers on which the might of the fleet depended, and the navy knew it would take ten years to replace them. Also in the summer of 1942, despite claims of total success, Hirohito was suddenly worried. The cause? A defeat at a tiny island in the Solomon chain, of which virtually no one had ever heard before. Its name was Guadalcanal.

18

The Juggernaut Stops

On June 6, 1942, Emperor Hirohito received his first news of a serious setback in the war. The Marquis Kido informed him of the defeat in the Battle of Midway and the loss of those four vital aircraft carriers. The Emperor was the first to know. Not even the army had been told; Prime Minister Tojo did not hear of the defeat for more than a week.

The Emperor took the news well. After the euphoric discussion of a few weeks earlier, Kido had warned him that reverses would come.

The Emperor's major concern was lest the men of the fleet become disheartened. He sent a message to Admiral Yamamoto telling him not to worry but to continue to do his best. In this instance Hirohito need not have worried about the men of the fleet. They were not to know the truth about Midway, nor was the nation at large, for many, many months, and even then the news would just seep out. But so enwalled was the Emperor that he did not even know that Midway was a secret.

Midway was only the beginning of the change. When the U.S. Marines landed at Guadalcanal, the Japanese believed the operation was a feint of the sort the Americans tried at the same time in the Gilbert Islands. Admiral Yamamoto soon enough moved his Combined Fleet flagship down to Truk, but the army completely misread the signals and tried first to achieve with a battalion what should have occupied at least two divisions.

Yamamoto's fleet won victory after victory over the Americans and Australians at sea, but the marines at Guadalcanal would not be dislodged.

Emperor Hirohito issued one rescript after another in honor of the navy, and demanded answers from the army. But he did not get them, because Imperial General Headquarters in Tokyo was as ignorant of the cause of the defeat as the Emperor. By the time the army realized what was happening, it was too late. Two divisions of troops were moved, helter-skelter, to Guadalcanal, where more men starved to death than were destroyed by the enemy. At the beginning of 1943 the Guadalcanal cause was lost, and not a single rescript could be written to honor the army.

The Emperor's worst fears were confirmed. Imperial General Headquarters told the southern commanders to concentrate on the capture of British New Guinea, but this campaign, too, proved disastrous. General MacArthur led his forces up the coast of New Guinea; Buna, Lae, Salamaua, all fell. In the Solomons, Admiral Halsey's troops and ships captured one island after another until they reached Bougainville, which gave them airfields that would make it possible to isolate the stronghold of Rabaul. By the end of 1943 Japan's southern empire was falling apart, harried by Allied aircraft and submarines.

The allies prepared to move toward the inner empire. That November the Gilbert Islands were the first to fall, as Admiral Chester Nimitz unleashed his Central Pacific drive. Also in November, General Tojo tried to stabilize Japan's weakening economy by organizing the Greater East Asia Coprosperity Sphere, which would enlist the aid of a new goverment established at Nanking, the captive government of Thailand, the puppet state of Manchukuo, the cooperating state of the Philippines, and the occupied state of Burma. Subhas Chandra Bose, the Indian nationalist leader who had cast his lot with Japan, was also involved, hoping that Japan would invade India. Japan tried but failed.

When the new union was organized, Emperor Hirohito welcomed his allies to Tokyo with a reception and banquet. Hundreds of thousands jammed into Hibiya Park for a giant rally. But all the hoopla could not conceal from his majesty the truth; the war could not now be won. It was as Admiral Yamamoto (killed in action in the spring of 1943) had said initially: Japan had the advantage of surprise and preparation, but at the end of two years there was a dramatic reversal.

By the end of 1943 Hirohito was relying mostly on his family for information about the war effort, and he was aware that General Tojo was lying to him, but there was nothing he could do about it.

The newspapers now told him how badly the war was going. Women replaced men as streetcar conductors, as bus drivers, and on street gangs so the men could fight. Student deferments from the draft were eliminated. The draft age was dropped to 19 and then to 18. School children were mobilized to work in factories. Most elementary school pupils were evacuated from the big cities to protect them from bombing. The geisha houses were closed down, and gardens and all open spaces were turned over to the growing of pumpkins and sweet potatoes.

From Hirohito's standpoint the most telling sign of the change was his personal disassociation from the imperial rescripts issued in his name. Through the Guadalcanal campaign the rescripts had been his own, based on information supplied by his military aides. Afterwards, his aides were discouraged from traveling to the fronts, and the rescripts became propaganda instruments of the military government. Tojo was the culprit.

By the spring of 1944, Hirohito knew the war was lost. The Allies had captured the Gilbert Islands and encircled Rabaul. They had captured the Marshall Islands and were moving up the New Guinea shoreline. Allied submarines ranged into Japanese waters. Allied aircraft controlled the southern skies.

But the military junta still retained tight control of Japan. The Emperor began to consider ways in which he could loosen that control, because he knew no one else could do so, so fanatical was the army leadership. He also knew that by moving in any direction except that prescribed by the army he ran the danger of dethronement or death, but by this time the burden of the war had become too great for him to bear without doing anything. All this he held inside, until long afterwards in his conversations with Terasaki, when it spilled out.

The Emperor mused on the reasons the war had been lost. In the first place, he considered the primary adage of that great Chinese strategist, General Sun Tzu: "First, know yourself." "In that we failed," said Hirohito. "Neither did we know our enemy.

"Second, we placed our emphasis on the spritual, ignoring the technical developments of weapons, a matter we should have learned about in the Nomonhan incident, when we were resoundingly defeated by the Soviets.

"Third, the army and navy had begun in disagreement on virtually everything, and they continued all through the war without unity.

"Fourth, we had experts as our military commanders, not leaders. These men did not have the vision or the abilities of leadership. In the Meiji era my grandfather had real leaders, General Count Aritomo Yamagata, General Iwao Oyama, Admiral Gombei Yamamoto. I had none. My generals were like the German generals of World War I—all technicians, no thinkers."

Then came the Allied attack on Saipan, and with its fall the realization that the inner gates of empire had been breached. Prime Minister Tojo had failed. The Emperor attributed the Tojo failure to three major factors. The first was Tojo's reliance on mysticism (the Imperial Way) and not on modern technology and military methods.

Second was Tojo's distrust of others, which made him believe he had to assume all major military tasks himself, as prime minister, war minister, munitions minister, and army chief of staff, with his toady Admiral Shimada as navy minister and navy chief of staff. Together they made one wrong decision after another.

Third was Tojo's reliance on coercion and fear, his use of the Kempeitai and thought control police to suppress opposition.

So Tojo had to go, and after a brief struggle in the corridors of power he did go. The problem then was to find someone to replace him. First came the cabinet of Koiso and Yonai, a general and an admiral, but it did not work because this general also wanted to be in charge, and he, too, wanted to be army minister as well as prime minister. The reason, he told the Emperor, was that he needed that authority over the army to bring an end to the war. He was prevented in this because he was a retired general, and the rule said that the army minister must be a general in active service. General Sugiyama, the current army minister, would not step down; the army balked; and Koiso resigned.

After Koiso, the Emperor sought a man of peace. He looked to Admiral Suzuki, once his chamberlain, who had been nearly killed in the attack of February 26, 1936. Suzuki was very old now and half deaf. He did not want to take the responsibility, and he so told his son, but the Emperor said that even though Suzuki could not hear, he was the man wanted for the job, and he must take it in the interest of the country. So Suzuki allowed himself to be persuaded.

The war continued. The Allied invasion of the Philippines came in October 1944, and the Emperor knew that the air force and the navy had failed completely. The nation was left with the bleak prospect of sacrificing its brave sons as human bombs!

Winter came, with the invasion of Iwo Jima and the more and more powerful raids of the B-29s over Japan which soon (March 10) became fire raids.

Tojo had become persona non grata in the summer of 1944, but so many things had happened by the winter of 1944–45 that in February he was admitted into the ranks of the Jushin, for what good his advice might be. At first Hirohito could not help but recall all the months of lying and was so angry with the general that he would not even allow him into the Jushin, which had replaced the privy council as the primary source of counsel. As noted, the Jushin included every other former prime minister then alive.

Early in 1945 the Emperor began to ask questions again, the impassable barrier of military control having been breached. Within his circle of advisors in recent months a definite peace faction had emerged, which included the Marquis Kido, the Marquis Matsudaira, Admiral Okada, and the former foreign minister Shigenori Togo. The army still controlled the mechanism of government, so the peace advocates met behind closed doors and planned secretly. Their effort was lauded by the Emperor; indeed, one of the most active of them all was Prince Chichibu, who was on the retired list of the army, suffering from cancer. Chichibu lived in the country, far from Tokyo. But that gave him the advantage of a new perspective, and he corresponded with Hirohito frequently, advocating that peace feelers be made through neutral countries.

On March 10, 1945, the Americans staged their first big firebomb raid on Tokyo. The atmospheric conditions could not have been more favorable to the Allies; the fires spread rapidly in high winds and soon became a fire storm, with hundred-mile-an-hour blasts whipping the flames to frenzy and sending them leaping five and six blocks at a time. The next day corpses were stacked like cordwood on the bank of the Sumida River. Hundreds of acres of busy city districts were still smoldering. No accurate figures of the dead could be assembled, but the total for that one grisly night may have been more than two hundred thousand.

Hirohito said he was going out to see what had happened, but he was restrained. Security again. It was a week before his guardians would let him go, but when he did manage, he saw from the destruction that all was lost and that unless some action could be taken to halt the slaughter, the Japanese people were going to suffer terribly.

The firebombings continued all that spring and summer, killing hundreds of thousands of Japanese, mostly women and children, and making millions homeless. Firebombs were ideal for destroying Japanese cities, since most of the buildings in those days were made of wood and paper.

The use of fire on this massive scale made Hirohito pessimistic about the sort of mercy the Japanese might expect from the Western allies, but by June he had definitely made up his mind to seek peace.

However, on June 8, without his knowledge, the military men of the government met and pledged themselves to continue the war no matter what happened. A few days later at an imperial conference the Emperor sensed this attitude, and it aroused him to such strong emotion to be so duped he fell ill with the digestive ailment that now troubled him so often. On June 14 and 15 he was sick in bed at the palace. But on June 16 he was up again and meeting with his advisors, asking what they thought about ending the war. They had broken down into two factions, a grouping that lasted for the rest of the war: Foreign Minister Shigenori Togo, Admiral Yonai, Prime Minister Suzuki, General Umezu, and, behind the

scenes, Lord Keeper of the Privy Seal Kido, all for peace, and on the other
side, General Sugiyama, General Hata, and General Tojo, the most insis-
tent on continuing the war.

On June 22 the Emperor called a meeting of the Jushin. The lineup
was the same as it had been before: the army men for continuation of
the war and the others all for a settlement as soon as possible. It was
established at this meeting, however, that there was not enough oil
coming to Japan from the south to carry on the war.

Hirohito then suggested that a deal be struck with the Soviets. Actually, Hirota, the former foreign minister and former prime minister,
had suggested it first: if the Soviets would supply the Japanese with
petroleum from their reserves in the Soviet Far East (North Sakhalin),
then the Japanese would turn over Manchuria to them and abandon the
whole Manchukuo adventure! But the Potsdam Conference, the meeting
at which the Allies, including Russia, were to determine the shape of
the war effort against Japan, was only a few weeks away, and the Soviets
did not respond to the Japanese overture.

Neither did they respond to the suggestion that Prince Konoye visit
Moscow and deal with Stalin for the future of Japan. Stalin had already
opted for war with Japan, and soon he was waging it.

More meetings were called by the Emperor. There was no further
pretense that the Emperor was to hide behind a silken screen. He was
working hard to end the war, asking incisive, embarrassing questions of
the military.

War Minister Sugiyama announced that the Japanese army was arming
women and children to fight on the beaches of Chiba against the invaders.
Hirohito had sent his relatives out before; this time he sent his sister to
Chiba. She returned to report that the women and children were still
drilling with sticks and staves. The Emperor taxed Sugiyama with this
information, and the general had nothing to say. The continued losses
in battle, the continued firebombings of Japanese cities had persuaded
the Emperor that the war must be stopped, and stopped soon. The army
leaders said they could win; why then did they not launch a drive for
victory? The Emperor suggested a drive in China, where the army still
had major strength, a drive against Yunnan Province, in the heart of
Chiang Kai-shek's Nationalist territory. The army had to admit it did
not have the oil to undertake the task.

As the Japanese position continued to worsen, the Emperor's activity
increased, revealing his deep concern for the national welfare. The government inaugurated a program to honor heroes. The courageous dead
were promoted two grades in rank and awarded a posthumous medal.

Once or twice a week the newspapers carried dispatches from the Imperial Palace, praising the people of Japan for their patriotic fervor. In this way it was made clear to the people that the Emperor was more than aware of the sacrifices being made on the fields of battle.

When the Allies had invaded Okinawa in the spring of 1945, the Japanese navy and army suicide squads had come out to meet them. The Emperor lamented the necesity of sending young men on suicide missions, but he did not question the matter publicly.

All of 1945 was terrible for the people of the Japanese cities. They foraged for food, trading their valuables in the countryside, mostly for sweet potatoes, for there was very little else to eat. But of course this sort of privation was not shared by the royal family, who continued to live much as before. The Emperor himself always was Spartan in his approach to food; aside from the English breakfast, he ate very simply, rice and fish and vegetables. But the imperial household consisted of 6,000 people, the size of a large village, and it demanded an enormous effort by the Imperial Household Ministry just to keep things going.

August came, and with it the greatest blows of all. The American carrier fleet ranged around the Japanese homeland, striking where it wished. The B-29s continued their firebomb raids on half a dozen cities. The Japanese air force still had hundreds of planes to oppose the fleet, but for the most part these were being saved for the great battle of the islands, a battle to the death, which the army had ordained as the fate of the Japanese people. As for the imperial household, it was to be moved into caves in the mountains. No one asked the Emperor what he thought of the army plan to sacrifice all the women and children of Japan to the army's desire for a last glorious act of defiance.

Early in August, when the first atomic bomb had been dropped on Hiroshima, initial reports were confused and the army scientists tried to make light of the new weapon. So the generals professed themselves to be unimpressed.

But Hirohito was not fooled. He pressed the government to make an attempt through the Japanese ambassador in Moscow to persuade the Soviet government to intervene on behalf of Japan. But this was naive; the Japanese did not realize that Stalin was keen to grab his share of the plunder from a shattered empire. So, having endured atomic bombing, firebombing, and the ravages of the U.S. fleet offshore, in early August Japan also had to face a powerful Soviet army pouring down from the north. This was Hirohito's Japan on August 10, 1945—a defeated nation whose headstrong military leaders did not know it was time to quit. Their uncompromising attitude was sustained by the unconditional surrender policy of the Western Allies and the threats concerning what lay in store for the Emperor, who had been painted as the principal instigator of the Pacific war.

Hirohito was certain that the war must be stopped quickly. Prince Konoye had come to see him and raised the specter of a communist revolution if the Russians got involved in Japan. Hirohito had first been incredulous, but then he saw the logic of it. Indeed, something had to be done, and done swiftly.

19

The Long Week

No one in the Allied camp knew it, but, as noted in the introduction, on June 22, 1945, Emperor Hirohito decided to bring the disastrous Pacific war to a close. The problem was to manage this drastic action under the noses of the generals. The Emperor was under no illusion about his personal standing with the diehards of the Imperial Way faction. They had subverted him for eight years. He had been threatened in the past with everything from exile to assassination, and there was every reason to believe the military conspirators would try to subvert him again.

Hirohito called Prime Minister Kantaro Suzuki and four other important officials to an audience. Suzuki, he knew, was totally loyal. The prime minister had been his chamberlain in 1936. Suzuki knew the dangers, for he himself had been shot down and left for dead on that fateful February 26 when the rebellious young officers had been put up to creating mayhem by generals Araki and Mazaki. Suzuki and Shigenori Togo were the key figures in the imperial plan.

Togo, the foreign minister who during the days of victory had courageously told the Diet he was ready to make peace, was back as foreign minister. Now he would have his chance.

The five officials came in their limousines, across the moat and past the outer palace and along the wall of the inner palace enclosure, where the Emperor lived and kept his biological laboratory and his experimental rice field, past pet cranes and peacocks and along the gardens, with their arching bridges and hidden lotus pools. The scene, as always, was serene. They assembled in the conference room of the Imperial Library, a Western-style building. The room had a long conference table in the middle, covered with yellow silk bearing the imperial chrysanthemum crest, and armchairs all around.

The Emperor, in uniform, opened the meeting brusquely. "We have heard enough of this determination of yours to fight to the last soldier," said Hirohito. "Now we want action. We want you to consider methods of ending this war." He gazed at them. "Don't be bound by anything you have said before. State your real opinions."

The five officials were dismissed and went back in their puffing, charcoal-driven limousines, to return to their offices and to contemplate the words of the Emperor.

He, in turn, was considering the destruction the last six months had brought to Japan. He was particularly repelled by the suicidal impulse that was draining Japan of its lifeblood. Frustrated by the destruction of the Japanese fleet and the steady increase of Allied power, Admiral Takejiro Ohnishi had started the Kamikaze Corps in 1944 at the Battle of Leyte Gulf, and the army was right with him, having planned suicide operations for six months. "One man, one bomb, one plane, one carrier" was their motto.

By now, in 1945, the kamikaze concept had gone much further. The original pilots were eager volunteers; now there was no more volunteering. Suicide duty was thrust upon the young fliers, most of whom knew nothing but suicide tactics. In fact, most were hardly trained at all, since theirs would be a one-way mission. The kamikaze tactic had been extended to small boats and submarines, and now women were being trained to thrust grenades and satchel charges under tanks.

As Suzuki and the other officials tried to find a formula for peace that would surmount the objections of the generals, the pace of the war quickened. With the defeat and occupation of Germany, the Allied leaders were able to turn their complete attention and force toward Japan. The next step was considered at a meeting in Potsdam, at the site of the old Hohenzollern palace where another emperor had sat. From there the U.S., British, and Chinese heads of state called upon Japan to surrender unconditionally or have the full might of these powers thrust against it.

Initially, the governors of Japan did not even consult the Emperor, for their inference of the message was that Hirohito would be held responsible for Japan's belligerence during the past eight years. They decided to dishonor the proposal by *mokusatsu suru*—that is, there would be no reply at all. Japan would fight on. Since it was inevitable that the Allied message would leak out, the cabinet information office instructed the controlled press to print excerpts of the declaration—those parts unacceptable to Japan—and to make no comment. All this was done to propitiate the warlords, headed by War Minister Korechika Anami and Navy Chief of Staff Soemu Toyoda, the architect of the disastrous Battle of Leyte Gulf, which had destroyed the Japanese fleet.

But within the Allied proposal, those of the peace faction now saw their one great chance to move. On August 9 Prime Minister Suzuki told the supreme war council that the time had come to accept the Potsdam Declaration, but with one proviso, a guarantee of imperial immunity. He and Navy Minister Yonai, always an opponent of the war, called for surrender.

They were met by obstinance on the part of the generals. Said War Minister Anami:

> I object to the premier's proposal. Who can be 100 percent certain of defeat in the coming battle on our seashore? We haven't even started to fight it yet. There is an old saying, "He who loses his life shall find it." We certainly can't swallow this Potsdam Declaration. I demand that at least three conditions be fulfilled: (1) that our military forces be disarmed by our own command; (2) that all war criminals be tried in Japanese courts; (3) that the occupation of Japan by the enemy be limited to some specific areas in Japan and be terminated as soon as possible.

Nothing was decided that day. The cabinet met to consider the issues. As the cabinet was in session, the second atomic bomb was dropped, on Nagasaki. As with the first atomic bomb, the military declared that it was not a matter of particular importance; they could live with the atomic bomb, particularly because they were sure the United States did not have many left.

Sadamu Shimomura, the government director of information, secured an audience with the Emperor and spent two hours persuading Hirohito that the time had come for him to go over the heads of the generals and appeal directly to the people. The idea was so foreign to Hirohito that at first he would not even consider it. But as he listened to Shimomura's persuasive arguments, the Emperor realized that he had an opportunity to exercise a new sort of power, concerning which no interdictions had ever been handed down by the men around the throne because the technology had never applied to Japanese imperial life before. Hirohito agreed that the idea was sound and workable, and that he could broadcast to the nation.

Now the meetings continued, though the Emperor had made up his mind what he would do. So the army could not defend the shores of Honshu, said the Emperor, and he questioned the generals about the state of their armored forces on the Kanto Plain. No, they did not have fuel for their tanks, they admitted. No, they could not defend Tokyo, they admitted.

What did the army want? the Emperor asked. The army wanted the national polity defended, with no disarmament, no trials for war crimes, and no disbandment of the army. Obviously these were all demands that would be unacceptable to the Allies, who by August 1 had called for unconditional surrender.

The army also wanted the Emperor to place himself and all the imperial family under the command of Imperial General Headquarters, to be prepared to move inland to fight the war as an army vassal.

Hirohito refused to consider such an idea. He told the members of the imperial family that the best thing to do was for him to sacrifice himself in the unconditional surrender of Japan.

The decision for surrender was made on the night of August 9, after a long and exhausting meeting with all the senior advisors to the Emperor, who had come to the palace at 11 A.M. At midnight the Emperor announced that this was his final word, and he refused to be moved by sobbing and importuning.

In the next few hours the palace telephone lines were cut, isolating the palace from the outside world. At the demand of Marquis Kido the Emperor repaired to the underground bunker behind the steel doors, which were firmly shut against the outside world and the expected invasion of Japanese army troops.

As noted, the argument over surrender dominated official Japan for the next week, while the Emperor waited impatiently for the generals to come around. When they did not, on the night of August 14 he decreed the surrender and prepared to broadcast the news to his people the next day.

That night, when the Emperor dismissed that last meeting of the imperial war council, the cabinet officers went to the official residence of the prime minister to begin drafting the surrender document. War Minister Anami came, signed his name, said good night, and then went to the war office. There, as he entered, he was besieged by young officers, faces taut, fists clenched, quivering with stress. Anami told them what had happened.

"And, sir, what is your opinion?" said one junior officer.

"The Emperor said to me, 'I understand your feelings. It must be very painful to you, but please bear the burden.' I shall obey him. What else can I do?"

No one replied, but one of the officers, a Major Kenji Hatanaka, rushed out of the room, unable to contain himself.

Information Director Shimomura sent a team of recording technicians to the palace, but the recording session was delayed as the Emperor wrote his own message to the people. It was close to midnight before Hirohito emerged from his study, went to the library, and placed himself before the microphone. He began to read in his high-pitched, feathery voice:

> To our good and loyal subjects: after pondering deeply the general trends of the world and the actual conditions in Our Empire today, We have decided to effect a settlement of the present situation by resorting to an extraordinary measure. . . .

He read the whole statement through twice, and a record was made of both readings. Then the Emperor retired to his underground bedroom sixty feet below.

Information Director Shimomura was not sure what to do next. The records should be taken to NHK and put away for the morrow's broadcast, but Shimomura had learned that a number of young officers were hanging about the outer palace, planning to ambush him when he came out and destroy the records. Who could keep them safe?

Just then, in came Chamberlain Yoshihiro Tokugawa, and Shimamura asked him to take over the records for the night. Tokugawa knew what risks he was running, but he agreed. Shimomura then went off gratefully, to be stopped at the entry to the palace, bulldozed, and imprisoned in a guard hut for several hours.

Meanwhile Chamberlain Tokugawa pondered for a moment, and then hurried to the office of the Empress, opened a small locker, put in the records, locked the door, and took the key.

After rushing angrily from the war minister's office, Major Hatanaka had plunged around army headquarters, trying to enlist support for a rebellion. He went to the office of General Shizuichi Tanaka, commander of the army eastern region, which included Honshu Island. Anticipating such an action by the Emperor, Hatanaka had approached Tanaka before, to sound him out. Now he opened the door and entered the general's room, to be greeted by a thunderous voice. "Don't talk to me about that stupid idea again. I know what you are going to say. The answer is no. Now go back to your unit."

After more impassioned discussion with the young officers, War Minister Anami dismissed them. In the quiet of his office, he sat for a long time. Then he went to Prime Minister Suzuki's house, presented him with a box of cigars ("One of our officers from the Philippines gave them to me and I don't smoke"), and thanked the prime minister.

Suzuki sensed that he was seeing the general for the last time, and he was right. Anami returned to his official residence, sat down on the veranda, and composed a poem of farewell.

> Having received from His Imperial Majesty
> Many great favors,
> I have no final statement
> To make to posterity.

Then he plunged the short samurai sword into his belly.

At army headquarters, Major Hatanaka was beside himself. Not one of the generals he approached was willing to disregard the will of the Emperor and join the rebellion. Finally Hatanaka spoke to Masataka Ida, a member of General Anami's staff. Ida agreed, and the two officers got onto their bicycles and pedaled to the headquarters of the Imperial Guards at the northwest end of the Imperial Palace. There they insisted on seeing Lieutenant General Takeshi Mori, a kinsman of Ida's. They arrived at the guards office at about 11:30 P.M., but were kept waiting an hour because Mori knew why they had come and did not want to see them. When he eventually consented, they demanded that he send the Imperial Guards to seize the palace and in effect imprison Hirohito to prevent him from making the broadcast. Meanwhile they would issue orders in the name of the Emperor to continue the war. All this was official, said Hatanaka. It came directly from General Anami.

General Mori did not believe a word of it; he demanded proof. Hatanaka set out for General Anami's house with a letter he hoped to persuade the general to sign, but instead he found the general dead. He went back to Mori's office to report that Anami had been so distressed by the idea of surrender that he had killed himself.

General Mori told him to go away. Hatanaka was so enraged at this that he drew his pistol and shot the general dead.

Then Hatanaka and Ida set about their revolution. They faked orders to seize the palace. But when the orders reached the guards division, someone informed General Tanaka, and he knew that something had gone wrong.

General Tanaka left his office and was driven to the palace. As he crossed the bridge he saw a number of young officers of the guards division milling about. He stopped the car. "What are you doing here?" he demanded.

"We have been ordered to guard the palace, to let no one in or out."

"Go back to your barracks." said the general. "This is your commander speaking."

Major Hatanaka, having delivered the faked orders, had gone inside the outer palace and was frantically searching for the records. He led a gang inside to the inner palace, where they came across Chamberlain Tokugawa. "Where are the records?" Hatanaka demanded.

Tokugawa did not answer. A sergeant with Hatanaka stepped forward and struck the chamberlain in the face, but Hatanaka told him to desist. The chamberlain escaped without further harm.

Meanwhile the navy was preparing to act. The telephone lines had been cut, but the navy aide inside the palace had been in communication by radio with the navy operations office. Warships were standing in Tokyo Bay, ready for action.

Since he could not find the records in the palace, Hatanaka went to the offices of the Japan Broadcasting Corporation (Nikon Hoso Kyokai). Either the records were there or they soon would be, he reasoned, and he would seize them. At NHK he was greeted by a polite night duty officer, who said the records were not there. Hatanaka believed him. He demanded radio time so he could tell the people that the Emperor's broadcast was a fake. But the duty officer politely refused him. There were no technicians on duty, he said. Nothing could be done.

Hatanaka had already been informed by his associates that General Tanaka had intervened and that his revolution was a failure. He returned to the outer palace and verified this. The Imperial Guards were gone. He walked to the plaza and shot himself.

Stragglers of the rebellion continued to act. They burned down the houses of Marquis Kido and Prime Minister Suzuki. But by 4:30 A.M. on August 15, all was quiet. The Imperial Guards were back, guarding the palace but not threatening it, and the rebels had vanished into the last shadows of the night. The principal conspirators were all dead by their own hands.

All morning long the national radio announced that the Emperor would make an important broadcast at noon, so millions of Japanese turned to their radio sets. At noon they heard a thin, piping voice that the vast majority had never heard before. "To our good and loyal subjects: We have resolved to pave the way for a grand peace for all generations to come by enduring the unendurable, and suffering what is insufferable. . . ."

The war was over.

20

Capitulation

As Emperor Hirohito was broadcasting to the people of Japan on August 15, 1945, Admiral William F. Halsey's U.S. Third Fleet ranged off the coast of Honshu Island, where it had been striking Japanese targets for weeks. The Third Fleet was the principal occupying force in the early days of the peace, and Admiral Halsey took over the Japanese naval base at Yokosuka. To all intents and purposes, then, Yokosuka base became a U.S. base.

Soon General Douglas MacArthur arrived to be supreme commander for the Allied Powers, and the demilitarization of Japan began. The army was demobilized. The navy was also demobilized, to such an extent that Japan did not even have a naval force capable of guarding its shoreline against smugglers and pirates.

The coming of this particular set of white barbarians, fresh from conquering Japan overseas, was a matter of enormous concern to the Japanese ruling community. They expected the conquerors to loot and take their young women. What guidance did the Emperor, who had invited the foreigners in, offer the Japanese people? Not much was apparent, but there were some signs of authority emanating from the palace.

Immediately after announcing the surrender, Emperor Hirohito appointed an imperial family council. Its first task, in those days just after the surrender announcement, was to make sure that the army and navy obeyed the Emperor's dictate and really surrendered. This was accomplished, although not without pain. Members of the imperial family traveled to the hot spots, to Atsugi Air Base, where a number of army pilots were threatening to continue kamikaze tactics, and to the naval bases, where young officers wanted to continue the use of the suicide submarines and suicide boats.

All these potential outbreaks were quelled, and by the time the Allies began to arrive, just after September 1, 1945, Japan was quiet. But whether it could remain that way would depend on the nature of the occupation, and the Japanese were prepared for the worst. Women were told to dress like men, so as not to arouse attention from U.S. troops. Young girls were sent to the country, if possible. If not, they were told to hide out anywhere they could.

And then the flood began. First was the painful ceremony of surrender aboard the U.S. battleship *Missouri*, on September 2. Two days later Emperor Hirohito left the palace, for the first time in many months, and drove to the Diet buildings. He was to open the Japanese Parliament, called into special session to hear his report on those events of the dreadful days of August. He did not know—no one in Japan knew—what attitude and what actions the new military governors of Japan would take.

It was an occasion for statesmanship, not facts, and the Emperor rose to the occasion.

> Some days ago We issued a proclamation of cessation of hostilities, and We sent our ambassadors and caused them to sign the documents relative to this event. It is Our desire that Our people will surmount the manifold hardships and trials which attend the end of the war, and make manifest the glory of Japan's national polity, win the confidence of the world, establish firmly a peaceful state, and contribute to the progress of mankind. Our people are continually directed to that end. In the consummation of the great task, beware most strictly of any outburst of emotion, which may bring needless complications, or any contention of strife, which may create confusion, lead you astray, and cause you to lose the confidence of the world. At home cultivate the ways of righteousness, foster nobility of spirit, and work with resolution to enhance the glory of the Imperial State and keep pace with the progress of the world.

Having spoken, the Emperor left the Diet, bowing low and then striding from the chamber. He had never appeared more confident of the future; yet at the time he had no idea of the attitude that would be shown toward him or toward Japan by the conquering Allied powers.

The occupation was not at all as the Japanese had feared. The Americans behaved themselves according to the code of military discipline. There was very little rape, very little looting, and much fraternization, particularly between the soldiers and young Japanese women. The Americans even provided some food relief, but even so that first winter was very hard on Japan.

The Allied powers were in disagreement among themselves as to the policy to be pursued regarding the fate of the Emperor and the dismantling of Japanese industry. Even within nations, as in the United States, opinions were divided. In the face of such total uncertainty, the confidence shown by the Emperor was nothing less than heroic, and it had its effect on the nation.

The fact is that in the late summer of 1945, almost anything could have happened in Japan. Some 3 million Japanese troops and auxiliaries were still armed and on duty, and all of them detested the thought of surrender.

For example, Mutsuo Saito, a kamikaze pilot at the Honjo Army Air Base, was waiting. He had not been one of the ardent kamikaze pilots, but one who had accepted the fate ordained for him as inevitable. But now what would happen?

Not waiting for the Allies, the commanding office of Honjo Base began demobilizing the pilots. They were given an allowance of 2,000 yen; some food, chocolate, and a large sack of flour, and were told to go to their homes immediately. The hope of the commander was that by sending them thus, as individuals, incidents could be avoided.

And so Pilot Saito started home. On the train he encountered a young cadet pilot he had met before, who engaged him in conversation about the surrender. What did Saito think of it? the youngster wanted to know.

Saito thought fast. He had already met some of the never-say-die fanatics at the base. He temporized, but said he did not like the surrender.

The other nodded and continued to talk about war, about the new weapons that were being developed to lead Japan to victory, and how they could drive the Americans away from Japan even now.

The train slowed at Saito's stop and he prepared to get off. The cadet pulled a pistol from his holster. It was loaded. "I'm glad you agreed that the surrender was wrong," said the cadet. "If you had said otherwise, I would have killed you."

With that sort of people on the loose, almost anything could happen. *Asahi Shimbun* coined a phrase to characterize the situation that existed in those earliest days: *ichi-oku sokyodatsu*, which means "a hundred million people in a state of shock." And that was Japan, September 1945.

General MacArthur arrived in Japan by airplane on September 8, 1945. Almost immediately the supreme commander for Allied powers (SCAP) took over the Dai Ichi Building, across from the palace moat, and the old U.S. Embassy in Akasaka. Still there was no discernable plan for the occupation. Was it to be military, or was it to be a military presence guiding a civil government? Within Japan there were many views. The left wing, of course, wanted many changes. The communists wanted to destroy the monarchy, the socialists to keep it as a constitutional monarchy. The right wing was very quiet, but nonetheless active, for maintenance of the status quo.

Even within the imperial family opinions were divided. Prince Higashikuni, a cousin, who had taken over the role of premier after Prime Minister Suzuki resigned on the morrow after the surrender ceremony aboard the *Missouri*, suggested that Hirohito abdicate in favor of 12-year-old Akihito, the Crown Prince. Prince Chichibu, the Emperor's brother, would become regent.

What about the Emperor? Was he, as some said, the primary war criminal? The Australians said so. So did the Dutch. So did some of the British, but not all. From America, too, came shouts of "Hang the Emperor." That sort of talk was a product of the war image. Searching for a symbol of Japan to match Hitler for Germany and Mussolini for Italy, the American political cartoonists had settled on Hirohito, with Tojo as a sort of stooge. The fact that there was no validity to the portrait did not disturb its wartime currency. The Soviets, of course, wanted the Imperial system destroyed, in the hope that this would help to bring about communism in Japan.

MacArthur frankly did not know what he wanted to do, but from his long experience and family background he had enough knowledge of Asia not to move too fast. Some of his aides wanted him to deal with the Emperor immediately and harshly. He demurred. September came, and still the status of the Emperor was hanging in the balance. There was no action and no news at the Imperial Palace that gave any indication of the future. The Emperor grew gloomy, and he developed an attack of jaundice.

The Japanese attitudes toward their Emperor ran the gamut, too. The communists, of course, were noisiest, and students and others also demonstrated against the Empire.

One day the Empress was out driving in Tokyo when a demonstration developed just outside the palace. Her car, with its distinctive markings, came back across the moat. As the driver made his way slowly through the hundreds of flag-bearing and chanting people, the Empress was frightened. But suddenly the demonstrators recognised the imperial flag on the hood of the auto, and as a group they turned and bowed low to her.

September dragged along. The Emperor's health declined further, from worry about the future. Finally he decided that he would go to see MacArthur. Through the Imperial Household Ministry an appointment was made, and on September 26 the Emperor donned civilian formal attire, with the cutaway coat, striped trousers, and top hat of diplomacy, and was driven in his limousine from the palace across the Nijubashi double bridge. The car moved along the streets to the U.S. Embassy, where the MacArthur family now lived. Hirohito was accompanied by his interpreter, Terasaki; by the court chamberlain, the Marquis Matsudaira; and, because the court was worried about him, by his doctor as well.

MacArthur's staff, not knowing what to do, adopted a cold and formal air that was most intimidating. General Bonner Fellers, a man who had much knowledge and many connections with Japan smiled, greeted the Emperor, and shook hands with him, but he was the exception. MacArthur was under one great misapprehension. He believed that the Emperor had come to deny that he was a war criminal, and even to plead not to be charged.

Hirohito's evident nervousness (his hand shook as he accepted a proffered cigarette) lent credence to that idea. "I come to you, General MacArthur", said Hirohito, "to offer myself to the judgment of the powers you represent as the one to bear sole responsibility for every political and military decision made and action taken by my people in the conduct of the war."

MacArthur, as he later wrote in his memoirs, was enormously impressed, because his staff had made a thorough investigation of all the charges of "war crimes" made against the Emperor and learned that they were all untrue. After that meeting MacArthur made up his mind: there would be no charges against Emperor Hirohito in the war crimes trials. He informed Washington of his deep opposition to any such move.

Of course, as the Japanese began saying openly forty years later, the war crimes trials were simply the trial of the defeated by the victors, and any neutral would see that in a moment. At a briefing session held for the foreign press on October 14, 1988, in response to an aggressive question from a foreign reporter, Professor Masakazu Amazaki made this point very clearly. Even forty-three years later, when Emperor Hirohito was terminally ill with cancer, and Japan was mourning, the Western press dredged up all the old charges of war crimes. If Tojo and the others were responsible for war crimes, and everything was done in the name of the Emperor, said this one reporter, then why was not the Emperor a war criminal? And, of course, the answer is that the Emperor was not aware of most of the wartime acts that were committed in his name. As the war crimes trials developed and the indictments were handed down, he told intimates that he had no objection to the trial of General Tojo because he had discovered that Tojo had inserted many lies about military affairs into the imperial rescripts, which the Emperor always accepted as his own responsibility. The trials that troubled the Emperor were those of such men as the Marquis Kido, Koki Hirota, and Foreign Minister Togo, all of whom, Hirohito knew, had done their level best to prevent war, and to vitiate its effects.

21

A Ray of Hope

The Americans who were sent to Japan came with instructions to occupy the country, eliminate the constitution and people declared to be obnoxious, and democratize Japan in the Western image. As a practical person, General MacArthur knew that it would take very little to make his occupation onerous to victor and vanquished alike. Had President Truman insisted on the trial of Hirohito as a war criminal, MacArthur observed, he would need at least a million more soldiers to occupy the country. So instead, left to his own devices, MacArthur chose to deal with those in the Japanese civil government, putting the SCAP directives through them. This, naturally, caused some consultation with the civil government, and so the U.S. military governors found their programs reduced in scale below what the radicals wanted, to the scale of the practical.

The particular bête noire of the Imperial family in the MacArthur administration was General Courtney Whitney, whose arrogance was superseded only by that of his commander. But MacArthur's arrogance was imperial, while General Whitney had wanted to humiliate Emperor Hirohito if he could not destroy him. Whitney ordered the palace staff cut severely—why, no one could quite explain, since the palace lived on the civil economy, which just then was getting nothing from the United States. So the staff was cut from 7,500 to 1,600 people. The cut created considerable hardship and did nothing else but assuage General Whitney's sense of the appropriate. In his view, a defeated monarch ought to be treated as though he were defeated.

The Emperor never complained. Rations were cut at the palace, and the Emperor, who had always been ascetic in his eating anyhow, became more so. His diet consisted mostly of unhulled rice and sweet potatoes, like the diet of his subjects. One effect on the 350-acre palace was to leave the grounds to fall to ruin. When the Japanese people learned of this, they organized volunteer parties from all over the country—"sweeping parties" to take care of the imperial domain. When the Emperor learned that 12-year-old Prince Akihito had developed some taste for Western candy bars and chocolate, he brought the youngster into the imperial office and chastised him. The Crown Prince must learn to live the life of the people.

Another direct result of the occupation of Japan was a basic change in the religious structure of the country. In the 1930s Shinto had been declared to be the official religion of Japan, and the Emperor to be Shinto's high priest. Actually it had ever been thus, but until the emergence of the military oligarchs Shinto had been a quiet, self-effacing religion, more concerned with the state of the crops and the weather than with human affairs. Under the militarists, Shinto had been made into an arm of Emperor worship, but with the ending of the war and the decline of the military it was moving back to its rightful place. The U.S. occupation helped it to do so, by forbidding subsidies to any Shinto institution.

Nevertheless, the Yasukuni Shrine, once the state shrine, continues to be an important part of Japanese religious and political life, and, thirty years after the war ended, a campaign was begun to restore its significance as of old, a campaign that by this writing has not been successful, although pressed by members of the Liberal Democratic ruling party.

One aspect of the occupation remains veiled: General MacArthur denied in his memoirs that the Emperor's declaration of his humanity was in any way prompted by the supreme commander. But that, of course, is nonsense. From the beginning of the occupation, senior staff members of SCAP talked about the need to strip the Emperor of his divinity as part of removing the mystique of the Emperor system. So while MacArthur may never have made a direct suggestion, the whole occupation was dedicated to the prospect.

The campaign to undeify Emperor Hirohito was a definite program of the occupation and was part of the campaign against Shinto. The Emperor was, by the entire Japanese polity, the chief religious officer of Japan, whose responsibility it was (and is) to propitiate the gods and explain to them the ways of the people. The people around the Emperor got the message, and they suggested that he issue a public declaration that he was only human.

To Hirohito this seemed to be of a piece with the army demand of the late 1930s that he declare himself, or allow himself to be declared, a god. He had not liked the one situation, and he did not like the other.

But to understand the pressures involved, one must also understand the shape and form of the Japanese government in the late days of 1945.

Admiral Suzuki's cabinet, which had presided over the surrender of Japan, resigned ten days after the surrender ceremony aboard the battleship *Missouri*. The new prime minister was Prince Naruhiko Higashikuni, a member of the Imperial family.

In those early days the prince did his best for the supporters of the government. The big war industries were paid off for the contracts they held. This move cost the Japanese government an enormous sum and virtually bankrupted the treasury, but what was the difference? The money of a defeated country is only as valuable as the conquerors say it is. So Higashikuni did not hesitate, and the result was the doubling of the money in circulation, the salvation of the profitability of the big corporations, and concurrently, the debasement of the currency and the impoverishment of the middle class.

After a few weeks the Higashikuni cabinet resigned and was replaced by a government under Kijuro Shidehara. It was to be his task to work with MacArthur's officials and to put into Japanese law the directives of the supreme commander.

Once the Japanese were disarmed, the five basic precepts of the occupation force were (1) the emancipation of women, (2) the unionization of labor, (3) the relaxation of national control of education, (4) the reform of the judicial system, and (5) the destruction of the *zaibatsu*, or giant economic holding companies. But if Japan was to democratize itself, what about the Emperor? How could a country become free if it were ruled by a god?

Hirohito could tell by the tenor of activity at the Dai Ichi Building across the moat that the officials of SCAP were only too eager to destroy the imperial institution if they could. The Emperor was determined to do something to relieve the pressure.

He had grown up with the concept of imperial divinity, but he had never believed it. Years earlier he and Prince Saionji had agreed that the trappings must be retained as part of the Japanese way of life, but that was all. All this had been perverted in the "die for the Emperor" complex that the generals had thrust upon Japan. Now that it was no longer dangerous, it was ridiculous.

One day Hirohito told a story to Prime Minister Shidehara about a previous Emperor of Kyoto days who had fallen ill and died because his illness was undiagnosed and untreated. The reason for that, said the monarch, was that the people around that Emperor had convinced themselves of his divinity, and would not allow doctors to come close enough to feel the imperial pulse.

So it was no surprise a little later when Hirohito began talking about drafting an imperial rescript denying the divinity of the ruler. The rescript was actually worked over in December 1945, and was issued as the Emperor's 1946 new year's proclamation. In it Hirohito said something he had long wanted to say:

We are with you, the people, and wish always to share common interests, joys and sorrows, with all of you. The bondage between Us and you, the people, is constantly tied with mutual trust, love, and respect. It is not brought about by mere mythology and legends. It is never founded on a chimerical conception which describes the Emperor as a living deity and, moreover, the Japanese as superior to all other races of people, thence destined to rule the world.

This rescript came to be known as the Ningen Sengan, or Human Being Declaration, because of this one paragraph.

That 1946 new year's rescript was designed to give the Japanese people comfort at a desperate time. The Japanese military oligarchy had fooled itself when it said in August that the war could be continued. The nation was economically exhausted. The payoff to the *zaibatsu* by the Higashi-kuni government had been the blow that almost brought destruction. In 1941, despite the high expense of the China war, which had worried many economists, the paper notes in circulation in Japan totaled only 4,700 million yen, and by 1945 the currency had only quadrupled, which was remarkable considering the level of expense brought by the war. But by December, courtesy of the big spending of the Higashikuni government, the currency had been inflated and 50 billion yen in notes circulated.

The amount of money in circulation was only one indicator of the misery of Japan. Three million people had died in the war, and another fifteen million were homeless. The rice bowls of Korea, Taiwan, and Indochina were denied Japan, and so was the grain land of Manchuria. Food was in extremely short supply; the official per capita ration came to less than 1,800 calories a day. One judge who believed in the rules insisted on living on the official ration; he died of malnutrition the next year. The vast majority of people turned to the black market. Even sweet potatoes and roots found their way to that market, so desperate was the need for food.

Here is the recollection of Mutsuo Saito, the young kamikaze pilot of a few months earlier. Then he was considering the manner of his death. Now he was struggling for survival.

> Food was very scarce. For a while my parents went off to Yamagata, because they knew that being farther away from Tokyo there would be fewer shortages there, and father thought that some of his relatives or friends might be able to sell him rice. When my parents found rice to buy, they wrote me to come and collect it. Then I would go and buy a black market railroad ticket to go to Yamagata to fetch the rice. You had to buy black market tickets because for ordinary tickets you needed to queue for days. The black marketeers would get waifs and strays to sit in the queue for them, and then they would sell the tickets for some vastly inflated price.

But even in the smaller cities and towns life was nearly desperate. Here is the plaint from those days of a young housewife from Kofu City, Yamanishi Prefecture:

> We consume ten days' ration of food in five days, supplementing the deficiency with costly food sold in the black market. People also say we should go and see the farmers in Chiba and buy agricultural products from them. They say even if we pay the train fare to Chiba, it more than pays off. But the trouble is we have no extra hand who can travel. We cannot afford the train ticket in the first place. We have no other choice but to go and find food in the black market. We have to eat somehow.
>
> My husband's salary is 200 yen, while our livelihood costs are about 600 yen every month. To make both ends meet, we sell everything we can. I know we cannot get along much longer this way.

The winter of 1945–46 was also a time of political disarray. The Communist party, which had been underground, emerged and became strong. The Socialist party also grew stronger. MacArthur and his people watched the growth of the left with alarm; they had spawned the social revolution, and now they did not know where it might lead. As relations between the United States and the Soviet Union worsened in the European occupations, the result was felt in Japan. All those promises of breaking up the *zaibatsu* now seemed to be an enormous error.

What the Americans decided to do was strengthen the Japanese economy, not destroy it as they had originally planned. Japan was not to be turned into a pastoral paradise, but rebuilt as a strong industrial economy, to be a bastion in Asia against the growing communist strength. This was not an easy task, because the Japanese were not quite sure what they wanted. The state of affairs in Japan was known as *kyodatsu*—lethargy.

The leftists were active, but the center was not, and the right wing continued in its old ways. The left was a political force driven by the hunger of the people, and that was very real. Outside the Imperial Palace the left organized its demonstrations. And, of course, the Emperor was seen as the symbol of all that was wrong in Japan. A demonstration of two hundred thousand greeted the efforts of Shigeru Yoshida to form a new right-wing government. The rally was put down by the force of SCAP, using U.S. troops. On May 19 the communists led an even greater demonstration, almost to the gates of the palace, demanding food and an audience with Hirohito.

"We are starving, how about him?" shouted Ryuichi Tokuda, leader of the Communist party. The governing group was saved by SCAP, which issued a declaration that order would be maintained by U.S. troops if necessary. And so the Yoshida government came to power to maintain the old ruling class.

By autumn 1946 SCAP and the government were beset: the Americans had demanded the organization of American-type labor unions, and of course the unions had turned to the left. By January 1947 the political scene was a nightmare, and the economic situation continued to be so desperate that many people expected a revolution. The demonstrations grew larger and more difficult to control. A general strike was called. General MacArthur said it would be put down with force if necessary, so the strike was canceled, but the atmosphere was like tinder. Thus, in the winter of 1946–47 the U.S. occupation reached a low point. Something had to be done by somebody, or Japan would collapse.

22

The Politics of Democracy

Although the first eight articles of the Japanese constitution of 1947 deal exclusively with the status and role of the Emperor, in daily Japanese political life since that time the Emperor has played almost no role at all.

After a period of ups and downs the reins of power went into the hands of the conservative Liberal Democratic party, which ever since has superintended a policy for Japan that emphasizes business, often at the expense of public welfare. If this is a matter of concern to Emperor Akihito, it is not one to which he can address himself directly, for his function is to be the conscience and the presence of Japan. The role he plays now is almost altogether ceremonial.

In one sense the change since the 1920s has been enormous. In those days Hirohito was in constant danger of assassination (and one attempt was nearly successful). He had to be protected from the public by cordons of guards and plenty of space. But in his declining years the Emperor found himself able to go anywhere he wished and speak to whom he chose, with no danger at all. Thus did Hirohito become emancipated and no longer the prisoner of the palace behind the moat. One of his early acts to show his humanity was to take the Empress to a baseball game. He did not do that again; baseball was not really one of his interests. Sumo wrestling, however, was something he had followed for years. After the autumn tournament the sumo champions were invited to visit the Imperial Palace as usual, even though the Emperor was dreadfully ill.

In the beginning days of the new position of the imperial presence, Hirohito embarked on one tour after another to make himself visible. Most of the tours, through bombed out areas or places where the people had suffered during the years of occupation, were unimpressive. Hirohito, never a loquacious man, confined his observations to "Ah, soo desuka," which means "so . . . isn't that so?" and not much else. To the press these tours became known as the "Ah, soo desuka tours."

But as time went on, the Emperor gained a politician's presence of mind and even developed a few tricks, such as the habit of wearing a crushed felt hat with the brim turned down, so unusual as to be a sort of badge of personality.

The Emperor's new visibility accomplished something the occupation authorities had certainly not envisaged, and the left wing of the Japanese political sector found very painful. The Emperor established himself, by his own efforts, in an entirely new position in Japan. His tours took on a presence of their own, and the Japanese people responded with evidence that they appreciated the interest of their Emperor and his gestures of goodwill. He was the spirit of Japan, and his visits meant that Japan cared about Japanese people. In all the machinations of the Diet politicians, none of them had ever achieved such a warm relationship with the people.

In the 1960s, once the new imperial presence was established, Hirohito and the royal family ceased making so many public relations gestures. The time of the fifteenth summer Olympic Games in 1964 was an exception. With noticeable pride, Hirohito presided over the opening festivities from the royal box, waving, chatting, and smiling, accompanied by the Empress, his two surviving brothers, his sisters-in-law, Crown Prince Akihito and his bride, and other children of the family. From that point on, the relationship between Emperor and subjects was distinctly easy without being overfamiliar.

In the days of the occupation, the result of this royal activity was to bring to the Japanese again a sense of oneness, but this time not accompanied by fanfare or military trappings. The Hirohito who had posed in his general's uniform each year atop his white horse, Spring Snow, was no more. All the military uniforms were long gone, and the presence was of a fatherly and later a grandfatherly figure. December 25, 1986, marked Hirohito's 75th anniversary as ruler of Japan. Akihito has never had his picture taken on a horse and has never worn a uniform.

More and more, as time went on, the people of Japan received glimpses of the life that went on inside the great palace. Like Buckingham Palace in London, the Imperial Palace stands at the center of the capital, lending a sense of security and well-being to Tokyo. In its moat live the royal ducks, and in the springtime the ducks nest in the little parks and garden spots of the huge office towers across the moat, and across the great avenue Uchibori dori. And every day in the springtime, thousands of Japanese come to Uchibori dori. When the ducklings and their mamas waddle back across the boulevard to the moat, the policemen stop traffic, as they do for nothing else, and everyone smiles and laughs—it is all symbolic of goodwill and national pride, and all associated with the royal presence.

To say that the Emperor today has no political influence would be wrong. Certainly, however, his influence is not the same as in the days when cabinet ministers could go directly to the Emperor. Through the Imperial Household Agency, no longer a ministry, as it was before 1947, the imperial attitude toward affairs of state is often transmitted to the ruling cabinet. Generally the Emperor speaks up, even though quietly, only on basic issues of national policy. He might, for example, counsel the government to go slowly in its efforts to get around those troublesome elements of the constitution and the basic law that tried to limit the Japanese military spending to 1 percent of the national income.

But his views are never forcefully imposed on the nation; indeed, there is no avenue through which they could be imposed, since it is no longer the Emperor who selects a prime minister, but the ruling party, and the Emperor's views are never openly sought by a prime minister on any subject.

Today it is all much more subtle than that. In a nation where the business image is of a man in a dark gray or black suit, black shoes, black socks, white shirt, and black tie, carrying a dispatch case, the Emperor has a special image. The palace and everything in it are a reminder of the Japaneseness of Japan. On a busy Tokyo street, where the bus stop or subway station may be flanked by a McDonald's hamburger restaurant and a Kentucky Fried Chicken establishment, sometimes the Japanese people feel the need for reminders that theirs is an ancient Oriental civilization.

As I write this on a word processor, in a room overlooking the university district, against the background noise of the Japanese baseball world series on television, with cars and buses speeding along the busy streets, only the Chinese characters and Japanese *furigana* of the signs and billboards make this appear any different from a European or American city. Half a block away, a new fast-food establishment, "Moskurgers," has opened. Fast food, fast pace, fast life, make Tokyo people, most of whom are commuters by American standards, although their homes and business offices may both be within the limits of the great Tokyo sprawl, feel very much part of the racing twentieth century.

Only the Emperor and the relative handful of temples and shrines bring a sense of continuity with the past. And to the Japanese, it is very important to feel their essentially Japanese nature and their oneness with other Japanese. They are extremely conscious that theirs is a small country, theirs a secondary language, and that their culture is unique. It is the Emperor and the occasional airing on television of one of the imperial affairs at court that bring all this home in a satisfying manner. Some of the functions of royalty—the opening of celebrations and the visiting of fairs and other events—are still carried out by members of the royal family other than the Emperor, but the problem is that in the rearrangement of Japanese society under the occupation, the peerage was dissolved, and in one generation or two the collateral lines of the royal family will become ordinary citizens. Thus the Showa Emperor's four surviving daughters are princesses, but their children are not princes and princesses. Indeed, in two or three generations the imperial system may collapse completely, from lack of stock to perpetuate it. As noted, Crown Prince Akihito married a commoner, although she would have been of the peerage had it not been destroyed. After death she will be known as the Heisei Empress. Perhaps after one or two generations of this sort of mingling the Japanese will see the monarchy as irrelevant. It is a definite possibility. But, for the moment, in the Heisei era, the imperial succession seems safe enough.

The present Emperor, Akihito, has two sons. Crown Prince Naruhito was educated at the Gakushuin, the special royal school established for Hirohito, whose lines he kept for Akihito. But then, this being a modern world, Naruhito spent two and a half years at Merton College at Oxford University, thus fulfilling another of Hirohito's dreams.

As for the succession of the monarchy in case Naruhito should be unable to take over, the Showa Emperor made provision some time ago. Prince Fumihito, the second son of Akihito, was in 1985 granted a coming-of-age ceremony, a traditional royal place function redolent of ancient times and involving hundreds of thousands of dollars worth of Imperial costumes, in which the robes of manhood were granted to the prince. The real significance of this action was not just to prop up the national morale, but to make sure that Fumihito could succeed to the throne if something untoward happened to his brother. Without this action, the imperial line would fall into a regency.

In the last half of his reign, Emperor Hirohito proved unusually thoughtful and farseeing. From time to time since 1945, and particularly in the hectic days of the 1960s, there were cries from the left, some greeted with public acclaim, for the abdication of the Emperor and the abolition of the imperial system. But a Japan without an Emperor would lose its cultural ties with the past, as China appears to be doing in the wake of Mao Tse-tung's disastrous revolution, and in the very nature of its communist society.

Without fanfare, and sometimes against the odds, it seemed, Hirohito worked diligently from 1945 to 1988 to adjust the imperial system to the needs of a new Japanese society, and the indications are that he did so successfully.

23

The Emperor

Emperor Hirohito's renunciation of his divinity was, and continues to be, a subject of controversy in the foreign press. In fact, the Emperor's life came under sharp scrutiny in the autumn of 1988, when Hirohito fell ill and began receiving multiple blood transfusions.

So many were the questions asked by foreign reporters about the events of World War II that the Japan Foreign Press Center, a foundation that is closely linked with the Japanese foreign office, presented a series of three press briefings to try to explain the Emperor and his position in Japanese society. The vast majority of reporters at these briefings chose to ask questions that in some way referred to Hirohito's responsibility, or lack of it, for the war against China and then the Pacific war.

What was remarkable about the briefers was their basic agreement, although they came from vastly different backgrounds. Unanimously they stressed Hirohito's lack of personal responsibility for the events of the Pacific war and the equal responsibility of the Western powers for that war.

The briefers were Noboru Kojima, a historian of the Pacific war and biographer of Hirohito; Mazakazu Yamazaki, a professor of drama at the University of Osaka; and Kanehisa Hoshino, a well-known Japanese journalist and television commentator. Their points of view were not those of the left wing, but very close to those of the mainstream of Japanese society, and probably close to the point of view of Emperor Hirohito.

The role of the Emperor was very much in the minds of the victorious allies as they pondered the future of Japan in the fall of 1945. The view that the Emperor ought to accept total responsibility for the war because all was done in his name was shared by Hirohito, who so told General MacArthur. But, as noted, MacArthur was shrewd enough to realize that if the Allies put the Emperor on trial there would be difficulties in Japan, and he told President Truman just that.

But while the Imperial Person was thus saved from the ignominy of a Roman-style victory orgy, nothing else about the imperial presence was. The cutback in the imperial household was accompanied by a seizure of the known assets of the imperial family. Known assets is the key, because there is a deep suspicion that most of the liquid assets of the imperial family were transferred shortly before the war's end to banks in neutral countries. But the Allies did seize the personal assets of the immediate royal family, estimated to be worth $100 million, leaving Hirohito with a net worth of $70,000, a figure no one could possibly believe.

What was apparent to reasonable leaders of the victorious world was the need to prevent a reemergence of Japanese militarism, and about this they were absolutely right. Accordingly, they took steps that they hoped would make such reemergence impossible. The Meiji Constitution, with its anomalies concerning the power of the imperial system, if not the Emperor, had to be scrapped.

A new constitution, cynically called the MacArthur constitution, was first discussed by the Allies and Japanese and then enacted by the Japanese government. In this constitution, the Emperor lost all of those powers that had so vexed him, and so troubled the Allies. The base of power was transferred from the Emperor to the people. The Emperor and his entourage would reign, not rule. He was no longer commander in chief of the army and the navy; that responsibility went to the prime minister, whose power came from the people through the Diet. So important was the matter of the imperial situation that the first eight articles of the constitution deal with it.

Privy council abolished, power transferred to the prime minister, Hirohito was placed in the position he had always wanted to occupy, that of his hero, George V of England. He who had been a symbol of power became a powerless symbol. He would remain the revered head of state, and the spirit of Japan. His position would rest on his duty to carry out the old naturalistic and ancient religious customs. And now that he had been declared to be a human being and no longer the Sun God, he was free to travel as no Emperor had ever been free to do before. Between 1947 and 1954 Hirohito journeyed to every corner of Japan, and in so doing brought about a metamorphosis in his relationship with the Japanese people.

To some Japanese of the Showa generation there could never be an entirely comfortable acceptance of the change. In 1988, seeking answers to the simple question "What are your thoughts about the Emperor?" I found that most people over age 60—the war generation—were unwilling to discuss the matter. It was far too personal with them; most had never quite overcome the shock of learning that all they had been told as children was false, and many did not know how they felt about the Emperor in his new role.

In the early years of the occupation the Emperor himself did not know exactly how he felt about the monarchy or his own role in it. From many remarks he made to people around him, it is clear that he carried a heavy burden of guilt for the war. This was not because he had wanted the war, for he had not, but because he had allowed himself to be persuaded by those around him that it would be a violation of tradition and the Meiji Constitution for him to take direct action contrary to the advice of his ministers and the privy council. It was not until 1952 that the Emperor finally made up his mind not to abdicate.

The monarchy did continue in the tradition of the past. Crown Prince Akihito had been sequestered from his family at the age of three, and thereafter lived an almost separate existence, staying first, as had his father, in a wing of the Akasaka Palace.

During the war years Akihito was sent outside Tokyo to escape the bombings. Afterwards he was established in a palace about forty minutes from Tokyo. Here he was allowed to mingle with children of the Japanese upper crust. For, although SCAP had brought democratization to Japan and an end to the Japanese aristocracy, the royal family could remember the lineage of its subjects.

So Crown Prince Akihito grew up and was educated. Hirohito had been set up in his own middle school, with a handful of the children of the elite to maintain some sort of balance. Akihito went to a public school, because in the postwar reorganization of Japanese education the public school system emerged as the best in the nation. Later Hirohito would again show his personal leanings, by sending the Crown Prince to Oxford University to complete his education.

In the spring of 1951 one link with the past of Japan was broken; the dowager Empress Sadako died. She had survived her husband, the Taisho Emperor, by a quarter of a century, the most violent quarter-century in the history of Japan. She was buried in the royal mausoleum in the Tokyo suburbs.

In November 1952, Akihito became of age and was installed as Crown Prince. The next year he was sent to England to represent the throne, gaining the same chance to see the world that his father had once had.

When Akihito came home from this trip, Hirohito once again had an opportunity to consider the past and remake the future. Only too well could he recall the furor that had surrounded his insistence on selecting his own bride. So with Prince Akihito only the broadest rules were laid down, and in the end the Crown Prince selected a young woman named Michiko Shoda, from a formerly aristocratic family. But the fact was that Akihito, who had met her at the resort of Kuruizawa, had been quite smitten by her, and so the match was really as much of a love match as an imperial family is likely to make.

The match might not have come off at all. The young lady had serious reservations about entering into a court life, and she expressed them to her family in a letter, which fell into the hands of a reporter and created gossip of the sort that the public in Japan likes to read as much as does the English public. However, the prince succeeded, and the engagement was announced on November 24, 1958. So the royal succession seemed to be assured for another generation.

24

A Dream Come True

When Emperor Hirohito contemplated the horrors wrought on Japan in August 1945, he had two visions of the future. One was a vision of a holocaust, in which the Japanese people would literally fight to the death, prodded on by the officers of the army. In that vision Hirohito foresaw the end of the Japanese people and the enslavement of his country.

The second vision, to which he referred in his surrender message and later in discussions with his ministers and others, was of a Japan that would dedicate itself to peace and to the improvement of the world. This peaceful Japan would rise from the ashes of the old militarist Japan and take its place in the leadership of a new and peaceful world.

In 1949 the Emperor's dream began to gain substance. The reason for this was a growing American concern over political trends in Japan and a major change in U.S. economic policy toward Japan.

Japan was badly in need of a helping hand, for inflation had virtually destroyed its economic development. The amount of money in circulation had jumped from about 30 billion yen in 1945 to 425 billion in 1949. The Yoshida party, the Democratic Liberals, had become the majority party of Japan, but how long this conservative group could hold power in the face of these economic difficulties was questionable.

The first moves were Spartan. The Truman administration sent a midwestern banker named Joseph M. Dodge, who introduced stern measures to stop the inflation. There were serious cutbacks in government spending and in employment. The inflation ended, but was replaced by a serious economic depression.

The real change came the following year, and was occasioned by something no one could have predicted, a glaring need of the Americans for help. On June 25, 1950, the North Korean army marched across the 38th parallel line that divided the Democratic People's Republic of Korea (DPRK) in the north from the Republic of Korea (ROK) in the south.

The U.S. force in Korea was minuscule, consisting mostly of advisors to the ROK government. There was virtually nothing it could do to stop the North Koreans.

UN troops, mostly from the United States, were rushed to Korea, but they had neither the equipment nor the skills to stop the North Koreans, who moved steadily south until they extended in a vast semicircle about fifty miles from the South Korean port of Pusan. Here the UN forces finally managed to hold the line.

This was Japan's opportunity and she was not slow in grasping it. The Japanese government might have declared neutrality. After all, the new constitution forswore war, and that might have been construed to mean helping any warriors. But the Japanese did not choose to follow that route. Within a week the government, with the support of the Emperor, although he was not officially asked, declared its backing of U.S. policy regarding the Korean War.

Almost immediately Japan began to prosper, and to recover its sovereignty as a nation. The Japanese were asked by the Americans to increase their defenses, in order to free MacArthur's men from occupation duties to fight the battle in Korea. And Japanese industry geared up to produce war supplies for the Americans. Japanese technicians also serviced U.S. vehicles and weapons. The irony was driven home in the Imperial Palace, where there had always been a nice appreciation of ironies, when the Americans sought Japanese assistance in sweeping mines from Korean waters, because the Americans had no minesweepers or men trained in the task in Eastern waters. Most of the American minesweepers were "in mothballs."

By 1951 Emperor Hirohito was gratified to see the signs of economic recovery appearing everywhere. In January, Prime Minister Yoshida consulted his Majesty before making a speech in the Diet about this.

The Korean War was a blessing to Japan. Among its other virtues in Japanese eyes, it rationalized the actions of American bankers and industrialists in investing heavily in Japanese enterprise, removing the stigma of "dealing with the enemy."

By 1955 the American investments were paying off in profits. The Japanese share of those profits had been reinvested in research and development, so that suddenly in 1955 Japan's economy enjoyed a spurt known as the Jimmu Boom, named for the legendary founder of the Japanese Kingdom. The secret of the Jimmu Boom was the agreement among government and business leaders that Japan's economic health depended on seizure of important export markets, and the willingness of the Japanese to make sacrifices to achieve those ends. The year 1955 showed the beginning of a series of economic surpluses in balance of payments that turned the country around.

Soon, in every aspect of Japanese industry, the world saw a vast investment, backed by a government policy of subsidy and low interest rates. This policy enabled Japan to forge ahead in industry at the expense of the Western powers, which did not have the same concern about rebuilding. For example, Japan began to capture an ever larger share of the international steel market, being able to respond to that market more quickly and at lower prices than the U.S. competitors. In the 1960s and 1970s American steel plants began to close down, and they were not replaced.

The same processes occurred in the Japanese automobile, appliance, and electronics industries, in farm machinery, and in chemicals. Much of the Japanese share of the industrial market came from the United States and Britain, where whole industries, such as the motorcycle industry, disappeared.

With this newfound affluence, Japan began to enter various enterprises in international areas, giving aid to third-world countries, while always expanding international trade. Japanese athletes began to compete in sports such as golf and swimming. Japanese tourists began to rove the world, becoming a major factor in the international tourist market. Japanese intellectuals began to appear at international meetings. In 1949, for instance, Professor Hideki Yukawa won the Nobel prize for physics. The Japanese were active in nearly every field, from the Boston marathon to the conquest of the Himalayas.

But what did all this mean in terms of Emperor Hirohito and the imperial system of Japan? To Hirohito it meant a dream come true. In 1947 he had been reduced to the status of a constitutional monarch, a change that, as we have seen, pleased him enormously and relieved him of much responsibility. To be sure, he would always carry a personal feeling of guilt for not having somehow prevented the Pacific war, but that guilt had lost some of its intensity. In the 1980s the Emperor presented a picture of a mild, grandfatherly, absent-minded scientist, and his scientific achievements, although not spectacular, were real enough to attract a constant flow of visitors to the royal laboratory on the palace grounds.

As Japan advanced steadily economically, to become the second greatest economic power in the world, and in banking the first, the prestige of Emperor Hirohito rose. In his later years he was depicted in the world press as a figure of dignity. In 1971, in response to Japan's enormous prestige abroad, the Emperor began to travel again, for the first time in

half a century. He and the Empress visited Denmark and Belgium. They
also made a return trip to the United Kingdom and the Federal Republic
of Germany.

Four years later Hirohito and the Empress achieved one of his lifelong
ambitions by making a state visit to the United States, where they were
entertained at the White House. It was just thirty years since the end
of a war in which Radio Tokyo had boasted that the peace would be
dictated to that White House from Tokyo. But all that braggadocio and
bitterness was forgotten in the mid-1970s, by which time Japan and the
United States, much to the approval of Emperor Hirohito, had forged a
strong political and military alliance.

25

The Last Year

For several days in mid-September 1988, Emperor Hirohito had been feeling ill. It was, everyone in the palace entourage knew, somehow connected with his illness of the previous year. He began to bleed internally and had to be rushed into the hospital facilities within the palace.

The only news made public was in the official announcement that the Emperor had been feeling some discomfort in his abdomen and that the doctors were following a prearranged plan to prevent the problem from getting any worse.

The Emperor had been staying at his summer villa at Hayama, but when he began vomiting that day, he was rushed back to Tokyo and the superior hospital facilities of the palace. The media were disinformed; they were told that the Emperor had come back to Tokyo because of the press of official business. But what was this official business? That the minister from Iceland had arrived in Tokyo and wanted to present his credentials.

By this time everyone knew the Emperor's illness was grave. He had vomited three times. X rays showed an intestinal blockage. But no one would give a name to the Emperor's illness. The word "cancer" was never mentioned.

Emperor Hirohito had the finest medical aid available, including the president of the Tokyo University medical school and specialists from France. After much consultation the doctors agreed that they should operate, and Hirohito was hospitalized.

The senior spokesman for the palace announced in flowery court language that His Imperial Majesty's official duties would be assumed temporarily by His Imperial Highness the Crown Prince. This meant that a visit to the United States by Akihito, planned for October 3, would have to be scrapped. To the media this indicated crisis.

On the morning of September 22 the Emperor left his apartments and

went to the imperial household hospital, located on the grounds of the
375-acre imperial palace. He moved with an entourage of 100 people.

The operation began at 11:55 A.M. on September 23 and lasted two
and a half hours. Afterwards the doctors reported "a suspicious inflam-
mation of the pancreas." They had also taken out a segment of intestine.

The next day there were some difficulties with blood pressure and body
temperature. Still, the doctors said all this was normal enough after
surgery and there was no need for concern. But the Emperor was not
taken back to the inner palace.

It was also announced that for the first time in fifty years the Emperor
would not celebrate the official coming of the autumn season, but that
the Crown Prince would do this. This is one of the most important
celebrations, one of the binding ties of the Japanese people.

The people began to worry, and the reporters began to speculate. Was
the Showa Era near its end? The Imperial Household Agency was giving
no clues to the seriousness of the Emperor's illness, and very little information. The media demanded answers, and at 5 P.M. on September
25 the doctors came forth. They gave all the vital signs to the press and
reassured them. But soon it became clear that the doctors and the Imperial
Household Agency were being less than frank. The media turned from
a quizzical attitude to an adversarial position.

That day the Crown Prince announced that he would go on to the
United States for his scheduled visit, but that he would shorten it to
eight days because of his father's illness. This was the most heartening
news yet.

On September 30 the reporters asked the doctors if the Emperor had
cancer, and the doctors denied it. But the Emperor was still not eating.
On October 2 the doctors had to report that fact, but denied that it had
any significance. He was being fed intravenously, they said.

On October 13 the Crown Prince went off on his trip to the United
States, and Grand Chamberlain Yoshihiro Tokugawa assured the press
that the affairs of state were in excellent hands and that there were no
outstanding problems.

The imperial palace reported that the Emperor had slept seven and a
half hours, taken nourishment, gone to the toilet by himself, and read
the newspapers and watched television. He was under the constant care
of four doctors and six nurses, the announcement said.

From that point on, the media carried that sort of report. The newspapers ran the imperial vital signs on the front page every day, and
television did the same with every newscast. Any slight variation in

routine was noted. The big news on October 11 was that the Emperor had eaten an omelette.

Hirohito improved, and by October 14 he was reported to be sitting out on his veranda at the palace. This was encouraging news, and it banished many doubts.

But to the journalists the attitude of the Imperial Household Agency was arrogant and infuriating. To the people around the Emperor, on the other hand, protecting him against invasion of privacy was the only important matter. But by November the tensions had died down. The foreign press had tired of the story, and the Japanese media also turned elsewhere, while maintaining an "Emperor watch."

On November 5 the palace staged a show for the media, with special attention to the cameramen and television people. The Emperor took a little walk, about a hundred meters. Shutters snapped and the television cameras were trained on the Emperor. The walk was an indication of recovery, certainly, and it caught the interest of the nation, which had previously been believed to be more or less uninterested in the royal family.

As the year came to an end, tens of thousands of greeting, goodwill, and get-well cards flooded the palace. Oddly, the leading religious figure of the Japanese Shinto religion was deluged with Christmas cards. It was during this month, December, that the Emperor resumed his national duties and the Crown Prince stepped into the background.

So the sixty-third year of the Showa Era began on January 1, 1988. The Emperor celebrated the coming of the New Year with all the ceremony demanded at this most propitious time. He prayed to the gods at the four corners, assuring them of the fealty of Japan and asking their indulgence. Later in the day he received special visitors on the palace veranda. Life really seemed to have returned to normal, and the press watch was relaxed.

On January 12 the Emperor was again watching sumo wrestling on television. These days he was receiving many visitors and chatting without apparent effort, and he seemed to be in excellent spirits and good health.

On March 6 attention was drawn away from the Emperor's health by news that the Empress had suffered a heart attack. This matter occupied palace, press, and nation for several days, until she was declared to be out of danger and on the mend. This second illness in the royal family emphasized to the nation the inevitability of change in the near future.

In the early months of 1988 the gradual weakening of Emperor Hirohito was obvious. After his good start on New Year's Day, his health slid downward. Occasionally he coughed or passed blood. He had a very bad spell in the spring, and the Emperor watch began again.

But it was up and down. On May 7 the great spring sumo wrestling tournament came up. Usually the Emperor gave a garden party to honor this event, but this year the party was canceled. Official business had ended, according to the palace announcement, and therefore the Emperor was going off on holiday to the Summer Palace. Before he left he did attend one day of the sumo tournament, but that was all. Obviously the Emperor's health had not recovered completely, and everyone knew it. He was, after all, 86 years old that spring, and what was to be expected? Already he had ruled for more than sixty years, longer by far than any other ruler of Japan.

Still, he moved back and forth from the Tokyo palace to the summer villa. He traveled by helicopter for the most part. Once again the nation relaxed.

But on September 18, 1988, the atmosphere changed again. Word from the Imperial Household Agency that day caused reporters to come scurrying back to Tokyo. The Emperor, said the agency spokesman, was very ill again.

The doctors came out to report: His Majesty was running a high fever. Next morning the imperial spokesman announced that the Emperor had spent a good night in his own bed and that he was eating and drinking. So jaded were the reporters that virtually none of them believed the spokesman. They went across Hibiya Park to the prime minister's official residence to see what the government knew about conditions.

The prime minister's staff would say nothing at all. Based on that, several reporters wrote that the Emperor's condition was growing worse and cited "elements close to the prime minister." This news infuriated the imperial household spokesman and started an argument at the press conference that day.

The Emperor had spent an hour and a half watching the final day's action of the autumn sumo tournament, the spokesman finally said. And again the press was querulous. It seemed odd that they had been told on the one hand that the Emperor's condition required total rest, and on the other hand that he was up watching sumo.

Some reporters began to ask if the Emperor was really conscious. Some asked if he was still alive. And more questions were asked that afternoon when a Toyota station wagon from the Japan Red Cross arrived at the palace bringing blood for transfusion. If the Emperor was in as good a state of health as the imperial household indicated, then why transfusions?

That day the Japanese people began to realize just how ill their Emperor really was.

26

The Heart of Japan

In the winter of 1987–88 Emperor Hirohito's illness seemed to have subsided, and the outside world was paying little attention to the affairs of the Japanese court. At that time I was in London completing research and beginning the writing of this book. I conceived of the idea of inquiring among the Japanese community of London about the popular feeling toward Hirohito, and also wrote to friends in Japan to get their impressions.

The results were most discouraging, making my idea seem puerile in the extreme. In Japan, generations identify themselves by the era in which they were born. "I am a Meiji person," for example, means born before 1912. Taisho means born between 1912 and 1926, and Showa, between 1926 and 1989. But Showa is sharply divided between the people born before 1945 and those born afterward. Those born in the early Showa years have a point of view colored by the Pacific war, and an attitude toward the imperial system of government that is indelibly stamped. Those who grew up in the 1950s have an entirely different view, and those whose teenage years have been spent in a totally prosperous, peaceful Japan have still different ideas.

Among the elder, the Meiji generation, the attitude toward the throne is one of unwavering adoration. No matter what Emperor Hirohito said about his "humanity" in the immediate postwar years, the older generation looked upon him as a god. They knew, of course, that he was made of flesh and blood and had all the bodily functions of a human being. But it was inherent in their whole lives and religious attitudes that the Emperor represented the unbroken line of Japan, and that he and all he did represented also the essence of Yamato, the ancient name for the Japanese kingdom.

Such a man is Admiral Hoshino, the last survivor of the fateful war council meeting in the imperial bunker on the night of August 14, 1945.

The admiral's loyalty to the Imperial Way is unshakeable. He has lived through three stages of imperial rule: the Meiji period of building a modern Japan; the Taisho period of World War I, and Japan's emergence to equality among nations; and the Showa period, which began with such high hopes of world peace only to have them blasted by the emergence of the militarists, and then saw the rise of a new Japan to world leadership in the last part of the twentieth century.

A Taisho figure is Seiichi Mura, now a grandfather and retired executive, in his eighties. The Japan into which he was born was thrown into World War I, which was exciting but not dangerous to the Japanese people. In that war Japan was never under direct attack.

Mura was in his teens in the 1920s, when the fact of Japanese life was economic hardship. That depression produced the ardent generation of young officers who, seeing corruption and misery all around them, were willing to sacrifice their lives for what they believed to be reform through a military government that eschewed politics.

In his formative adult years Mura worked for the city government of one of the suburbs of Tokyo. By the 1930s he had a manufacturing business, and he spent the 1930s and early 1940s fulfilling war contracts for leather goods. He was touched by the war in the same way that all who stayed at home in Japan were touched. He felt the excitement, the feeling of strength and prosperity in the early days, and witnessed the turn of the tide and the deprivations and the knowledge of the bombings, even if, as was the case with Mura, his own home was outside the bombing and air attack zones and he had no personal experience of the hardships. He was, of course, shocked by the manner in which the war ended, but he did not blame the Emperor. He was further shocked when the Emperor declared his humanity, but, as with Admiral Hoshino, it really made no difference in his attitude.

Another Taisho child is Masao Harada, a public servant of Nagaoka City, on the north shore of Honshu Island. When I asked him how Harada felt about the Emperor, he refused to reply. He was upset that the question had been raised, because it stirred up too many old memories. Harada had been born in 1921, and he was 10 years old when the army moved into the public schools with its program of Imperial Way, beginning with the morning prayer to the Emperor, the honor to the Hinumaru (Red Sun) flag, and the singing of the national anthem "Kimogaya." Harada and his friends grew up being told every day that the Emperor was a living god.

When Harada was 18 years old, in 1939, he went for his two years of compulsory military service, but by the end of that period the Pacific war had broken out and with ever more soldiers needed at the expanding front lines there was no way he could be released into the reserve. Harada went to China, where he served along the Yellow River.

When the war ended Harada was repatriated from Tianjin by ship and brought home, filled with that sense of emptiness shared by millions of Japanese servicemen. Scarcely had he begun picking up the shards of his life, when the Emperor announced his humanity. No wonder this was not a matter that Harada wanted to discuss.

Noriko Shimoda is a Taisho person, but just barely. Hirohito became Emperor when she was very small. When she was 8 years old the Mukden Incident occurred, and her life was changed completely. Her father took the family to Manchuria because of opportunity in the construction business. They prospered as Japan exploited the new colony. Then came the disaster of the surrender and the Russian occupation. The Shimodas were lucky; they fled to Korea and came down into the U.S. occupation zone. And what of Noriko? What does she believe? She never considers the subject. During the first years after 1945 she was too busy building a new life. Since then she has married and her family is her life. To her Emperor Hirohito is simply a stick figure.

Sadayoshi Mutsuo, a Showa person, was a member of the army suicide flying corps. He was waiting to kill himself in a flight against the enemy when the war ended. He had been told that he was going to die for the Emperor and for Japan. When the surrender came, at first Mutsuo could not believe it; he blamed the Emperor for being gulled by the people around him. Later, when he had found a job, married, had children, and watched them grow up, he realized that his children blamed him and his fellow soldiers for the war, not the Emperor. This was a matter he had not considered, but he then tried to explain to his children that he and the soldiers of his generation had absolutely nothing to say about what happened in higher circles. But he did not blame the Emperor for the war.

Not all the early Showa generation were of the same mind. Mutsuo Saito had a different view, as was shown in the story of his early years. Saito was another suicide pilot not called to make the last sacrifice. It was popularly believed at the time that the suicide pilots all went to their deaths with the Emperor's name on their lips. Not so, said Saito.

I never believed during the war that I was fighting for the Emperor, and I don't think that any of my friends believed it either. Of course people talked about "dying for the Emperor," but we didn't feel that way. If it was necessary I was prepared to die for Japan and the Japanese people. That was something I could understand and identify myself with. But I did not want to connect the fact of my death with some abstract cause like saving the Emperor.

And when in 1946 Saito heard the Emperor's Human Being declaration, he wondered what the Emperor was talking about. He had never for a moment imagined that the Emperor was anything but a human being.

As for the later generations, in London and in Japan I spoke to a number of people in their forties and thirties, and twenties. Shimoda, then in her forties, had come to London some ten years earlier and carved out a career as a go-between, serving Japanese and British firms. She had become so anglicized that she admitted she could not think of going back to Japan and trying to fit back into the highly structured Japanese society.

"The Emperor?" she said, "I never think of him at all."

That attitude was mirrored by many young people in their thirties, the first postwar generation. The Emperor was so far removed from their lives that they gave no thought to him as a person or as a symbol. Even in Japan, to much of the younger generation the Emperor symbolized Golden Week, at the end of April, when the Emperor's birthday, combined with two other national holidays, made up an almost solid week of festivity and freedom from work.

And yet not all the young people of Japan ignore either the Emperor or the traditional Shinto religion of the country. To be sure, Shinto was outlawed as a state religion by the Allies, and the ban continued in the Constitution of 1947. Among the older generations many still worship Shinto, and many still worship the Buddha. Most of them are more than sixty years old. When the young go to the temples it is usually for a wedding, or a coming of age ceremony, or a funeral. But they go. The father of a bride will spend a small fortune to hire a a palanquin or a ricksha and footmen, to have his daughter married in the Japanese tradition.

Something happened in Japan in the autumn of 1988, however. When I arrived in Tokyo, on September 24, it was odd to see all these attitudes change before my eyes.

I found a Japan in a deep state of shock. Hirohito's picture was on the front page of every newspaper. Every magazine carried a major article on the Emperor's illness. Every television newscast opened with a report on the Emperor's condition. Long television programs were overlaid with subtitles showing the Emperor's vital signs.

On the day the doctors confirmed the gravity of Hirohito's illness, a typhoon whirled down on Tokyo. But at Hibiya Park and Nijubashi, the entrance to the Imperial Palace which had been set aside for the people to come and offer prayers for the Emperor's welfare, thousands of Japanese with umbrellas and rainwear fought the storm and were soaked while paying their obeisances. They came every day by the thousands; at the end of the week six hundred thousand people had signed the prayer book.

At the end of that week the sun came out, and even more people went to Hibiya park, forming up in long lines at the many tables in their long tents, where the staff of the Imperial Household Agency supervised the signing of the book of those who came to pray. Hundreds of others walked up to the gate of the palace, which was manned by soldiers of the Imperial Guard. These soldiers were fine-looking, trim young men, polite and friendly. They were also tough, no-nonsense soldiers, the spiritual descendants of those guardsmen who had protected Hirohito in the militarist years.

Near the fence that protects the inner palace grounds I saw one girl who seemed overcome with emotion. When I asked about her sentiments, she paused, hurled me a look of disgust, put her handkerchief to her mouth, and went off toward Hibiya Park, sobbing.

I looked around more closely then. The vast majority of these people at the palace gate were exhibiting strong emotion. There were very few gawkers.

And yet, once away from the palace gate, the mourners were not without humor. I saw one old gentleman in country clothes, heading up toward the line of those who prayed. In a rich Kyushu Island accent he said with a twinkle, "I am going to pray for the Emperor, just as soon as I pee." And he turned off the path and headed for the men's toilet building behind the bushes.

27

The Role of the Emperor

Mutsuo Saito, who grew up in the darkest years of Japan, 1931–45, had every reason to resent the Emperor and the imperial system, for they had taken away his childhood, and had nearly killed him as a suicide pilot in the last days of the war. And yet he had no resentment. "The funny thing is that if I were ever to meet the Emperor face to face, I would bow down to him—I know I would. That's the power of education for you."

But is the power of education the whole reason for his reverence for the Emperor? If that were so, then the younger generation of Japanese, educated in a system to which the imperial family is largely irrelevant, would have no such reverence. However, the iron strikes deeper, as the events of 1988 proved. In Hirohito's terminal illness, Japan recognized the bond that had never ceased to exist between the governed and the symbol of their government and national way of life.

That is not to say that Emperor and imperial system do not have their opponents within Japan. For example, Peter Gill of the *London Sunday Observer* found an old soldier in Tokyo who had spent three years at hard labor in a Soviet prison camp at the end of the war. He was bitter, and he held Hirohito personally responsible.

The far left opposes the imperial system, although the socialists are ambiguous on the subject. During the Emperor's illness, students tried to put up posters around the Imperial Palace, protesting the national concern that had brought business and official Japan to a virtual stop. The students were arrested, but they were not detained.

At the Gokoku Shrine in Fukuoka, an organization calling itself the Revolutionary Workers Council put up posters opposing "the rightist fascists who support the Emperor system."

And on the other side are the organizations of the right wing, who were speaking broadly of taking over the government again, once Crown

Prince Akihito ascended the throne. I met one young woman who claimed that everyone who visited the palace to pray was a right-winger.

Those who recall the 2–26–36 Incident and the young rebels who disrupted Japan's government for a week worry about the possibility of a right-wing insurrection. But how would it come about in the Japan of 1989? Gone are the days when the army and the navy were largely independent agencies, claiming responsibility only to the throne.

Japan could swing to the right. But if this were happening the signs would be unmistakable, as they were in the 1930s, when the Western powers stood by and let the Japanese army swallow Manchuria. The Japanese Defense Force is a tightly controlled organization with civilians at the top, responsible to the people, through the Parliament, not to the Emperor. There is no sign within the defense agency of any incipient rebellion.

There is a certain validity to the fears of the center about violence from the right wing. Japan's history is full of such actions, and many people still recall the tales of the 1930s, full of "government by assassination."

In 1985 I published *The New Militarists* in the United States. The book tells of the problems of a Japan pushed into heavy rearmament by the United States and suggests a danger of a new militarism. This book cannot be published in Japan, because no Japanese publisher is willing to take the risk.

As the Showa Era drew to a close, a new view of the Pacific war was openly espoused in Japan: a denial of sole Japanese responsibility for the Pacific war. The Japanese bore the burden of guilt for forty years, but many Japanese now refute the standard Western view. Millions of Japanese have felt this way for a long time. It was impossible during the occupation years to admit it, but Westerners cannot expect the Japanese to wear sackcloth and ashes forever.

Some Japanese believe that with the passing of Emperor Hirohito there came a big change in Japanese attitudes. "The end of guilt," said one man. This view is shared by millions of Japanese, and it varies. Hideki Kase, a publicist, admits to being a Japanese nationalist. He believes in the unique position of the Emperor as half god–half man, and symbol of Japan. He wants the Japanese constitution rewritten, with elimination of much of the material inserted at the insistence of the Americans, such as the no defense clause, which is already violated daily. Deep in the hearts of Japanese nationalists is a desire to clear the record, to absolve Japan from the burden of total guilt that she has borne for more than forty years.

It is this view and variations of it that have brought about the raging argument among educators and historians as to how World War II should be treated in textbooks for junior high school and high school readers. The fact is that in Japanese education there is little space given to history at all, and the war must perforce be slurred over. That being the case, some educators believe a general textbook is not the place for discussion of such matters as the Rape of Nanking. This atrocity, one of the many committed by both sides, has become symbolic of the whole approach to the war, and the role of Emperor Hirohito in that war. Several government officials, including Cabinet Minister Sosuke Okuno, lost their jobs in the 1980s for expressing the view that the Rape of Nanking is irrelevant, and that the Tokyo war crimes trials were victors' justice upon the vanquished. They are not the first in the world to feel that way, however. Perhaps the most prominent Westerner to hold that view was the late U.S. Supreme Court Justice William O. Douglas.

Such men as Kase hold that the death of Hirohito was a liberation, and in a sense that must be right. For, as the Emperor lay bleeding to death internally, kept alive only by so many transfusions that his body was like a pincushion, it was apparent that because Hirohito was the last of the heads of state of the World War II years to remain alive, the Western press was determined once more to raise the specter of Japanese responsibility for the Pacific war.

This barrage of accusations in the Western press was typified by the American successors to Britain's penny press, the *Sun* and the *Star*, which began in September to rehash once more the old charges that Hirohito was responsible for the Pacific war, that he was a "war criminal." This even though the Pacific "tribunal of international justice," as the war crimes prosecutors termed their court, and also General MacArthur, had refused to bring charges against Hirohito.

The Japanese government responded with a formal protest regarding the insult to their head of state, but the world press began its old litany of complaint against Hirohito as the architect of the war.

The complaints were always vague. "He must have known about all the war crimes, like the Nanking massacre," said one Englishman resident in Japan. "I remember reading somewhere. . . . " Perhaps he read it in Bergamini's *Japan's Imperial Conspiracy*. But more enlightened views are those of Edwin O. Reischauer, a historian and former U.S. ambassador to Japan, who holds that the Emperor was a prisoner of the system, and Hugh Cortazzi, who was British ambassador to Japan from 1980 to 1984. According to Cortazzi, Hirohito never had autocratic power and . . . had to accept the recommendations of his ministers and advisors.

If he had attempted to protest publicly against the war, his views would have been suppressed and he would have been removed from the scene. His decision in 1945 to support the surrender was an act of courage at a time when his advisors were divided.

And so, as Alexander Chancellor noted in a column in the *London Sunday Observer* on October 1, 1988, the debate outside, as well as inside, Japan about the Emperor and his roles continued as the Emperor lay dying. As Chancellor said, times have changed. War Historian Hugh Trevor-Roper (now Lord Dacre) praised the Emperor, whereas previous generations of historians had damned him. Surray Sayle, in the *Independent Magazine*, called Hirohito "the god who made good" and denied that he was either dictator or war criminal.

For an enlightened, intimate Japanese view of Emperor Hirohito, I sought an interview with Yoshihiro Tokugawa, a man who had served Emperor Hirohito in a personal position for most of his life. Tokugawa is a member of an illustrious Japanese family of ancient origin, from which came the Tokugawa shoguns (1603–1867). He joined the imperial household in 1936, just about at the time of the 2–26–36 Incident, and continued in service, rising to the post of grand chamberlain, or director, of the imperial household and one of the Emperor's chief advisors, until the summer of 1988, when he retired. He is also notable as the person who saved the recordings of the Imperial surrender message on that dangerous night of August 14, 1945, when the young rebels were trying to stage their palace revolution—and by doing so, Tokugawa may have prevented the continuation of the war for more bloody days or weeks.

He was not giving any interviews at all, said the former grand chamberlain, but he consented to see me on condition that nothing he said would be published before this book. By that time, it seemed safe to say, the crisis of the imperial illness would be long past. And so I went to see Grand Chamberlain Tokugawa at his home in the suburbs of Tokyo.

I had submitted a list of seven questions in writing. Obviously there was no point in asking the journalists' sort of question (e.g., Do you think the Emperor was a war criminal? How much did he know about what was done in his name?). Such questions have already been answered over and over by various Japanese authorities, and yet they were still, in the fall of 1988, being asked by the journalists.

The seven questions were designed to elicit real answers and, if possible, lead to further conversation. They were also designed to remove Tokugawa's concern lest the interview result in another attack on Hirohito.

During your years of service, what was the major change in the imperial relationship with Japan?

"The major change was stipulated in the new constitution of Japan, drawn in 1946 and enacted in 1947. The Emperor was very pleased with this constitution because it clearly defined the Emperor's duties and obligations and indicated his role as the symbol of Japan. They say that the Americans forced Japan into this constitution, but as far as the Emperor was concerned it was a welcome change. The problem under the Meiji constitution was that there was far too much emphasis on the role of the Emperor, and far too much was done in his name."

How did the Emperor regard his own position under the MacArthur constitution?

"The Emperor Meiji had stipulated the five areas of his responsibility, and in his New Year's address of 1946, Emperor Hirohito also stipulated the five items of responsibility. The idea of declaring his humanity was not prompted by General MacArthur but was Emperor Hirohito's own wish. The Emperor was pleased, however, when MacArthur let him know that he applauded the imperial statements as very helpful and very democratic.

"The Imperial wish in the beginning of 1946 was to discard all the old Japan and bring to Japan human liberty of thought and action, and justice for all. That was Emperor Hirohito's hope for the course that would be adopted by the modern Japan."

Did the Emperor ever discuss the Imperial Way years with you?

"To me, Imperial Way is a misnomer. The Emperor never had imperial power in the absolute sense, nor did his father or his grandfather. If you are referring to the situation of the army, it was badly riddled by factions, the Tosei Ha and the Kodo Ha being the main ones. These went back to the old days of the Choshu-Satsuma clan quarrels. But the settlement really made no difference in the course of the Empire in this period.

"As to the end of the war, there was no chance of the army's rebellion succeeding, even from the first moment. The palace was cut off from the outside only for a short time. At 4:30 on the morning of August 15 the navy sent us a message by radio telling all about the incident and its resolution. The navy had been standing by to act at any time if that would have been necessary. Admiral Hoshino was fully aware of what was happening, and was in touch with Vice Admiral Nakamura on the outside and with Captain Hiroshi Nagasawa, the director of policy and planning. They were on top of the situation and there was no way the army plot by Hatanaka could have succeeded. The navy would have intervened, and Captain Nagasawa was at navy headquarters, ready to act. He had already been in communication with General Tanaka, the director of eastern sector defenses."

In recent years how much time has the Emperor spent on his marine biology work?

This question was asked to divert the grand chamberlain from heavy matters, but it produced a most interesting result. The chamberlain brightened and began to produce a litany of all the work the Emperor had done recently, and it was considerable. (The foreword to a 1988 scientific work by the Emperor is added to this book as an appendix. It is used with the permission of Mr. Tokugawa.)

It was apparent from the grand chamberlain's discussion that no aspect of Emperor Hirohito's life was dearer to him than his scientific studies. During his last years, freed of the responsibility of keeping track of the army, the navy, and every aspect of government (although he had none but the highest veto power), the Emperor's life was a happy one. He was always glad to greet scientific visitors to his laboratories, and they were not a few. Sometimes he was known to spend an hour or two with them. What one of his courtiers said years ago certainly was true: The Emperor would have been happiest had he been born an ordinary citizen and allowed to spend his life with his hobby.

How has the Emperor felt about the emergence of the New Japan in recent years?

"Emperor Hirohito has been pleased with the progress of Japan toward leadership in a stable, peaceful world. Because he was relieved of the great responsibility (without authority) placed on him by the Meiji Constitution, he has now spent as much time on governmental detail as in the past, but has paid more attention to his constitutional duties."

And what are these?

"He appoints the prime minister, as designated by the Diet. He appoints the chief judge of the Supreme Court, as designated by the cabinet.

"Nowadays, under the postwar constitution, the Emperor of Japan has duties which are very similar to those of the reigning monarch of the United Kingdom:

"He convokes the Diet with advice of the cabinet.

"He dissolves the House of Representatives.

"He proclaims general elections.

"He makes the appointments and dismissals of ministers of state and other officials, as provided by law, and he gives powers and credentials to ambassadors and ministers.

"He signs, as provided by law, the general and special amnesties, commutations of punishment, reprieves, and restorations of rights.

"He awards honors.

"He signs treaties and other documents as provided by law.

"He receives foreign ambassadors and ministers.

"And last, he carries out the ceremonial functions of the chief of state and principal priest of the Shinto religion. Although Shinto is no longer the official religion of Japan, it is still the leading ceremonial recourse of the Japanese people."

What is the Imperial attitude toward the American pressure on Japan to rearm even more?

"The Emperor has never talked much about the rearmament of Japan. But he has been very observant about such affairs as he travels around the country. I think he thinks that defense is enormously important."

I asked a subsidiary question: If the Emperor had his life to live over, what would he change?

This gave the chamberlain a chance to escape the sensitive issue of rearmament, and soon he was discussing the Emperor's feelings about his job, his gloom in the immediate postwar years, and his near-abdication. Several times Hirohito spoke to the chamberlain about resigning the imperial post. But then he would remember his grandfather, the Meiji Emperor, who had the same inclinations but resisted them, and decided it was his responsibility to continue in office, no matter the personal hardship. At times this link with his grandfather seemed to be all that kept Hirohito from abdication.

The closest he had come to quitting was in the 1960s, when there were bitter complaints about the defense alliance with the United States. But he did not, telling the grand chamberlain that he had decided to carry the burden and hand it over to a successor.

How would you assess the Showa Era in terms of Japanese history?

Actually, the grand chamberlain did not assess the era, leaving that
for the historians. But he did have some words about Emperor Hirohito's
hopes, fears, and longings in the last months of his life.

After World War II, Emperor Hirohito's concern passed to a more
spiritual level than before. He saw himself as the symbol of national
unity of Japan, the nucleus around which the people's hearts and minds
could unite. The chamberlain indicated that this was no change. The
Emperor had always believed in the people, he said, and the ultimate
triumph of the people's will. The new constitution had made no difference in that way; Hirohito had obeyed the Meiji Constitution, and when
the constitution of 1947 replaced it, he was eager to follow that law.

As the Emperor saw it in his last years, one of Japan's major problems
had been the overidealization of the Emperor by government officials in
the 1920s and 1930s. That was his major reason for issuing the imperial
rescript of January 1, 1946, in which he denied his divinity.

The Emperor became an ardent environmentalist, seeing in the hap-
penings of these years dangers to the world environment that he also
saw as dangers to the human spirit. On the sixtieth anniversary of his
reign, he established an international prize in genetics. He also continued
to work in his experimental rice plot, and he took a great interest in
reforestation and would always go out of his way to attend a tree-planting
ceremony.

He lamented the coming of the atomic age. The spiritual progress of
humanity had been lost in atomic research, he believed, and he worried
for the people of the future. His concerns were now world concerns. The
great East Asia war was long behind him; he regretted it, just as he had
regretted the Japanese desertion of the League of Nations in 1932. He
attributed most of Japan's subsequent troubles, and the war, to this act
and the subsequent isolation of Japan.

He saw an emerging Asia as the wave of the future, with particularly
close cooperation among Japan, China, and Korea, in a great enlightened
society.

Hirohito noted two high points in his postwar political life. First was
the signing of the 1947 constitution, which pleased him so enormously
that to commemorate the day he wrote a poem about the coming into
force of the new constitution. In the poem he said how happy he was
that Japan's national law had been established, comparing it to a new
dawn.

The second political event that prompted Hirohito to poesy was the official end of World War II in 1952. On the day the peace treaty became effective, he wrote of his pleasure that spring had come to Japan, which had endured so many trials. His nation had endured the unendurable, and the Emperor's relief and pleasure were overwhelming.

For all practical purposes, the Showa Era ended on the day that the power of the regency was handed over to Prince Akihito, who began to perform all the imperial functions in the fall of 1988.

And what would come next to Japan?

Heisei (Akihito) Japan is searching for a way of the future. Some leaders have said that the death of Hirohito "ends the era of shame" and that thereafter there will be no more apologies for the past.

The issue was very much alive in the beginning of 1989. Just weeks earlier, Sanseido Publishing Company, Japan's largest, had deleted a chapter in a high school textbook referring to the Japanese massacre of Malaysian civilians during World War II. The change was made by editors in response to a complaint by the ruling Democratic Liberal party to the Ministry of Education that such a chapter "was inappropriate from the standpoint of proper education." The left wing of Japan protested, and the right wing cheered.

That is a part of Japan's essential problem of direction, finding a base on which to assess the past.

However, Japan is not the first country that has suffered embarrassments in its history. Germany is certainly another, and the Japanese could take a page from the German book and simply ignore the past, instead of trying to justify or explain it.

Perhaps now that Hirohito is dead the world will stop trying to remind Japan of that embarrassing past. That would be a good idea in the interest of international amity. For if Japan feels isolated, then its proclivity for consensus could become the capital of the right wing, and Japan could become as dangerous to world peace in the 1990s as it was in the 1930s. Japan has the economic power now; its economy is the strongest in the world. In the same way, Japan could become a major military power again, and it is no use saying the people do not want that, because when the people of Japan did not want military power in 1936 and voted overwhelmingly against it, they only succeeded in precipitating the military takeover. There were plenty of signs of that danger in the early 1930s, and such signs are what the world is watching for in the emergence of the new Japanese era.

Appendix

A 1988 Scientific Work by Emperor Hirohito

Over the past long years, since the beginning of the Showa Era until today, I have been continuing my study of hydroids, collected mainly in the sea area of Sagami Bay, making use of the leisure hours spared from my official duties.

I began my study of the Hydrozoa initially on the advice of the late Dr. Hirotaro Hattori. During the first twenty years, I continued my research under his guidance; and, as of 1945, with the advice of the late Dr. Itiro Tomiyama as well as with the assistance of Mr. Hatsuki Tsujimura. During this period, the late Drs. Tadao Sato and Kenzo Kikuchi also offered their valuable advice.

Up to 1944 the research work on hydroids had been conducted in the eastern part of Sagami Bay and at Okinose, in the Gulf of Sagami. After that, however, owing to the difficulties concerning marine research work, the operations were suspended for a time. In 1949 the work was resumed using research vessels. And I continued my research whenever I stayed at my detached palace in Hayama up to 1971, and from 1972 in Suzaki, the southern part of the Izu Peninsula.

As to the research vessels, *Hayama Maru* was employed after *Miura Maru* in my research operations, which continued up to 1956, except during the period from 1945 to 1948. *Hatagumo* replaced *Hayama Maru* in 1956, and continued its service up to 1971. The above-mentioned vessels were used in research work during my stay in Hayama. From 1972 *Matsunami* came into service, and it has been used in my research work at Suzaki.

A number of people, including mates and engineers as well as the captains of the research vessels, members of the Biological Laboratory, and fishermen, have worked together in close cooperation in my research work. The means of collecting materials was mostly by dredging.

In the early days of research vessel operations, the late Mr. Hachiro Saionji, an unattached imperial household official, and the late Mr. Masanao Tsuchiya, a chamberlain, used to help the captains and the other crew of the vessels. Especially, new trawl nets invented by Mr. Saionji were of great use in collecting specimens. In the case of the late Mr. Hiroo Sanada, a member of the Biological Laboratory, he succeeded in overcoming his seasickness by training his body and mind, and finally got used to his duties. Fishermen not only drew a dragnet but also helped to collect materials, and specially trained divers were employed.

The collection was done sometimes in mud and sandy places such as Nakabukari, but mainly in such rocky spots as Amadaiba, and therefore the dragnets occasionally suffered damage.

Two small Japanese-style rowing boats, *Take* and *Momo*, were used to ferry people over to the beach or to the research vessel, but later on, in 1947 and in 1948, these two boats were also brought into use in the research work, in order to make up for the lack of larger vessels.

I have decided to bring out the results of my study on the hydroids of Sagami Bay, dividing them into two parts. This volume is Part 1, and Athecata are treated.

The late Dr. Tohru Uchida, and Drs. Syoziro Asahina and Mayumi Yamada, were asked to examine the results of my study. Mr. Hatsuki Tsujimura has assisted me all the time in preparing this report.

I am indebted to Mr. Hiroo Sanada and Mr. Tatsuya Shimizu for making permanent slides, to Mr. Tsugio Saito and Mr. Yasuo Omi for photographing, and to Mr. Sanada and Mrs. Hiroko Daba for drawing sketches.

Grateful acknowledgments are due to foreign colleagues, Drs. E. Stechow, E. Jaderhol, C. M. Fraser, and E. Leloup, who conducted the study of hydroid specimens of Sagami Bay and on each occasion kindly took the trouble of examining the specimens sent by me.

I wish to express my deep thanks to those concerned in the above-mentioned research work and to those who have given me valuable cooperation in my study.

I hope that this volume not only will contribute to the study of hydroids but also will help to elucidate the condition of the biota of Sagami Bay.

Finally, my best thanks are due to the members of the Maruzen Company for the trouble taken about printing and binding of the present publication.

Hirohito
January 1988

Chapter Notes

Introduction   Long the Imperial Way

In the fall of 1988 in Tokyo I attended several press briefings dealing with the health and status of Emperor Hirohito, who lay dying of cancer in the Imperial Palace. The briefings were arranged by the Japan Foreign Press Center because the foreign press was exhibiting so much interest in the Emperor and the imperial family. They were conducted by the distinguished historian Noburo Kojima, Professor Masakazu Yamazaki of Osaka University, and a television commentator, Kanehisa Hoshino.

After more than thirty years, in which the Emperor had been stripped of his divinity by the new constitution (a matter which pleased him) and had been relegated to the role of constitutional monarch who reigned but did not rule (which also pleased him), the Japanese and their friends were rediscovering the imperial presence.

There was another element, well represented among the media people who attended the briefings. This was the Hirohito-the-unindicted-war-criminal claque, which still held the view that the Emperor was responsible for the war and for every action taken by Japan in that war, and that he ought to own up and admit that he was a Class A war criminal who had struck it lucky, and that General Douglas MacArthur had refused to prosecute him only because it would stir up the Japanese people and make the occupation more difficult. Because these media representatives had kept asking, "What about Hirohito's war guilt?" the Japanese government had arranged for these several briefings to try to explain the role of the monarch in Japan under the old Meiji Constitution, and specifically the role of Hirohito and the limitations on what appeared to be his absolute power during the prewar and war years.

It was apparent that the briefings changed no minds. While the Japanese and friendly press absorbed material they knew already, the "war criminal" advocates listened but did not hear, and all the old charges remained, to be brought up again in Emperor Akihito's first press conference. There they were squelched, as far as the new Heisei Era was concerned. But the residue remained, and perhaps it always will.

Chapter 1   The Emperor Speaks

In recent years many accounts of the final meeting of the imperial supreme defense council in August 1945 have appeared in the diaries and accounts of various officials who were present on that historic occasion. As of this writing, only one of these officials, Admiral Hoshino, was left alive. I interviewed Hoshino on this subject a number of years ago, and he guided me to a magazine article he had written on the subject.

According to Hoshino, Hirohito spoke about his hope that the war would end after the capture of Singapore and his suggestion to General Sugiyama to that effect. But the army was swollen with victory, and since the suggestion was made through the Marquis Koichi Kido and was not a direct order, Sugiyama chose to ignore it.

As noted herein, the Emperor had tried to set the wheels of the peace mechanism going several times after that, but each time he was frustrated by the army conspirators.

As the Terasaki notes published in *Bungei Shunju* indicated, the Emperor had decided in June that peace was essential and had after that taken the actions that pulled the rug out from under General Tojo. But in July he found that this was not enough. The army continued to dominate Japan, even though he had stipulated that the new Kuniaki Koiso–Mitsumasa Yonai cabinet was to share the authority between the army and navy. So more had to be done. Koiso resigned when he could achieve nothing against the hard-liner army generals. Admiral Suzuki, who succeeded, according to Terasaki did not have the personal magnetism for leadership, and the army stubbornly held its ground.

So in the end it was up to the Emperor to make peace, and he was ready for the responsibility, although in his heart he felt that by taking power into his own hands, he was for the third time in his life violating the Meiji Constitution. For this, Admiral Hoshino and the other peacemakers would always revere him.

Chapter 2   Perfect Harmony

The *Mainichi* effort in ferreting out the name of the new era and breaking the story was quite in the tradition of the Japanese free press of that period, which was aggressive and not very responsible, much like its American counterpart of the 1920s. Much of the material for this chapter comes from the *Mainichi* series of books on Showa (see bibliography). *Yomiuri Shimbun* did a similar study, and so did *Asahi Shimun*. Like Americans, the Japanese have an insatiable interest in their own history.

Most of the historical material in this chapter comes from Sir George Bailey Sansom, Edwin O. Reischauer, and Ruth Benedict. The passage about the Japanese extreme right wing and book publishing comes from an experience of my own. In 1985 I published in the United States *The Militarists*. I wanted the book published in Japan, but several Japanese publishers and an agent told me it was impossible: no Japanese publisher would dare issue such a book at the time, for fear of having the publishing house burned down by extremists, who made such threats against any books they considered to be antirearmament.

The material in the last part of the chapter about the samurai and the daimyo comes from Sansom and my own studies in Japanese, from a study I made of the American whaling industry when I lived on Nantucket Island, Massachusetts, and from the official account of Commodore Perry's mission to Japan.

Chapter 3   Emperor Meiji: A Modern Man

The material for this chapter came largely from the Sansom and Reischauer works and from the *Mainichi* series *Showashi*—a history of the Showa Era. This *Showashi* series begins with a volume on the Meiji restoration. The story of Saigo Takamori has recently been revived in Japan by NHK, the Japan Broadcasting Corporation, which televised a series of historical dramas in 1990 and 1991 that captured the Japanese imagination. All this is mirrored in the *Mainichi Showashi* series and also the series on the same subject by *Yomiuri* and *Asahi*.

Chapter 4   Hirohito Enters

The various series of highly illustrated volumes about the Meiji and Taisho and Showa eras tell a great deal through pictures about social life in Japan in the last years of the nineteenth century and the early years of the twentieth century, as noted in the opening paragraphs of this chapter. This chapter depends largely on the early chapters of the *Showashi* series issued by *Mainichi Shimbun* and *Fifty Years of Light and Dark: The Hirohito Era*, issued in English in 1967, also by *Mainichi Shimbun*. Also, the biography of Foreign Minister Wakaho Togo was useful here, as were Prince Kimmochi Saionji's memoirs. The quarrel within the palace about Hirohito's future, was related by Saionji and by the Marquis Koichi Kido.

Chapter 5   A Voyage of Discovery

All his life Hirohito cherished the memory of his trip abroad in 1921 to England and Europe, mostly for his experience in the British Isles. When he returned to Japan, he adopted the trappings of an English gentleman. His favorite breakfast was an English country breakfast of fruit, cereal, bacon, eggs, toast, and coffee. His personal office was decorated with English artifacts. The story of the voyage to England comes largely from the Japanese press of the day, where it was a sensation. The story of Hirohito's stay at the palace came from several of his aides, who leaked it to the press. The later attitudes of the prince toward his voyage comes from his own statements through the year, which show a nostalgia for those days that was quite unusual in a Japanese.

Chapter 6   Violence in Japan

The story of the Black Dragon Society and that period of Japanese history comes from Reischauer and from Hugh Byas. The story of Hirohito's Western-style party comes from *Fifty Years of Light and Dark*. The story of the great earthquake of 1923 is from the Japanese newspapers. The excesses of the Kempeitai are described in Leonard Mosley's work on Hirohito.

Chapter 7   Emperor

The material about the machinations of the army in the 1920s is from my research for *Japan's War* and includes army records and interviews with Japanese military men. The story of the new Emperor's trip to Hayama comes from newspaper files from the period, as do the descriptions of Hirohito's apartments. Details of his way of life are from the old Imperial Household Ministry, now the Imperial Household Agency. The material about Hirohito's religious obligations comes from papers supplied by the Japan Foreign Press Center. Events in Shandong Province in China are related in Liang Chin-tung, *Sinister Face of the Mukden Incident*. The material about the Manchurian incident comes from several diaries published in 1990 and 1991 of people close to the army and the Imperial Palace in the 1920s and 1930s. The story of General Tanaka's fall is from the Makino diary, as noted in the text.

Chapter 8   The Rape of Manchuria

The story of the Manchurian incident comes from materials arising from the war crimes trials of 1947–48 and from the Honjo diary and other diaries. Liang, *Sinister Face*, was very useful, as was Yoshihashi's book on the Mukden and Manchurian situations.

Chapter 9   Against the Emperor's Will

Captain Shin Tomonaga, a retired Japanese naval captain, explained to me the complicated Japanese system (both army and navy) of entrusting staff work to young officers, to a degree unknown in the Western world. The material about the advice from Hirohito's advisors comes from the Saionji and Kido memoirs and the Konoye diary. The material about the Japanese army in China comes from Shanghai newspapers and materials I gathered for *The Rise of the Chinese Republic*. The story of the Chapei incident is from the Japanese and Chinese newspapers of the period.

Chapter 10   The Struggle for Power

As noted in the preface, the diary of Nobuaki Makino (*Chuo Koron*, August–September, 1990) is an important source for this book. Makino's influence on

Hirohito was very strong, and so, for a time, was that of General Honjo, although Honjo's conduct in the February 26, 1936, incident (Chapter 12) cost him the confidence of the Emperor. It was unfortunate that Honjo and the Emperor came to part, for Honjo was probably the best and most open aide that Hirohito ever had, and the one most inclined to tell him the truth no matter how much it hurt. Even Prince Saionji, that old cynic, would try to sidestep truth to avoid troubles.

One thing that did not become apparent until after the end of the Pacific war was the growing degree to which the Emperor had to rely on members of his private imperial family for information, as the army tried to keep him insulated from the facts of Japanese life in the 1930s and 1940s. The army did not really succeed; the various imperial princes did keep the Emperor informed. However, he was constrained by his advisors to accept events, and by 1941 he was concerned, quite properly, as it proved, that if he went up flat against the army he might very well be deposed. If this happened, the whole imperial system would be destroyed in favor of an army oligarchy, or at best a monarchy so weakened as to be meaningless. That is why he allowed himself to be persuaded, first by Saionji and then by Kido, against interfering openly in decisions. He also had some very bad luck, as will be seen, in the last days before the Pacific war began.

Chapter 11   The First Crisis

The Imperial Way, as opposed to the Emperor Organ theory of government, dominated Hirohito's life during this period. He detested the Imperial Way idea and always had. He considered himself a man just like other men, one who put his pants on one leg at a time, as the expression goes, and that his position was due to fortune. His job was to serve Japan in his constitutional position, just as it was the Diet's task to serve in its position. He was not a god, he maintained, and it was ridiculous to worship him. For its own purposes, the army disagreed. To have a God Emperor made the task of molding the nation to the army will that much easier, and that is why they insisted on the Imperial Way.

Chapter 12   Four Days That Shook Japan

The violence that was erupting within the army was a matter of serious concern to Hirohito, and he talked it over with the imperial princes, but they did not have much to offer in the way of solutions. The major problem was the split of the army into its two factions, Kodo Ha (Imperial Way) and Tosei Ha. As noted in this chapter, the Emperor had a great deal of quiet influence. He managed to move divisions around by suggesting the moves through his military aide, but he soon learned to his chagrin that it did not make much difference, because the army had become so politicized by this time.

What was not apparent in the Imperial Palace, but was very apparent in the

army ranks, was that the country was still being run by the same clique of
nobility that had been in power since the days of the Meiji reformation. Really
it was still the clans. Some were army and navy officers; some were noblemen
and politicians. But they were still the old clique, and this is what the army
wanted to break up. When the soldiers (particularly the young officers) talked
about the corruption of the political system, this maintenance of power in the
hands of the old nobility is what they meant. Hirohito, who accepted that
system completely, was unaware of this feeling; indeed, he was shocked when
he finally did begin to understand what was going on. The understanding began
on the night of February 25, 1936, when the young officers of the First Division
were goaded into their rebellion, because this was what the young officers were
saying in the manifesto that preceded their grisly murders of the Emperor's
servants.

The sources for this material are the newspapers of the day, the Honjo Diary,
and *Fifty Years of Light and Dark*. When the rebellion was all over, the Emperor
chose Koki Hirota to become the new prime minister precisely because he was
not a military man. Hirohito told Hirota that his primary responsibility was to
protect the nobility—the precise group which had been under threat from the
young officers, who found in the Japanese nobility the roots of all Japan's evils.
The source for this analysis is Saburo Shiroyama's *War Criminal: The Life of Koki
Hirota*.

Chapter 13   The China War

The isolation of Hirohito by the army was planned by the cabal led by Generals
Terauchi, Nakoyushi Muto, and Hajime Sugiyama. Although the army faction
was unpopular with the people and the Diet, it won out in the end by sheer
power politics, and there was nothing that anyone, including the Emperor,
could do about it, because by this time Hirohito had no one to whom he could
turn except the members of the imperial family. The coming of Prince Konoye
to the prime ministry was the next to last act in the drama.

Chapter 14   Incident or War?

In the spring of 1937 Hirohito sent members of the imperial family all over
the Far East to ascertain the facts. Prince Chichibu went to London on the
Emperor's orders, a matter he recalled later in his talks with Hidenari Terasaki
(Terasaki notes). The idea was to resurrect the Japanese-British alliance, which
had served Japan so well in the first part of the twentieth century but which
had been allowed to lapse in the 1930s because of the navy's insistence on
rebuilding to meet the size of the British and U.S. fleets. Now Hirohito wanted
to undo what had been done, but the British showed no interest, and Prince
Naruhiko Higashikuni received no encouragement at Buckingham Palace.

Hirohito always had something to say to a new prime minister, asking him to look into the matter that was closest on the Emperor's mind at the moment. When he asked Konoye to form the cabinet, he told him he must do something to stop the Japanese army aggression against China. This Konoye did try to do, but he failed completely and had to tell the Emperor that he had failed. The army simply would not listen. The technique was for the Tokyo headquarters to say that the Tianjin garrison and the Kwantung Army in Manchuria would not obey orders; but Tokyo headquarters did not ever seem to be enough concerned about this failure to do anything about it. The fact, however, was that the Gunbatsu, or army commanders, in Tokyo were orchestrating the activities in Tianjin and Changchun, and the Lukouchiao incident (Marco Polo Bridge) was proof of it. The Emperor knew it. He later told Terasaki so, but what could he do? He was a prisoner behind his moat; the proof was the failure to deliver the message to him from President Roosevelt on the subject, a message Hirohito would not know about for years.

Chapter 15   The Strike to the North

The reality of the Nomonhan Incident is that the Japanese army was testing out the Soviet defenses, in the highly mistaken notion that Japanese military power was superior to any in the world. The most interesting thing about the experiment was not that it proved a disaster for the Japanese, who were resoundingly defeated, as noted in the text, but that for a short time, downcast by their disaster, the army leaders were responsive to Hirohito. He ordered, and they obeyed. But only for a moment. After Nomonhan they recovered quickly, and all the old arrogance was soon back. The net was that the army did not learn anything from the experiment. As Hirohito observed later, the Japanese army continued to believe that "spiritual power" would defeat modern technology, although they had just had a lesson to the contrary. They chose to regard the lesson as an anomaly, peculiar to the Soviets but not shared by the Western powers. Gulled by their successes against the badly armed and badly trained, although brave, Chinese armies, the Japanese continued to believe that they had the best army in the world. They had a great deal to learn, and the learning was to prove disastrous to them in the next eight years. To Hirohito the army was complete anathema. They did not listen to advice; they did not listen to criticism. The only way to deal with them was through confrontation, and that the Emperor was afraid to do because the power in Japan was in their hands, not his.

Chapter 16   War!

The materials for this chapter come from studies made for my books on Hideki Tojo (not yet published) and Admiral Isoroku Yamamoto and for my *Japan's War*. The study of the imperial conferences and liaison conferences was very useful for material about this period. Marquis Kido's diary was also useful, as were the notes by Terasaki. Hirohito's later polling of his advisors was recalled in his conversations with Terasaki.

Chapter 17   Days of Victory

The message from President Roosevelt to Emperor Hirohito actually arrived in Tokyo in plenty of time, but because of collusion between the young officers of the imperial general headquarters and the censorship office it sat for three days in a bin and was not delivered to the palace.

The source for the quotations about the early hours of the war is the daily Japanese newspapers of the time. The quotation from *Mainichi Shimbun* comes from *Fifty Years of Light and Dark*. The comments about historians in this chapter are my own, stemming from readings of David Bergamini and similar "revisionist" works. The Kido diary was the source for Kido's remarks. The Kotara poem appeared in the *Japan Times* (Dec. 20, 1941). The conversations with Terasaki are the source of Hirohito's remarks to Kido about ending the war. The quotation from Admiral Kurusu comes from his memoirs. The discussion of President Roosevelt's message to Hirohito is from U.S. State Department diplomatic papers and the Grew memoirs.

Chapter 18   The Juggernaut Stops

The source for the material about the war and the Emperor is the Kido diary. The sources for the material about the Greater East Asia Coprosperity Sphere are the "secret diary" of General Tojo's secretaries and the Tokyo press. The source for Hirohito's trip to see the damage of the firebombing is the Kido diary. Other materials come from the Konoye diary and the Terasaki notes.

Chapter 19   The Long Week

The decision made by Hirohito at this time was reflected in his later conversations with Terasaki. Part of the material here comes from *Japan's Longest Day*, from William Craig's *The Fall of Japan*, and from interviews with Admiral Hoshino in 1987. The interview with former grand chamberlain Yoshihiru Tokugawa was conducted at his home in Tokyo. The information about General Tanaka's behavior is from notes for my *Japan's War*.

Chapter 20   Capitulation

The story of the Japanese capitulation comes from Craig, *Fall of Japan*, from research for my own *Closing the Circle*, and from the newspapers of the period.

As noted in the text, I heard Professor Amazaki discuss the war crimes trials. The Japanese, more than forty years after the fact, still feel that these were trials of the vanquished by the victors, and so does much of the rest of the world. In considering future wars, then, would not the world be better advised to find some less abrasive method of dealing with the question of guilt or innocence, if there is such a thing in war?

Chapter 21   A Ray of Hope

I was in and out of Japan in 1945 and 1946 and observed the progress of the U.S. occupation. The undeification of Hirohito was in progress then, and what the Japanese at first called the MacArthur Constitution was being drawn. As noted, Prince Higashikuni served the nobility well in his brief term as prime minister, when he virtually turned the Japanese treasury over to the task of protecting the big industrial companies from the problems they would face in the early months of the occupation.

The story of Mutsuo Saito is from the Morris-Suzuki book.

Chapter 22   The Politics of Democracy

The material for this chapter depends largely on personal observation and study of current affairs in Japan over the years since the occupation began.

Chapter 23   The Emperor

As noted the briefings during the illness of the Showa Emperor were taken very seriously by the Japanese, if less so by the foreign press at whom they were aimed. To the Japanese they explained much that had hitherto seemed inexplicable about their Emperor's degree of responsibility for World War II in the Pacific.

Chapter 24   A Dream Come True

Again, from Japan, Korea, and China, I observed these changes over the early years of the occupation.

Chapter 25   The Last Year

I spent much of this last year of the Showa Emperor in Japan, where I observed the changes mostly through television and the newspapers.

Chapter 26   The Heart of Japan

The early part of this chapter is drawn from my personal discussions with Japanese friends in London and Tokyo. As noted in the text, Mutsuo Saito's tale comes from Tessa Morris Suzuki's *Showa*. Most of the rest of the chapter is the result of my own observations and speculations. The material about

Chamberlain Yoshihiro Tokugawa came from a long interview with the chamberlain and his wife in Tokyo in the summer of 1988.

Chapter 27   The Role of the Emperor

The interview with former grand chamberlain Tokugawa was conducted at his home in Tokyo.

Appendix   A 1988 Scientific Work by Emperor Hirohito

Hirohito's statement about his last scientific work was given to me by former grand chamberlain Tokugawa, with the Imperial Household's permission to publish it.

Selected Bibliography

Documents, Pamphlets, Primary Sources

International Society for Educational Information. "The Japan of Today." Tokyo, n.d.
————. "The Japanese Emperor through History." Tokyo, 1984.
Japan Foreign Press Center. Press briefings by Kanehisa Hoshino, Noboru Kojima, Kinko Sato, Shichihei Yamamoto, and Masakazu Yamazaki.
Makino, Nobuaki. Diary. *Chuo Koron*, August–September 1990.
Terasaki, Hidenari. Notes of conversation with Hirohito. *Bungei Shimbun*, Winter 1991.
U.S. National Archives. Department of State diplomatic papers, December 1941.

Books

Benedict, Ruth. *The Crysanthemum and the Sword*. Boston: Houghton Mifflin, 1946.
Bergamini, David. *Japan's Imperial Conspiracy*. New York: William Morrow, 1971.
Blond, Georges. *Admiral Togo*. New York: Macmillan, 1960.
Butow, R. J. C. *Japan's Decision to Surrender*. Stanford, Calif.: Stanford University Press, 1954.
Byas, Hugh. *Government by Assassination*. New York: Knopf, 1942.
Fifty Years of Light and Dark: The Hirohito Era. Tokyo: Mainichi Shimbunsha, 1967.
Honjo, Shigeru. *Honjo nikki*. Tokyo: Hara Shobo, 1967.
Hosokawa, Morisada. *Joho tenno ni tassezu*. 2 vols. Tokyo: Osobe Shobo, 1967.
Hoyt, Edwin P. *Closing the Circle: War in the Pacific: 1945*. Van Nostrand Reinhold, 1978.
————. *Japan's War: The Great Pacific Conflict*. New York: McGraw-Hill, 1986.

————. *The Militarists: The Rise of Japanese Militarism since World War II*. New York: Donald Fine, 1985.

————. *The Rise of the Chinese Republic: From the Last Emperor to Deng Xiaoping*. New York: McGraw-Hill, 1988.

————. *Yamamoto: The Man Who Planned Pearl Harbor*. New York: McGraw-Hill, 1990.

Ike, Nobutake, ed. *Japan's Decision for War: Records of the 1941 Policy Conferences*. Stanford, Calif.: Stanford University Press, 1967.

Inagaki, Masami. *Tenno no senso to shomin*. Tokyo: Kokusho Kankokai, 1975.

Inoue, Kiyoshi. *Tenno no senso sekinin*. Tokyo: Gendai Hyoronsha, 1975.

Iriye, Sukemasa. *Tenno-sama no kanreki*. Tokyo: Asahi Shimbunsha, 1962.

Isamu, Kanaji. *Hirohito, Japan's Compassionate Emperor*. Tokyo: Kao Corporation, 1989.

Japan's Longest Day: The Last Twenty-Four Hours through Japanese Eyes. Ed. Pacific War Research Society. Tokyo: Kodansha, 1980.

Kadoya, Fumio. *Showa jida.*. Tokyo: Gakuyo Shobo, 1973.

Kanroji, Osanaga. *Sibiru no tenno.*. Tokyo: Tozai Bunmeisha, 1967.

————. *Tenno sama*. Tokyo: Nichirinkaku, 1960.

Katsube, Mitake. *Tennosei*. Tokyo: Shibundo, 1973.

Kido, Koichi. *Kido Koichi nikki*. 2 vols. Tokyo: Tokyo Daigaku Shuppankai, 1966.

Kojima, Noboru. *Tenno*. 5 vols. Tokyo: Bungei Shunju, 1974.

Konoye, Fumimaro. *Konoye nikki*. Tokyo: Kyodo Tsushinsha, 1968.

Kurihara, Ken. *Tenno*. Tokyo: Yushindo, 1955.

Kurzman, Dan. *Kishi and Japan*. New York: Ivan Obolensky, 1960.

Liang Chin-tung. *Sinister Face of the Mukden Incident*. Cambridge, Mass.: Harvard University Press.

Mitsuda, Iwao. *Showa fuunroku*. Tokyo: Shinkigensha, 1940.

Morris-Suzuki, Tessa. *Showa: An Inside History of Hirohito's Japan*. New York: Schocken, 1985.

Mosley, Leonard. *Hirohito*. Englewood Cliffs, N.J.: Prentice-Hall, 1966.

Nakajima, Kenzo. *Showa jidai*. Tokyo: Iwanami Shinsho, 1957.

Nakamura, Kikuo. *Showa rikugun hishi*. Tokyo: Bancho Shobo, 1968.

————. *Tenno-sei fuashizumu-ron*. Tokyo: Hara Shobo, 1967.

Nezu, Masashi. *Tenno to showaashi*. Tokyo: San'ichi Shobo, 1974.

Oya, Seichi, ed. *Nippon no ichiban nagai hi*. Tokyo: Bungei Shunju Shinsha, 1965.

Reischauer, Edwin O. *The United States and Japan*. New York: Viking, 1968.

Sakuda, Kotaro. *Tenno to Kido*. Tokyo: Heibonsha, 1948.

Sansom, Sir George Bailey. *A History of Japan*. 3 vols. Stanford, Calif.: Stanford University Press, 1958–63.

Shinoda, Goro. *Tenno shusen hishi*. Tokyo: Tairiku Shobo, 1978.

Shiroyama, Saburo. *War Criminal: The Life of Koki Hirota.* Tokyo: Kodansha, 1983.

Showashi. 18 vols. Tokyo: Mainichi Shimbunsha, 1984.

Showashi no shunkan. 2 vols. Tokyo: Asahi Shimbunsha, 1966.

Showashi no tenno. 18 vols. Tokyo: Yomiuri Shimbunsha, 1972.

Suzuki, Hajime. *Tenno sama no sain.* Tokyo: Mainichi Shimbunsha, 1962.

Takemiya, Tahei. *Tenno heika.* Tokyo: Kantosha, 1951.

Yuri, Shizuo, and Asuma Kunihike. *Tenno goruku.* Tokyo: Kodansha, 1974.

Periodicals

Japan

Asahi Shimbun
Bungei Shimbun
Bungei Shunju
Chuo Koron
Japan Times
Mainichi Shimbun

Great Britain

Independent Magazine
London Sunday Observer

Index

About the Author

EDWIN P. HOYT is a writer and journalist who has written widely on the Pacific war and Japan and China. He writes a weekly column on current Japanese affairs for *The Daily Yomiuri* of Tokyo. He is the author of *Japan's War*, *The Militarists*, and *The Rise of the Chinese Republic*. He is currently at work on *The Last Kamikaze*, the story of Admiral Matome Ugaki and the Imperial Japanese Navy.